Faraway Campaign

John Wrake

Faraway Campaign

Experiences of an Indian Cavalry Officer in Persia & Russia During the Great War

F. James

LEONAUR

*Faraway Campaign: Experiences of an Indian Cavalry Officer
in Persia & Russia During the Great War*
by F. James

Published by Leonaur Ltd

ISBN: 978-1-84677-422-5 (hardcover)
ISBN: 978-1-84677-421-8 (softcover)

http://www.leonaur.com

Contents

1916

1917

1918

1919

1916

"Came out by the same door
as in I went."

CHAPTER 1

The East Persian Cordon

A dilapidated mud fort adjoining a crumbling serai backed to the north by a line of bleak rocky hill; at one side a stony water-course along which trickled, with every now and then a pool, a stream crystal clear, but salty and evil smelling. To the south, as far as the eye could see, an infinity of stony desert. Such was Bandan, a halting-place on the Seistan Trade Route in Eastern Persia for caravans moving up and down the hundreds of miles of that inhospitable waste, some forty miles to the north of Nasratabad, the capital of Seistan. A few inhabitants, ragged Persians with their attendant half-starved goats, completed the picture.

It was from the turret of this fort that I watched the officer, whom I had relieved the night before, ride away southwards with his escort to rejoin Regimental Headquarters. When the little dots representing their figures became no longer discernible, merged into one with that far horizon, I turned to take stock of what was my first real "halt" for many weeks of travel after leaving the Indian Cavalry Corps in France. The stock-taking was soon done. I occupied the turret, and below me lived my little garrison of a troop of my regiment—an Indian officer and a machine-gun section.

Very pleased was I to be back with these, my old friends. There is, in an Indian Cavalry regiment, a tremendous esprit de corps. With practically no exception, the regiment consists of men who enlist with the object of serving as many years as they can, and to all intents and purposes it resembles a great family. And so, having rejoined my family in this appalling spot, I was happy.

I read and reread my orders as post commander—to do so-and-so, to see to this and that, and to achieve "the destruction or capture of any parties working actively" against the interests of the Allies in Persia.

To make the situation clear, I had better give a brief account of the reasons leading to the presence of our troops in Persia at that time, and explain the meaning of these sinister "parties working actively" against our interests.

The preparations made by Germany before the war had included all that might induce Mohammedan States to become her allies. What better, then, encouraged by her success with Turkey, than to turn especial attention to Afghanistan, thereby pinning down in India a great number of British troops? Not too easy a task with Russia on the north; on the south and east, Britain. The neutral country of Persia therefore represented the only way open.

Directly Britain entered the war, German agents of first-class ability already in Persia began dealing blows at British prestige and attempting to force themselves or their emissaries into Afghanistan. At this time Persia was divided into "spheres of influence" between Britain and Russia. The Russian sphere, from Russian Turkestan in the north southwards to Birjand, contained sufficient troops attached to the Russian Consulates to patrol the Afghan frontier and keep a watch for German agents. The British sphere south of Birjand had no such troops, the Indian cavalrymen who formed our consular escorts being totally insufficient. It became therefore essential to place our consulates on the same footing as the Russian, and Persian agreement to this was obtained.

So it came about that a British Force consisting of a complete regiment of Indian Cavalry and one of Indian Infantry, known at the time as the East Persian Cordon, was occupying a chain of posts hundreds of miles long, and widely separated, from Birjand to the south of Robat, the latter place being actually a distance of some five hundred miles across the desert of Baluchistan eastwards to India and civilization.

Along this route and northwards to Birjand the camel caravans had to crawl, bringing vital supplies for our troops.

To the south of Robat lies a great tract of mountainous country, dominated by a semi-extinct volcano over 14,000 feet in height known as the Koh-i-Taftan. This wild and grim expanse, with which I was shortly to become acquainted, and which somehow always made me think of Alan Quatermain, is inhabited by Baluch tribesmen, lawless brigand shepherds, armed to the teeth, picturesque and strangely suggesting the warriors of childhood's imagination straight from the pages of the Old Testament. Completely indifferent to any Government, they have from time immemorial varied their normal occupations by sallying forth in lashkars (large armed forces) to raid Persian territory. Mounted on their fast trotting camels they would sack a few villages, returning to their fastnesses in the hills with all the sheep, camels and slaves they could secure. These excursions, entailing treks of many hundred miles through desert country, much of it impassable to ordinary human beings, could not be dealt with by the Persian Government who had simply no resources effective against them.

It did not take long for the German agents to influence these tribesmen, and persuade them that our convoys on their long lines of communication—convoys containing supplies, ammunition, in fact many luxuries and riches unheard of by these "Biblical" raiders—were worth their attention. I take off my hat to the pluck of these Germans, nearly all picked officers, who had to travel so many thousands of miles through incredibly difficult country, in constant danger from our patrols and spies. To win the help of the raiders must have entailed great danger, for it mattered nothing to them whom they looted. What was a German to them, and what was a Britisher? People of whom they had probably never heard and whose throats were equally worth cutting for whatever could be looted.

I believe that one tribe was completely won over to the hostile cause by a German officer with his little party who told its members of Germany and the war, and of Britain, and who actually had the cheek to rig up with poles and boxes an imitation wireless station, pretend he was in communication with the Kaiser himself, and mention unheard of rewards; also that the

11

Kaiser had become a Mohammedan. He got away with it, gallant chap! Later on I met several of these officer agents.

The "parties working actively" against the Allied interests in Persia, therefore, were these adventurous Germans bound for Afghanistan across Persia, and their dupes—the "Biblical" ruffians intent on reward and the spoils of raiding our convoys.

Before turning to events and experiences in the years that elapsed until we returned to civilization, some impression of the general scene will make my story more clear.

Leaving Quetta, the second largest garrison in India, one takes the railway southwards to Spezand, where the line branches off westwards through a maze of hills down to Nushki, ending there in a tin hut station and a mud bungalow used by political officers. As the train crawls between the hills, this desolate spot far below can be seen for miles before arrival. Here civilization ends, and the great desert of Baluchistan meets the traveller's eyes.

We were a small party who started from Nushki, bound for Seistan; myself and two brother officers going to rejoin our regiment on the East Persian Cordon. Little did I think, as we trotted out, that this venture would take me by horse and camel, during the next few years, from Robat southward half-way to the Persian Gulf and northward beyond Merv in Russian Turkestan to within a few miles of the river Oxus. It is about four hundred miles to Robat along what is known as the Seistan Trade Route. "Route" sounds definite enough; but the way is marked only by the skeletons and bodies, in varying stages of decay, of the unfortunate casualties among the camels of passing caravans.

To Robat is a matter of some twenty stages, each marked by a water-hole and tiny mud bungalow. One hacks quietly along the daily twenty to thirty miles through sheer "nothingness"—the dominant note is desolation; and at first the immensity of space, the complete absence of vegetation, the sameness and stillness of it all, with no sign of human being or animal life, inspire a sense of oppression and dread. Yet after a while the scene begins slowly to develop a queer charm of its own. I remember so well the evenings at the end of the day's trek, waiting for the arrival of our little camel convoy; the rare beauty of desert, bringing a

great sense of peace; the infinite variations of colour in the tree-
less rocky ranges; the grandeur, the silence. Those were happy
evenings in the little mud huts which marked the day's trek.
Every officer who came out to the Persian Cordon brought
with him tinned supplies, as rations were few, and the chances of
augmenting them locally, negligible. There are outstanding and
queerly shaped rocky landmarks in this four hundred miles, that
can be seen for days, ever approached, yet betraying no signs of
growing nearness; one seemed at times to make no headway.

Not a living soul or animal did we see in this stage beyond an
occasional great lammergeyer, high in the air, winging his way
from one range of mountains to the next. The scarcity of water
in this stretch is perhaps less trying than its abominable quality
when found. The climate is more than trying, summer being
marked by winds and sand-storms hot as the breath of a furnace,
winter by repetitions of them, but icy cold.

So, in due course, we came into Robat, the south-west corner of Afghanistan. I remember, that day, meeting the first India-
bound caravan. Seated on his camel was the first German officer
captured on the Cordon. There had been a cavalry skirmish up
the Line—a long, cross-country search—a gallop—and the end
of activities for that particular enemy party. I remember, too, the
man's name—Winkelmann. Well, he had done his best and lost.

For the last sixty miles before turning up the Robat ravine
we had been riding on a stony track across the foothills of a barren rocky range. And here was Robat with its little garrison—a
well-built political officer's bungalow, two turreted serais, and a
few huts to accommodate the troops; all in a great ravine about
a quarter of a mile wide overlooked by towering rocky hills. An
unlovely and grim spot; but this meeting with the detachment
of my own regiment—the first since leaving them in Quetta to
go to France at Christmas, 1914—made it seem even more than
worth while to have come out to this comfortless land.

It was extremely pleasant to make a two days' halt in Robat,
as we were all suffering from the effects of the abominable water. The drinking water at Robat itself was brought daily from a
spring up in the hills; though brackish, we welcomed the change.

The view of Afghanistan to the north is extensive, a long expanse of sheer wilderness forming the south-west corner of this country. A stretch of almost snowy white, centred with pale blue, can be seen; this is known as the Gaud-i-Zirreh, a salt water lake in the midst of a huge pan of nitre.

Away on the northern frontier in the Karakoram mountains rises the river Helmund bearing the water from the melting snows of the mountains, never reaching the sea, but spreading out in Seistan into a vast inland lake, sometimes, according to the season, one hundred miles long by fifty broad though only eight to ten feet in depth. The water at the south end of this lake becomes salter. This is the great Hamun which in ages past made Seistan the richest province of that part of Asia until the vengeful Tamerlane sacked its towns and destroyed its irrigation system.

The overflow of this mighty basin is formed by the bitterly salt river Shelagh, which after a few miles, loses itself in this salt pan—the Gaud-i-Zirreh.

It was here that a tragedy occurred during the years of this faraway campaign. A party of Pathan soldiers, escorting a convoy, decided to desert to their homes in Afghanistan with their rifles and ammunition, in the hope of refilling their water bottles and making the Gaud-i-Zirreh a halting-place. These unfortunates did actually reach the banks of the salt pan and spent the last night of their lives there.

Testimony to this was the report of the Baluch Levies who had been sent to search for them, and found fourteen naked bodies contorted round holes in the sand which had obviously been scratched out by agonized fingers in the hope of digging to where fresh water might be found.

In Robat I heard all there was to hear concerning the Cordon, the story of the scrap ending in the capture of Winkelmann, and of the terrific marches and counter-marches in search of these "parties hostile" to our interests.

It may seem easy to imagine a small party getting through by night, or even by day, unobserved, considering the hundreds of miles to choose from and those protected only by a handful of Indian Cavalry in garrisons fifty to one hundred miles apart.

To get through from the west, to begin with, entails crossing the great Lut desert, waterless and grim, over which certain definite lines must be followed owing to the distance apart of the water-holes. A system of spies, locally enlisted, ensured that the nearest posts received news of any who might halt at these water-holes. Days and nights of hard riding followed for the garrison concerned, searching for these human "needles in haystacks." So far the tribesmen—the ruffians from the Old Testament—were quiet, but rumours were afloat of their lashkars (armed gatherings) mustering for trouble. In India nobody had even heard of this undertaking. My regiment, I was told, had been whisked out of Quetta to an unknown destination. It had been considered impossible to take horses to this inhospitable arena, and so they had been mounted on camels!

Each man was provided with a green gauze veil, in addition to other unusual equipment, to protect him from the biting winds and the glare, not to mention the biting winged ones. Such precautions in the case of hardened Indian troopers may serve as an indication of the charms of this corner of Asia.

Before I arrived, however, it had been discovered that camels were unsuitable for many reasons, and I was glad to find that our horses had been sent out, with very few casualties—a remarkable achievement on the part of the British officer and handful of men in charge. Incidentally, despite shortage of rations, incessant trekking, and the worst of water, they throve throughout the years we were there.

It was cheery, that two days' halt in Robat, meeting again the first detachment of my regiment. The future was full of interest, possibilities and novelty. And so, leaving one of our little party detailed to command that post, we trotted out once more to cross from Baluchistan over its frontier and into Persia.

CHAPTER 2

Bandan

Out of the ravine, bearing slightly right-handed for a mile or two, we came upon a water-hole with a few mud huts adjoining, Koh-i-Malik-Siah, "The Black Mountain." But more prominent than all else stands a tall mud pillar, marking the actual spot where three Empires meet—Persia, Afghanistan, and British Baluchistan, through which we had been journeying. At this point, the end of our westward trek, we turned north into Persia, parallel with the Afghan western frontier. About a thousand miles north lay the Russian frontier, which, later, I was also to cross, though I little anticipated such a journey.

Riding on, I called to my mind my previous ideas of Persia. Carpets, yes, and cats, and comforting philosophies of Omar Khayyám; gardens with fountains playing in the moonlight; nightingales, roses, wine; dignified old turbaned and white-bearded gentlemen in flowing robes; stars of enormous size gleaming from a firmament north, south, east and west to a horizon, and against them the silhouette of distant mountain ranges; soft, sandy desert in the foreground. All these, in due course, I was destined to see, except the cats. I shared many a Persian hut with its attendant cats, but they were just good, honest, short-haired tabbies, exact replicas of our pets in England.

That scorching hot wind meeting us suddenly from a rocky corner brought an end to my imaginings. Ahead lay four trying days' ride to Nasratabad, our destination, Headquarters of the East Persian Cordon. Mile after mile we covered, now dismounting to lead our horses, then a mounted trot, then a walk. Soon we came through a defile and before us stretched the flat desert, as far as the eye could see, bearing ever the same landmarks of camel skeletons, ever exhaling that foul stench of camels who were not yet skeletons. . . . Poor, foundered ships of the desert, their carcasses being stripped by hungry lammergeyers and vultures. It is said that these birds soar for thousands of feet into the air with a camel's bone, drop it to be crashed to pieces on the rocks, and follow it down to get what goodness may be in it.

The sun is low in the sky as we come to our halting-place for the night—a water-hole; no more of those mud huts now for a night's shelter. The water is impure and brackish, and we are grateful for the arrival of our little convoy, and our bivouac tents. In an incredibly short time we are all settled down—there is still a little whisky left to drown the taste of that abominable water. Life seems good as we turn in, and the last sounds we hear on the way to a dreamless and tired sleep are the occasional snort and stamp of a restless horse, the fidgeting and quaint grumble of the camels.

For two more days we travelled quietly along over the dead level desert, but on the second a scattering of tamarisk relieved the distressing glare of the sun. For stretches of miles the surface was hard, and as flat as a billiard table. Looking forward, the mirage concealed all, and that strange feeling of being in a treadmill, of making no perceptible progress, was stronger than ever, the regular clop-clop of our horses' feet being the only indication that we were moving at all. The water had the effect of rousing a terrible thirst, even the camels jibbing at it. But in spite of all drawbacks I enjoyed that trek with our little escort of my own regiment again, the space, the novelty, the possibilities.

A ride of perhaps some five hundred miles—how I should have laughed if I had realized what child's play it was to what the future held in store; a mere picnic!

Approaching the great oasis of Seistan on the fourth day, we rode into it to Nasratabad. A marvellous change: we revelled in the fresh Hamun water irrigating a land with cornfields and hedges, dwellings, human beings, animal and bird life. Gone was that horrible thirst. After the death-like stillness of the desert, to hear the whistling wings of lines of wild geese overhead, the call of plover and sandpiper and many other denizens of that great oasis, was incredibly refreshing.

Two squadrons of my regiment were in Nasratabad, and a large proportion of that fine Indian Infantry regiment with whom we were destined to share so many adventures. What a joy it was to walk into the officers' mess and greet so many old friends! I spent two days here, thoroughly enjoying the luxuries of fresh water, good food and pleasant quarters, and cheery company. Domed Persian mud huts had been built for quarters and a large mess; the men were all comfortably housed, and the horse lines consisted of rows of what looked like mud pillars. In the top of each of these was a hole into which a horse could put his head and neck to get at his feed, which was inside, and it was strange to see, at first, a line of apparently headless horses at feeding time.

Seistan is known as the land of the wind of Sad-o-Bist Roz, which means the wind of a hundred and twenty days: a scorching hurricane which literally achieves this record, and more. Hence the pillars and headless horses, for unless thus protected their food would be, in the space of seconds, half sand. There was also, at the time of my arrival, a plague of fleas which necessitated all kinds of traps and gadgets to keep their loathsome attentions at bay. Later, in the summer, comes the plague of horseflies, which would mean a change of station for the cavalry, for these pests are fatal to horses imported from elsewhere. Yet it all seemed marvellous. The "town" itself is but a medley of mud hovels, though there are two or three bungalows, occupied by the British and Russian Consuls and the manager of the local branch of the Imperial Bank of Persia. The Russian Consul had already left—yet here we found the first traces of Russia in the packets of cigarettes obtainable in the Bazaar—made in the usual half-cardboard way with Russian writing in the little boxes.

The Seistanis themselves are a miserable-looking race. The men wear curious, dome-shaped, felt, brimless hats, with baggy blue clothes; the women are dressed in dark blue and black, heavily veiled, with yashmaks, and always turn modestly to the nearest wall and wait motionless while the "unbeliever" passes by.

An unexpected meeting, and one peculiarly pleasant to me, occurred here. As I rode into the horse lines and dismounted, out ran a little figure with wizened, smiling face and short, grey, pointed beard, his eyes beaming under his wisp of turban. He held my horse with one hand and with the other wrung mine until I thought it was coming off. This was Suleiman Khan—a character known, liked, and, though a humble syce (groom), respected throughout the regiment; known to all of us as "old man syce." Like Sinbad, he seemed—a living character from a fairy story.

We first met some years before the war, in India. I was trekking with my ponies, across country, to some polo and racing week, hacking quietly along through the Central Provinces and spending each evening shooting, or hunting jackals and foxes with my long dogs—a delightful time. One evening as I was walking back to my camp, up came this strange figure. He looked at least one hundred years old then, with the exception of his bright little eyes and brisk movements; and even now there was no perceptible change in the little man. He was carrying a bird which I had shot. Interested in his unusual appearance, I asked who he might be. "Sahib," he said, "I am one of your syces." I had never seen him before, but there he stood smiling. I asked my orderly, in charge of my ponies, if he knew who this was. No, he knew nothing. So, discovering his name, I said, "Very well, Suleiman, one of my syces you shall be." Whence he came that day, what he was doing, he would never tell. He had a wonderful way with horses and always took charge of anything "difficult" that I owned. Unmoved, imperturbable, outwardly completely indifferent as to whether his special charge won its race, jumping competition, or what you will, he volunteered to come with me to France.

I can see him now, the ship pitching and rolling in a rough sea, seated on the top of a coil of rope, looking more like a fairy story figure to be summoned by rubbing a magic ring, laughing at the discomforts of sea-sick troopers—and, catching sight of me, smiling the wider and saying, "Your turn next, Sahib."

He was always a mystery. The ordinary syce is a humble, low-caste worker, who would not think of addressing even an Indian

19

trooper unless spoken to. Not so Suleiman—I had actually seen him holding the hand of that great autocrat, the Risaldar Major himself, the senior Indian officer, laughing up into his face. And that king of kings was laughing too!

How that little old man worked for me. In France it was the same. He was a regimental "character" at once with everyone from the Commanding Officer downwards. I watched his face when the first aeroplane he had ever seen flew over. The old Sinbad was adjusting a bandage on my horse's leg; he betrayed no excitement—there was nothing to get excited about!

Then came the day when all Indian servants had to leave the Indian Cavalry Corps in France to be replaced by "batmen" from the British Cavalry regiment in the brigades. Suleiman with the others stood before the CO. while each gave the address of his next-of-kin as his heir in case of being torpedoed on the way back to India.

The old man had no answer to this. "No, Colonel Sahib, I have no heir—no next-of-kin."

Well, then, what to do?

"I make James Sahib my heir," said Suleiman. (I am quite sure he said "Jimmy Sahib.") The last I had seen of him was his short figure seated in the back of a lorry, his little thin legs dangling, disappearing down the main street of Abbeville, laughing and waving till out of sight.

And here he was in Seistan. Yes, he had come out with the regiment with another sahib. He would leave that other sahib that moment and come along with me. I have asked my greatest Indian friends, with whom I served for over twenty years—Mohammedans, as of course was Suleiman—again and again what was the story of this strange little gnome man, whence had he come, who he was; but nobody could or would ever tell me. He was a humble syce, man to man with everybody.

The two days' halt over, I found myself riding out of this "oasis," alone now, to relieve the British officer commanding the outpost of Bandan, where this story began. My orderly, old man syce and myself. Crossing the Hamun on reed rafts at a narrow part, our horses and camels splashing alongside, that wild desert assaulted us again all too soon. Myriads of duck, geese and swans, disturbed by our crossing, rose in their thousands with almost a thunder of wings. It is a long and tricky passage, and a day's trek. We camped on the far bank, and the noise of a huge flock of swans—obviously new arrivals—made, sleep impossible through a mosquito-infested night.

For miles, the next day, over that abominable stony desert. For hours before arrival the little Bandan fort could be seen which never seemed to get nearer; and again came that futile impression of unavailing effort to which, later on, we were to grow accustomed.

The following morning, from the turret, I saw the officer whom I had relieved fade into the distant mirage. I reread my orders; there was no one to talk to. This had been a longish ride, of course, but before the war I had ridden with my regiment on changing stations from Saugor in the Central Provinces to Multan—those were good days—then on from Multan up to Quetta; and now to this execrable Bandan.

The sun, higher every hour, made the heat more than uncomfortable. At every turn one was followed and pestered by clouds of flies. I was in this place for a month and never till sunset did I take off my turban. That, at least, kept these torments off one's head and the back of one's neck.

Here, once more, water was the chief difficulty. My small garrison, who had been in Bandan for only a few weeks, were in a bad way—even camels could not stand that fluid. Rations were hard to come by in those days—the difficulty of regular convoys and supply meant an absence of any vegetable, not to mention of many things necessary to life itself. There were men in my troop whose teeth were loose, racked with the purgative element in the water. The rare convoys coming southward brought with them from our northern posts between Bandan and Birjand wrecks of men suffering as mine were, from scurvy, en route for India. It was, in truth, the survival of the fittest. Few of these unfortunates ever again were passed medically fit to rejoin the regiment.

We existed on goat—always goat, with rice, which we usually had, chupatties (a kind of unleavened bread), washed down with tea, the flavour completely obliterated by the only water obtainable. I can see those poor little goats now, being led away to have their heads chopped off by the troop sabre expert. The supply of tinned food was exhausted, and we were lucky if occasionally we could buy an egg or two.

Later this post, justly looked upon as the vilest one of all, was abandoned. Half-way to the Hamun, some twenty miles south, was the nearest decent water contained in what is called a hauz—a well-made cemented tank, sometimes twelve feet deep, to catch the rain, and roofed over to prevent evaporation. One of our duties was to maintain a permanent patrol night and day at this spot, as being an almost certain refilling place for any crossing hostile party; just after I left a scrap occurred there between some Afghan raiders from their western frontier and one of our few convoys. They had the worst of it; but they retaliated later by throwing the corpse of one of their casualties into the tank. That hauz was always eagerly anticipated by any of our patrols, men and horses alike. Imagine the feelings of the next party to arrive, finding that precious water, such as it was, fouled by this dead body. Fortunately it did not fall to me to pull the poor devil out.

Another duty was the escort northwards of convoys carrying Persian silver coin from Nasratabad up the line to Birjand. These travelled by night, leaving Bandan about four p.m. Crawling at about two miles an hour until seven o'clock the next morning, we too crawled alongside, slipping and stumbling over the rocks and stones. From time to time a camel would fall, and with luck could be got going again. Camels sometimes have a habit of just sitting down and dying—hence the bone-strewn trade route. Always I associate Bandan with the clanging and ringing of camel bells, and great unwieldy shapes lurching on silent feet through the night.

Relieved by an escort from the north in the morning, we would feed and water our horses and try to get some sleep amongst the sand and fleas, under what cover we could find from the burning wind; then back again to our fort in Bandan.

On other days we used to patrol for miles to get an idea of the lie of the country towards the distant Afghan frontier.

Sometimes, taking a rifle, I walked out into the desert on the chance of a shot at Persian gazelle, occasionally to be seen in the neighbourhood; one day I stopped and sat down. That eternal wind saw fit to stop at the same time, and I was out of sight of the fort. The absolute stillness, gigantic nothingness—no other words describe it—made me feel as if I must have finished this life and be in some other world. Reality only returned when, back in the fort, old Suleiman brought me my plate of goat and rice.

The one great excitement of the day occurred at the hour of communication with Headquarters. From Nushki, the end of the Indian railway, out through Robat and up north through Seistan, Bandan, Birjand and Meshed, stretches a single line of telegraph wire owned by the Indo-Persian Telegraphs. This is occasionally met with in the trade route, but in many parts it takes short cuts, not requiring water like men and animals. In my little turret stood the instrument, and at a certain hour each evening I had to connect with Headquarters in Seistan, for news and orders.

It might be thought that hostile tribesmen would interfere with this, but only once did this happen as far as I know. These worthies held it in awe, and feared to touch it. Incidentally some of the Persian operators were probably not disinclined to use it to the tribesmen's benefit. However, every evening the Bandan operator, Abbas Ali, would come in and with ear-splitting yells on the ancient mouthpiece gain connection with his chief in Seistan; then, with the utmost difficulty, my orders from Head-quarters would come, generally concerning expected convoys. When, occasionally, some secret order was transmitted in cipher, the fun began. I had nothing, of course, to read, and deciphering these messages was a joy. But to succeed in hearing them was another matter, what with the antediluvian mouthpiece and the eternal howling wind.

"Yes, I got that last one. Yes—A for Arthur, B for Bandan, W for Whisky (thank you very much)," . . . and so it went on. . . . The tribes round Robat were preparing a grand Persian raid. . . . Our convoys had been attacked between Robat and Nushki.

...A hostile party had been reported moving westward, so pay special attention to the hauz.

The sun rose, circled, and fell; the wind scorched and blew— day succeeded day. Again and again those nightly escorts alongside the groaning, bubbling, bell-ringing ships of the desert. Sand and fleas, fleas and sand.

The view from the turret was never brightened by the sight of a living, moving soul; such a glimpse then would mean trouble, instant action, and a galloping out to investigate. Would nothing ever happen? I need not have worried. It would. And it certainly did.

CHAPTER 3

Mohameddan Raiders

At last, one evening, when Abbas Ali, at telephone hour, after his ear-splitting greetings with his co-operator in Nasratabad, passed me the ancient instrument for my daily turn, I heard to my joy that one of our subalterns was due to arrive in Bandan on the following day, and that I was to rejoin Headquarters immediately I had handed over.

And so, having completed this welcome task, two days later back again with a small escort trotted my orderly, the "old man syce" and I, passed the hauz, to be lost to sight from my turret back in Bandan, in the mirage. Crossing the Hamun on the second day, we found ourselves once more in the congenial surroundings of Nasratabad.

News had been received of a party of German agents making for Afghanistan by a route south of Seistan; also of a large raiding lashkar from below Robat moving northward. Regular raids such as this thoroughly appealed to the inborn love of cruelty and greed possessed by these ruffians. They would sally forth hundreds strong, and cover incredible distances in a day. The wretched Persian villagers would be robbed of every goat and sheep they possessed, and many of them would be seized, both men and women, and taken back as slaves. The return journey of the raiders to their hill fastnesses was of necessity a slow one, as they had to drive these wretched people and animals back. They have no real dwellings, but move according to the season with their herds, their only real riches, and pitch their black tents accordingly.

I received orders to set out on the following morning with

some twenty-five lances and to occupy a post about twenty miles south at a well-known water-hole, scouring the country daily for the expected party of Germans. With us went a convoy of one hundred and fifty camels carrying rations for three weeks for men and horses. Off again then, alongside our bell-ringing, lurching, shuffling food-carriers; a good day's trek.

Our destination proved to be the usual smelling water-hole and one or two flea-ridden mud huts. Swarms of flies, as before; but here I had to wear my turban all day, and in addition to bind the loose end round my mouth and nose. There were one or two likely lines where the enemy might be expected, and these were watched day and night by standing patrols. The remainder of us waited, ready at a moment's notice to get into the saddle and away to any point from which reports might demand action.

We rode over every inch of country within a ten-mile radius to gain some idea of the nature of the land in case we had to undertake a night ride. This, at any rate, was better than Bandan; but day succeeded day and nothing happened—we rode and rode, the flies buzzed and swarmed, the fleas did their worst. The suspected German party was quite evidently not coming that way. We longed to get into touch with them and fight it out; but that was not to be.

Meanwhile our spies reported that the raiders were definitely on the move and looting northward across the desert, some hundred miles parallel with and west of our Cordon. These ruffians were divided into four or five distinct tribes, each with its own chief, but paramount was one Jiand Khan, who took the lion's share of all the booty, and was king of the Sarhad, as this mountainous waste south of Robat to the Persian Gulf is called. Later on I was to know him all too well. The present raiders were a clan known as the Ismailzais, led by one Juma Khan, said to be several hundreds strong.

Nearly all such parties are armed with modern rifles, purchased from gun-runners of the Persian Gulf; they literally bristle with knives and swords and bandoliers of ammunition. As a rule, tall and magnificently built men, and picturesque to a degree, with clean-cut, almost fair faces and black, glossy hair under their coloured turbans, they are capable of enduring astonishing hardships and covering, on foot or camel, distances that seem incredible. With their flocks and herds, their feuds and battle-cries, flowing white clothes, their general surroundings, in this desolate, far-away country they present a picture which cannot have changed since the times of the Old Testament.

Welcome orders arrived to move again some thirty miles west to another water-hole, there to join up with a detachment of the local Seistan Levy Camel Corps, forty or fifty strong, in conjunction with whom we were to do our utmost to intercept Juma Khan on his loot-burdened return to the fastnesses of the Sarhad—if we could find him.

It may seem easy to locate a marauding army of hundreds in a vast desert, but it isn't. It is as bad as looking for a needle in a haystack, so colossal is the emptiness and space, so infinite are the distances. This time, however, we were successful.

The next day found us with our convoy of rations at this water-hole, having been called off our search for the German party; the usual day's trek, but all of us greatly heartened at the prospect of coming to grips with the Ismailzais. We had every reason to feel encouraged. This tribe, and others—the Gomshadzais, and the Yar Mohammedzais—had been attacking our caravans on the Seistan Trade Route, and had killed many of our men escorting them. In short, inspired by German propaganda, they had become thoroughly "above themselves." British prestige was at the lowest ebb and it was high time to "get our own back."

One felt always, as was indeed true, that unseen eyes from rocky hills were watching every movement of companies such as mine; watching to take advantage of any carelessness, ready to pounce if one's back were turned. In these days, and for weeks afterwards, the faintest cloud of dust, barely discernible in the distance, meant a hostile camel scout—watching—always watching. News too, travels in the desert at miraculous speed. A scrap takes place and is known almost at once many miles away—somehow. And yet one travels day after day with no sign of human being, except that hardly visible cloud of dust—the watcher.

To my great joy I found an old friend in the officer commanding the Levy Camel Corps detachment. I will call him A.; we had last seen one another years before. He had already heard that the raiders had started their homeward trek, and we figured it out together that they might conceivably pass southward, some eighty miles away to the west down a certain wide valley. We calculated that some days must elapse before they could possibly even enter that valley, and so decided to give my men and horses two days' rest before we moved to intercept them. A fine type of soldier was A.—the most imperturbable warrior that I have ever met. He had been doing his utmost to teach his men to shoot. During those two days we held a great competition, instructing those wild levies, whose only idea of shooting was to pull the trigger and shout war-cries; they settled down with comic determination to knock over any old target we could invent—and what tense rivalry and jealousy prevailed!

To reach this valley where we hoped to catch the raiders meant going across country—leaving any recognized route for nearly eighty miles. Studying the map was not very helpful as each inch represented nearly forty miles of nothingness, and the name of every water-hole—this always amused me—took up at least three quarters of an inch, representing thirty miles on paper, but in reality a few square yards of probably fetid pool. One thing we did know, that the end of this eighty miles would bring us to a defile through the eastern or nearer range of hills forming the valley.

Followed a consultation with our levies. Yes, they knew the way, and, about half-way to the defile, there was a water-hole in a pocket of the hills where we could halt for the night.

The two days' rest over, off we went towards the promised water over miles of rolling open desert, with our levy guides in front—I shall always remember that day, riding easily along, my men in line at wide intervals behind and a light head wind carrying the dust where it did not matter. At the flanks were the levies on their camels, and behind all came our precious transport with forage and rations, such as they were, A. and I side by side discussing our chances.

No communication with anybody now. This was our very own show, and nobody could even know where we were. Not a living soul was seen; not even that little cloud of sand on the horizon.

Late that evening the guides pointed out the water-hole concealed in a defile of a range of hills we had been approaching all day. Halting, we sent forward a small patrol to picket the high ground surrounding this. All clear being signalled, that precious, though putrid water was soon being eagerly drunk by all of us; it had been a long march, the pace, of course, for safety's sake, being regulated to that of the convoy.

Choosing a suitable piece of ground, we settled down for the night with pickets posted at danger-points. The next day we wound in and out of low hills—a very trying march, and necessarily slow through having to "make good " the many defiles, not to mention constant halts to unload, pick up, and reload unfortunate camels slipping and falling on the rocks. Dusk, however, found us at the defile overlooking the valley which we hoped would be the homeward route of the raiders. We fitted ourselves into a sheltered ravine, which held the water; a most satisfactory camp, hidden from both the valley and the route by which we had come. This water-hole was on a recognized line by which a few, very few, supply convoys crossed the valley to an isolated post some twenty miles distant named Dehana-Baghi, which was held then by a company of Indian Infantry.

A. and I gazed down over this marvellous desert view. To north and south ran the valley, and away opposite to the west showed the silhouette of bleak hills forming its western barrier. A magnificent sunset flooded the sky, and we sat till dark searching with our glasses. To raise our hopes, we actually perceived on the northern horizon a sign of dust clouds. . . . Was it merely a sand-storm?

We sent out a few camel levies to form a chain of posts towards the west across the valley to give us timely warning in case the raiders passed during the night. But, to illustrate how news travels in those parts, some of our Seistani levies in camp, on our return, told us there had been trouble where we saw that dust cloud. We did not listen to them. How on earth could they know? They had been with us all day. But they did know—and they were quite right.

The last thing I remember looking at as I drifted into a sound sleep in a hollow scooped in the sand was the glittering North Star, that one permanent and fixed beacon among those millions of ever moving lights which we call the stars. And how soundly one slept after those long and thirsty rides! Dreaming we were back in India, pig-sticking . . . the most enormous boar in Asia had turned to charge ... we must not miss him—grand. . . . Then a rough awakening. A. was shaking me out of sleep. Behind him stood one of our levies who had hurried in from his post in the valley.

The raiders had just passed below us in the plain. It was barely dawn.

Within a few minutes twenty of my men were ready and mounted, the remainder being detailed to stay behind and look after the camp. A.'s levies were mustering on their camels. The last thing that had happened the night before, and a godsend, was the unexpected arrival of a rare convoy bound for Dehana-Baghi with an escort of a platoon of Indian Infantry in charge of an Indian officer. A quick consultation ensued; we decided that I should gallop in pursuit of the raiders; close with them, and hold them pending A.'s arrival with the slower moving camelry and infantry.

Over the shoulder of the ravine and down into the plain we clattered across the rocks, and, sure enough, there were the fresh tracks of the passing enemy.

These were easy enough to follow. Here and there lay an exhausted sheep or goat—part of the booty—unable to keep up and mercilessly left to die in the scorching heat. The vultures were already assembling, waiting to tear these unfortunates to pieces, as soon as, or even before, life had left their pitiful little bodies. At last I looked back to signal my men to follow me on this track, and laughed to see the smiles of anticipation on the faces of these Rajput cavalrymen longing to try conclusions with the Mohammedan raiders.

The going was good and the enemy's tracks became ever plainer. Each man could pick his own way and at the same time be well in sight of myself and my signals. After what seemed miles of galloping I topped a rise to see in the distance this lashkar, hundreds strong, with great flocks of goats and sheep, and countless camels.

Sighting us, and completely ignorant of our numbers, they made, as all tribesmen will, for the hills, to secure the advantage of being the "upper man," and of cover. It was too far to cut them off, but it was a grand gallop. We reached the foothills only about a couple of hundred yards behind the last of them.

From above they started firing wildly at us. A narrow ravine was our only chance, so galloping into it we dismounted, and leaving the horses under its cover, ran up to its crest to see the raiders still climbing higher. Those not already hidden made good targets, and as we got down to it I saw, one by one, those fluttering, white-clad figures crumple and lie still against the hill-side. But now they had our range; bullets were spitting round us, kicking up the dust and flattening on the rocks.

Looking back at the led horses I heard the sickening sound of a bullet that hits not sand, nor rocks. A horse plunged, reared, and fell over backwards.

"Mount!" And down that ravine we clattered and crashed, now under cover. One has to think quickly on these occasions. The raiders had no idea of our numbers; to them we had disappeared. Attack as quickly as possible from a new angle was the best idea. Our ravine favoured us by circling left-handed. We reached a position directly facing their hills.

"For action dismount" again, and unhurriedly we left our horses in the ravine and kept up a steady fire on those of the raiders who could be seen. Soon, however, a too unpleasantly accurate return of our compliment meant another move. A. and his little force were following our tracks; why not try to get beyond these villains so that they come between us? This meant a gallop over the open plain and into the hills behind them—up some nullah.

They made good shooting at us as we went, but luck favoured us. Once my horse crashed to his knees, but recovered,

31

and when protected by the nullah that fortunately presented itself, I found he had been shot right through the nostrils. Our start from this last dash had been under cover so I hoped we looked like yet another body of cavalry.

Luck again, as we reached the nullah crest, to find ourselves on the other side of the enemy facing the way we had come. And now to wait for A. Through my glasses I saw, high above all the others, a patriarchal figure, hands above his head, his shouts of encouragement plainly heard above the battle-cries of the rest, oaths and imprecations hurled at us. A Rajput recruit was lying next to me— grinning with delight. "Put your sight to 700," I said. He took careful aim at the patriarch and fired. The old man kept his hands and arms uplifted. I was trying to remember who it was in Biblical history held aloft his arms, the lowering of them to mean defeat for his army.

"Sight 800," I said.

The figure swayed, tottered, and crumpled. Down the slope it went head over heels, out of sight.

Now was heard firing from the far side. A. had arrived and we had them between us. To climb higher for them meant coming under our crossed fire in the open. The raiders had had enough. Down the ravine I had first used they came in full flight, some, leaders, I suppose, on their riding camels, the rest on foot, a howling, frenzied mob making across the open to the far side of the valley, in hundreds, making a line which would pass some four hundred yards from a small mound standing up in the desert. And now, what to do with my twenty delighted Rajputs?

"Mount!" again; and a gallop to this mound to fire all the ammunition we had left into the retreating horde. A few replied as the winging bullets overhead testified.

Then, silence!

The looted sheep, goats and camels, were now wandering all over the desert between A. and myself. Giving orders to my men to round these up, I was trotting across to greet A. followed by my orderly. White-clad corpses marked our way.

"Look, Sahib," said my orderly, pointing to one lying on his face, his head nothing but a bloody mask.

I looked. A few yards farther on something made me look again. The "corpse" had reached for his rifle and was swinging it towards me. He became a "corpse" again as my orderly turned as well, galloped up to him and pinned him with his lance to the ground, where he twisted like any butterfly pinned to cork by a thoughtless boy.

Over two thousand five hundred sheep and two hundred and fifty camels were collected.

What worried me among the spoils was a complete British officer's kit, sleeping-bag, everything. Even some mess stores, including a bottle of whisky and cigarettes! There were boxes and boxes of Government ammunition, bayonets, equipment. The explanation comes later.

Though I did not know it then, that cloud of dust on the horizon had not been incorrectly diagnosed by the levies.

A. and I rode over the battlefield.

Searching for the "patriarch" I found him still alive with a neat, round hole straight through his stomach, staring with glazing eyes into the sky. He died very soon. A., his levies and infantry platoon had done marvellous work hemming in our raiders. Only three were wounded; one of my troopers also, slightly, and two horses killed. We counted over forty enemy dead before our return to the water-hole.

As the sun was setting, over the shoulder we went into the ravine to blessed water; and to compete with those thousands of sheep, goats and camels was no easy matter.

It was over. A. and I shared a sheep, the whisky and the cigarettes. The bleating, gurgling and grunting of our newly acquired live-stock made night hideous.

Before darkness came I selected two camels and two goats as personal property; the former to carry my belongings, the latter to supply me with milk. For weeks they did so until I myself, with these my friends, tasted defeat instead of victory. I christened these ships of the desert P. and O., the goats, Fortnum and Mason. P. carried my kit. O. carried Fortnum and partner. I can see those nodding heads now confidently looking at me from O.'s back.

At last I sought my sleeping-bag, but to think too much.

Nobody knew where we were; we had no doctor, only our first field-dressings. And what, should the day have gone against us?

What was Juma Khan thinking about, too? He had escaped with the mob. He told me later when I met him. They must have had scores of wounded. "But why think of useless questions?" I asked myself. Said good night to the North Star, and fell asleep.

CHAPTER 4

The Captured German

I know of nothing more desolate than a camping ground "the morning after the night before." This one was particularly depressing.

A sheep or goat had been divided by every two men, and the flocks in their hundreds and the camels captured the day before made sunrise hideous with their ceaseless animal talk.

However, we got them going back down that tortuous ravine, hour after hour, myself with my twenty lancers "making good" as well as possible our homeward trek towards Seistan, and from time to time galloping ahead to investigate the meaning of rifle shots which turned out to be nothing but expressions of triumph on the part of our accompanying Seistani camel levies. How we cursed them!

P. and O., my share of the loot, headed the convoy—P. carrying my kit while O. followed with Fortnum and Mason comfortably ensconced on his back. I wonder if they envied the rest of their kind struggling along through the dust in their unhappy hundreds.

A tired cavalcade straggled in to the water-hole on the homeward route that night, and it was difficult to prevent all those thirsty animals from stampeding and ruining what putrid water existed there. We had sent a report of our doings ahead by camel to Seistan, so settled down for the night. A. and I sat up late, long after our "circus" had bleated its last bleat and gurgled its last gurgle and a great full moon assisted by a cool breeze had turned that silent emptiness into fairyland. It seemed so unreal, yesterday's struggle and confusion of infinitesimal units—we had been responsible for sending at least fifty of these units to an emptiness even more silent than this. And by what right? Why had somebody started this meaningless strife all over the world? Some assassin at Serajevo. . . . But what a scrap! And what a hunt!

In the morning P. and O., with their great disdainful faces and beautiful eyes, lurched groaning and complaining to their feet. Fortnum & Company had provided milk for the tea. Off we went. It was fairyland no longer.

Some hours later a cavalry patrol from Seistan met us, having ridden day and night, bringing orders; I was to turn back with my Rajputs through our late battlefield and on to Dehana-Baghi. Raiders of another clan were reported farther west of that place. Disentangling our transport, I said good-bye to A.

And so, he to his adventures and I to mine.

An uneventful three days' ride followed with a compact little unit—a troop of cavalry and its attendant hundred odd camel transport with forage and rations. Through that ravine again, back to the water-hole, the bleak, lifeless and barren day followed always by that fairyland night.

No sign of the "watcher," though doubtless he was not far off, and every precaution must be taken. Back over the battlefield. . . . No sign of a corpse now; only a collection of drowsy vultures on the rocks, gorged after their hideous meal.

Another two days across that vast valley and we entered Dehnna-Baghi, our farthest western post on the fringe of the great Lut desert in Central Persia. Here was actually a little mud bungalow, fresh, clear water, and a neatly laid out little camp; also from the single strand of telegraph wire I could get my orders. A night in great comfort lay before me with the little garrison of a company of Indian Infantry with its British officers, old friends.

Things had gone hard with them, and the mystery of that cloud of dust on the horizon which A. and I had watched was cleared up. But how on earth could our levies have known what it meant? Trouble, they had said; and trouble it was. The Company Commander, B., told me the story as we settled down for the evening in the comfort of his little mud hut.

With his subaltern and about a hundred rifles he had set out to intercept Juma Khan and his lashkar, and on that very evening when A. and I were scanning the distance they came face to face with these ruffians over a spur in the hills. Without any attempt at parley a determined attack was made on them.

Hopelessly outnumbered and caught in the open, B. and his command got down to what cover they might to fight it out. Closer and closer came the tribesmen, hotter and hotter the fire. One after another B.'s men were shot, one of the first to fall being his gallant subaltern.

In that pitiless sun, with no earthly hope of reinforcements, resolved to fight until the last round was expended, their plight can be imagined—the whistle and scream and sickening smack of the bullets, the shouts and curses of the tribesmen, the savagery of it all.

As the sun was setting, the tribesmen drew their swords, left cover, a half moon of frenzied, bloodthirsty fanatics, and charged down on those gallant riflemen. B. and his men, however, held their ground and this charge never came home.

About that time a sand-storm set in, and the enemy, working round in the rear, captured our transport containing all the reserve ammunition, supplies and kit. Content with this they left B. and about forty of his men who were still unhurt, having no further stomach for fighting such a tough outfit.

They then moved southwards but their triumph was short-lived; by the next morning they were a howling mob of fugitives leaving loot, stolen cattle and camels, and their dead in the hands of my old friend A. and myself. But what colossal luck we had! What a fight our riflemen put up! Still, that was to be expected of such a fine regiment.

My orders were due the following morning. I could not help thinking of that night in the ravine, and of the sharing of whisky and cigarettes with A. to the tune of that goat and camel orchestra. Did those unexpected luxuries belong to that cheery subaltern whose death hid in that very dust cloud we watched? Poor chap! He would be the first to hope that we enjoyed them.

Instead of coming in the morning, orders came through that

night for myself and my troop to march at dawn for a water-hole, Nasratabad Sipi—a tiny oasis reported to be already occupied by Baluchi raiders, thirty miles south-west. Rounding a spur of the Dehana valley, whence a view was obtained of the oasis, we extended in line, about thirty yards between each man, and galloped in— to find not a living soul! Many times our spies would thus try to justify their existence by sending in false reports. There was nothing to do but to camp here under the few scraggy trees by the putrid water, detail a patrol to report that all was quiet, and ask for further orders. No harm was done, for the horses needed a rest.

Farther to the west, as far as could be seen, stretched that barren Lut desert. The camel-men crossing it from west to east would whisper in their animals' ears before starting, "Lut," "Lut," hoping they would drink their fill.

Those ragged herd men with their affection for their camels appealed to me. Even more so those disdainful, snarling, gurgling ships of the desert. They would stop, lie down and scatter their burdens, and just die, as though to spite everybody and everything; they could be bothered no more with life, it seemed, would leave their little two-legged guardians and go.

Over the Lut tall, whirling columns of sand were constantly travelling, pillars rising into the sky. One of these drifted towards our camp when I was sitting in my bivouac tent, on my sleeping-bag. On it came, just missing my horse lines, straight at me, lifted my little tent instantly, ropes, pegs and all, and carried it hundreds of yards over the desert, leaving me clutching what I could of my belongings in the open; and my cheery Rajputs had great fun chasing the scattered treasures.

My patrol returned in a few days with orders to leave for Dehana-Baghi again. At the remains of an old fort at Nasratabad Sipi we had amused ourselves by digging, and had unearthed a beautifully carved, incredibly ancient cannon. Its history is unknown, but to this day it holds a place of honour on the verandah of the officers' mess of my regiment in India, a souvenir of the desert.

Back I went to Dehana-Baghi and its little mud hut, to

the companionship of the Company Commander, and the anticipation of what was to come next. Somehow there was a charm in being entirely on one's own, in defying these sinister "watchers," in the uncertainty of every day. And it was pleasant to see these Indian troopers, men with whom one had served in peace time for ten years before the war: like a big family. Could one ask for more?

Here, at Dehana-Baghi, news came that our convoys between Nushki and Robat were being constantly attacked. The raider trouble had become so acute that a General Officer had been sent out to Robat with orders to deal with these tribes as best he might. The Cordon had been formed to prevent the German parties crossing into Afghanistan, and we must not be distracted by these tribesmen.

This General Officer was Dyer, one of the finest soldiers I have ever known—hail-fellow-well-met with all ranks and fearless to a degree; the man whose name became associated after the war with the Amritsar incident. The man who saved countless lives there, faced by a situation which would have daunted a weaker character.

Like the sportsman he was, he made his way over the desert in a motorcar! At Robat he collected a few men, and with, a host of camels and his car bluffed his way two hundred miles south of Robat right to the raiders' stronghold, the fort at Khwash, and occupied it. This astounding feat he has ably described in his book, The Raiders of the Sarhad (Sarhad meaning a border or frontier).

There he was, surrounded by thousands of well-armed tribesmen, with a tiny force. Every available man and horse from all the posts was under orders to get down to Khwash as soon as possible before his bluff was called. He had cowed these brigand leaders by sheer courage. "Where was this white chief's army?" they were saying. So from all directions we were converging on Khwash as fast as we could. As luck had it, we were just in time.

Tied down to the pace of our food-carrying convoys we made the best speed we could. As regards distance, it was merely the customary ride of a hundred miles or so, through nothing-ness, as usual, and terrific heat. At Robat, on the way, I joined up with the remainder of the Rajput squadron and another of our squadrons from Seistan, bound, as I was for Khwash, the centu-ries-old fort and stronghold of Jiand Khan, lord and chief of all the Sarhad tribes surrounding the intrepid Dyer and his handful of men. With the squadrons were officers of my regiment who had been north of Bandan and Neh, and it was good to meet again for the first time since 1914.

Through this Dante's Inferno we moved, the twin peaks of the volcano Koh-i-Taftan ever in sight; a story-book setting, reminding one of Alan Quatermain; and here may be told the story of the capture of the German officer, Winkelmann, just as J. told it to me during this journey towards Khwash. The squadron ahead—a cloud of dust; the one behind us—a line of extended horsemen; the sharp sound of an occasional hoof striking a rock; the sun catching now and again the lance points: such was the setting of his adventurous tale.

J. was in command of the post at Neh when a spy reported that a party of twenty men, three of whom were Europeans, had arrived at a little oasis known as Deh-Salem (the village of Peace), fifty miles south-west, well out in the formidable Lut. Farther west from Deh-Salem lies an absolutely waterless re-gion stretching to Khabis, whose snow-capped mountains can in winter be just seen a hundred miles distant.

Setting out with two troops at midday, by nightfall J. had reached a water-hole twenty miles on his way, where another of our spies confirmed the news.

Nobody can cross this country without halting at these wide-ly separated wells, and from north to south of the Cordon each well had its spy, so that even in this vastness one or more of our posts would gain news of strangers and take suitable action.

There were still more than twenty miles to be covered, but by hard riding J. and his men at dawn were within a mile of Deh-Salem. Extending in two lines, the troops galloped straight through the little oasis but found no enemy; the birds had just flown, and were making for some hills about three miles away.

A race ensued, but our horses were exhausted after their forty miles forced march, and it was impossible to cut the enemy off before they reached a commanding position in the hills.

"For action dismount." Deducting his horse-holders, J. had but twenty men, so after the first exchange of fire he decided to split up his command, surround the raiders, and deprive them from access to water.

The day passed, and at night the separate posts were drawn in closer, but the German party had managed to worm their way through in the darkness by one of the many ravines in the hills. Enemy reinforcements were reported to be arriving; J. and his men, who had been without food or water for a day and a night, therefore put Deh-Salem into a state of defence, having sent word back to Neh. The report, however, proved to be false. The next night one of our sentry groups saw a man approaching stealthily. After a struggle he was overpowered, and turned out to be a German—Winkelmann. He owed his capture to having stayed behind to cover the retreat of his comrades; lost in the darkness, he was creeping in, exhausted, for water. The remainder of his party, with the exception of one or two casualties from our rifle fire, were known later to have gone all the way back across the Lut to Kirman, which they reached in an absolutely beaten condition, suffering severely from thirst and exposure.

Winkelmann claimed to be a lieutenant of the Potsdam Guards Artillery. At any rate, he was a sportsman; and that is how his war ended.

That was an enjoyable march down to Khwash. We knew that the news of our move in that direction, followed in a day or so by what infantry could be spared, was being passed with lightning speed from "watcher" to "watcher" to Jiand Khan and his braves. Needless to say, our own spies were spreading rumours of great armies coming to support Dyer. A moving speck in the far distance would mean an enemy camel scout, lost in a few minutes as he wheeled to carry the tidings.

Old Suleiman, old man syce, had met me again at Robat, coming along with the squadron from Seistan. That wrinkled little grey-bearded face wreathed in smiles at the idea of accompanying me again. Riding along with the transport on my second charger, smoking a cigarette, with a joke and a laugh for everyone, he might have been on his way to the polo ground in cantonments. My horse and saddlery, mysteriously, were perfectly groomed and cleaned.

At last, passing through a winding defile, in the distance, in the middle of a wide valley, we saw the turrets of Khwash fort— the green of the oasis. An hour over this level plain, and the two squadrons were watering their horses in the delightful fresh stream below the fort; our great camel convoy coming on in the distance. Over the lower slopes of the Koh-i-Taftan the water is peculiarly loathsome, tasting and smelling of sulphur; it can be imagined how we revelled in this freshness, and how the eager animals rushed to its luxury.

Dyer was as delighted to see us as we were to find him and his little force upholding their bluff. Spies and watchers had cowed Jiand and his ruffians—but only for the time; one could almost sense the unseen ones from behind the rocks of the hills to east and west; could picture their nightly conclave, their disputes as to whether this little force was to be attacked before reinforcements arrived. Dyer, however, was under no delusion about this.

CHAPTER 5

Dyer and the Fort

It was a queer situation. The tribesmen under their various leaders, realizing now that Dyer had marched right through their country with a tiny force, but with an army of camels carrying as much rations and forage as could be collected at Robat, reputed by spies of ours to be almost an army, had been gathering behind the hills that commanded Khwash with every intention of saving their faces by an overwhelming night attack.

Two squadrons of cavalry had arrived, and, as they well knew, further reinforcements of infantry were following. The defeat of Juma Khan's lashkar, greatly exaggerated, of course, as regards casualties, made them think. A kind of checkmate followed—a temporary lull, a calm that could not last.

Dyer played the first card.

Envoys were sent to the tribal leaders summoning them to a durbar (council). This they agreed to, and on the following day in they came, each with his respective "staff." Mounted on the most beautiful trotting camels, armed to the teeth, with bandoliers, modern rifles, and jewelled swords and daggers, they came from round the hills and over the horizon.

Inside the three sides of a square formed by our own men they squatted down, a semicircle of eagle-eyed, hawk-faced villains, as picturesque a gathering as one could wish. The fourth side of the square was formed by the British officers of our force, and in the centre General Dyer faced this most Biblical-looking assembly.

With the gravest attention they listened to what Dyer had to tell them, interpreted through the medium of his personal political agent, a Baluchi, whose services were invaluable to us. The import of his message was that we had no intention of interfering with them; that they had brought upon themselves, as the dupes of Germany, the casualties they had suffered; that it would be to their advantage, and to ours, to help us by refusing those German parties passage through their country. In short, he persuaded them to throw in their lot with the British Raj, emphasizing the financial appeal, and not allowing them to lose sight of the fact that refusal would mean that we should most certainly wipe them off the map.

That last made me smile. I wondered whether the minds behind those inscrutable, handsome faces realized that they could eat us in one mouthful. I wondered whether they believed that a host of British troops could possibly be spared from far-away India, as that wily Baluchi told them, to appear on the instant, as if by rubbing the magic ring, and perform this "wiping off the map."

Yet, after the time allowed for deliberation, one by one they salaamed to Dyer and swore on the Koran to be our allies; swore by their beards, their fathers and mothers, never to raise hand against us. Never should a hostile party cross their territory. Could they provide forage for our horses? In short, everything that was theirs, was ours. One of them, a spare, well-knit man, who had been eyeing me throughout this ceremony, came up, salaamed, and held out his hand.

"Sahib," he said, "I am Juma Khan."

He told me that the arrival of A. and myself on the scene was a complete surprise on that early morning, and inquired with great interest of what our force consisted.

I told him. He cursed himself when he knew, and said that he would have done for us all; but in his way he was a good fellow, Juma Khan, however many his crimes. I inquired who might be the patriarch who held his arms aloft. His uncle, he said. It was all Kismet, fate, the will of Allah.

He told me that it was no good for British officers to think that the disguise of a turban and kurta (Indian Cavalry long-coat) made them indistinguishable from their men.

Still smiling, the handsome villain gave me his hand again, and turned to mount his camel and trot off over the horizon with his little group of followers. And from that date Juma Khan and his Ismailzais never lifted hand against us.

One after the other the remaining chiefs disappeared, and we were left in our fortress—or rather theirs.

We had every reason to think that with the assistance of our new allies a cordon might be formed reaching southwards as far as the Persian Gulf. We could return, we thought, to our posts northwards as far as Birjand.

"Don't you believe it," said our wily Baluchi political.

Dyer certainly did not, and on the following morning summoned his staff to discuss the future.

It was too dangerous to return to our northern posts, leaving our lines of communication from Robat to India to the tender mercies of those brigands. Khwash must be occupied by a garrison and made tenable. The infantry came in, augmented by two mountain guns. After our durbar the tribesmen, of course, came and went as they pleased; but there was a great deal too much "coming." Now, instead of the unseen watcher, there were visible watchers on all sides, armed to the teeth, ostensibly about their own business. Outwardly peace seemed the chief note.

The first thing we did was to set about building a mud fort, one capable of holding us all and satisfying the requirements of modern warfare. The ancient stronghold of Khwash itself was useless, made as it was to repel the hand to hand fighter and invader of olden days. This was blown to pieces by gun-cotton one evening at sunset, and despite the necessity, there was a sadness in seeing those thick walls and turrets crumbling for the last time.

In our new quarters life was reasonably pleasant; rations were good, as fresh meat and eggs were easily obtainable. I had been appointed O.C. vegetable garden, and had sent to India a large order for seeds, etc., according to a catalogue that someone miraculously found. We all had our jobs; one officer acted as architect, another organized livestock and meat; a third attended to eggs and poultry. For a time affairs went well; but it took weeks by camel for any order—if lucky—to reach India, and weeks for the journey back. Transport was scarce, and soon the situation became acute as regards forage for our horses. Messengers were sent out, with the necessary payment, to neighbouring oases to induce the inhabitants to collect what we wanted; in due course they returned—all was well. The forage had been collected and stacked in the oases, and we only need send our camels to collect it.

It was just too easy to come bluffing our way in there and take everything for granted. There we were, amateur gardeners, livestock proprietors, poultry fanciers, proud as babies watching our fort grow up—and astoundingly cheery. Old man syce insisted on looking after everybody, utterly unmoved by the sequence of events. Koh-i-Taftan grumbled; everything remained as it had been since the beginning of the world. We babies laughed; the sun shone through the grilling days; but the nights were gloriously cool.

A sudden summons came one night. Dyer told us that the badly wanted, paid for, and heaped up forage in the neighbouring oases had been deliberately burnt. The babies all stopped laughing, and things happened at once.

In addition to this, a large gathering of tribesmen at the site of the burnt forage was reported. So much for the protestations, the swearing by the Koran, by the beards of their fathers and all the rest of it. Still, having bluffed out way into that country, the only thing to do was to uphold our bluff. If these oath-breakers were asking for trouble they should certainly have it.

Arrangements were made, then and there, for a column to proceed at dawn the following morning, leaving behind in our half-finished fort the minimum of troops required to protect it. Details were worked out, and in the dark of that night we separated to give the orders to our various commands.

Our burnt forage heaps, so urgently needed, and paid for in good silver Persian coin, were but a few miles away. Without this, or commandeered stuff, we were checkmated; our horses and camels would starve.

Jiand Khan and his friends had shown their hand. Their humiliation can easily be understood. They had been tricked out of their fortress, and their womenfolk had taunted them with cowardice in allowing this to happen.

Very well then, war it was, and let the best man win.

At dawn next morning Suleiman had my horse ready outside my tent, imperturbable as ever. We might have been in the paddock of some Indian racecourse, the old man seeing me off to the post. "Good luck, Sahib! " That bearded old face creased in smiles as we moved off to see what Jiand Khan and his followers were after. Did they want to fight it out?

Dyer led the infantry; behind them came the two mountain guns, and behind them again the transport. The distance was not great.

I had a squadron out on the flank of this force to get round an enemy, if engaged, or to pursue if they broke. It was a marvellous morning, and half-way to our destination we halted; the sun was by now well up and Dyer called in the Unit Commanders. Any sign of hostility or resistance and we were to go straight for it. Good orders those! The scene was set, the enemy were but an hour's trek away. We all knew what to do.

On again then, as before, from my point of view a column of dust denoting the main body, the infantry on my right, and the sun glinting on the lance points of my advance and flank patrols. A few miles down the valley, turning south, we obtained a view of our objective, the oasis, on a long commanding ridge. As our little force wheeled we could plainly see that the place was strongly held. It was obvious, too, that our being able to see this meant that the tribesmen, despite watchers and. spies, had not expected us in such force, or so soon.

Instantly our infantry deployed for attack, and the guns took up positions for action. My patrols came galloping in, and I was already mapping out the best route to get on the enemy's flank when down from the ridge came a small party on trotting camels, conspicuous with white flags. From our position we could just see them ride straight up to Dyer. Followed the "officers call."

I galloped across with my orderly, to find that the visitors consisted of Jiand Khan himself and one or two local chiefs.

Dyer was furious, and ordering a guard for those "white flaggers," directed me to go ahead in extended line, with the infantry immediately behind, straight over the ridge, where a council could be held under the palm trees. We rode straight through, pushing ahead of us those hawk-faced rascals, who were too nonplussed to resist as their king, Jiand Khan, was riding almost hand in hand with me.

Over the crest Dyer ordered the main body of the infantry and the guns to form a camp close by the water supply—good fresh water, too.

The remainder of us made for a clump of palm trees a mile distant. Here my men formed three sides of a square, in which seated themselves Jiand and his chiefs. We had seen en route the burnt stacks of our promised forage. In front of us stood a large expanse of tall, uncut crops. It was a mistake to have left our main body away there to make a camp.

The "white flaggers" seemed to increase in numbers.

Dyer dismounted, faced this assembly, and accused them direct of breaking their oath, of burning our forage, and of treachery. Jiand Khan immediately lost his temper, and in a second the scene was changed. Armed men sprang from the cover of the crops. We were surrounded.

Without an instant's hesitation Dyer seized Jiand Khan and forced him to the ground. In the wild scrimmage our men grabbed as many of the tribesmen as they could, wrenched their rifles from them and forced them into the square. Dyer's action saved the situation.

Seeing their chief disarmed, uncertain what to do, those not yet arrested faded into the tall crops and left us with our bag, which included nearly every man of importance in the Sarhad.

It was a close thing. Had those tribesmen not been momentarily cowed by the humiliation of their leader, had they then and there opened fire from their cover, they could have finished off Dyer and the rest of us easily.

Back we went to our newly formed camp with our prisoners, stripped now of their rifles, bandoliers, swords and daggers. A cavalry patrol was sent direct to Khwash to announce that we should return on the following morning and to order a suitable kraal for our captives. The oasis was combed for forage. We found plenty, and camels too.

Every possible precaution was taken that night to prevent attack by would-be rescuers. Nothing, however, happened, and in the morning we went slowly back to our "Dolls' House" in Khwash, armies of camels carrying forage. Our prisoners, to whom we had returned their jewelled swords and daggers—not their firearms—rode with us. A most ingenious kraal had been improvised, and into it they went like so many caged hawks.

So far, so good. We had our forage, we had the ringleaders. It was too much to imagine that this would close our troubles with the tribesmen and allow us to continue our search for those needles in the haystack, German intruders bound for Afghanistan.

News was instantly sent to India, two hundred miles by patrol to Robat, and thence telegraphed. We had therefore a long time to wait before orders could arrive directing the disposal of our prisoners. Great precautions were necessary, as we were soon surrounded by their friends, smarting under a sense of defeat. The longer we kept these rascals, the more it would be interpreted as a sign of weakness. While awaiting orders we spent our time completing the building of the new fort, the cavalry patrolling in all directions on the alert for hostile concentrations.

It was from Khwash fort, about this time, that my regiment lost one of its most popular and efficient officers, a former Indian civilian, attached to us for the duration of the war. A hostile party had been reported at a water-hole some distance down the valley, and he was sent out with a troop to investigate. As they approached, the enemy were plainly visible encamped there. Leading his troop at a gallop, this gallant chap went bald-headed for them. I can visualize the scene. Straight through they went, lances down, spearing some half-dozen, their leader accounting for one with his sword.

This weapon is popularly supposed to slice off heads, arms and legs when wielded like a battle-axe. As a matter of fact, unless the edge is kept exactly horizontal and used with a drawing,

cutting motion, no more harm is done than if it were a walk-
ing-stick. It is an expert's job. But when used with a firm grip
as a pointer it is absolutely deadly. There is a sickening groan or
grunt and it passes into and through a body like butter.

They wheeled, and came back through again. This time our
friend was shot at close quarters right through the body. Several
more of the enemy were speared; the remainder reached the
cover of the hills.

A gallant episode, but an end to the life of one of the best.

These tribesmen, like most others, are very difficult to find
in the open. They have a very healthy respect for the lance and
sword. One quite appreciates their objection. A steel point is a
peculiarly unpleasant thing when it is doing its best to find its
way through your system.

With these, too, as with most other uncivilized peoples, to
be taken prisoner means certain death preceded by torture and
mutilation. They will even dig up and chop into small pieces the
dead bodies of their foes. To pass into the next world with a full
complement of limbs and organs to them is paradise. Hence the
ghastly mutilation, indescribable, practised by those savages.

A particularly loathsome incident occurred with Juma Khan's
lashkar the night before our encounter. One of the slaves, a female, could no longer keep up with them; she was almost due
to give birth to a child. A circle was formed and the wretched
woman was slit up, the child wrenched out. ... I wished, when
I heard of it, that patriarch had taken longer to die. I was glad
that man was pinned to the ground. I can still see his hands fren-
ziedly gripping the shaft that had pierced him, his feet with their
toes curled in agony.

We were all in our "Dolls' House" Mess one evening discussing the future and what orders would come from India; Suleiman, as usual, hovered round, smiling as we laughed, waiting to
get us drinks. Our orderly came in, saluted, and told me that the
General Sahib wished to see me immediately.

CHAPTER 6
Prisoners & Escapes

I found Dyer in his quarters with his Staff Officer and the Baluchi political agent. Orders had arrived at last from India.

The situation in our fort was becoming daily more acute. Our cage, containing nearly every leading man in the Sarhad, was more than a white elephant. Their followers were watching day and night from every conceivable piece of cover, and would certainly attack in masses before long. They knew well enough what a stalemate it was, and interpreted only as weakness our forced inaction. Rations and forage were running short. Further supplies could only be obtained by a sortie in force, and a sortie meant a weakening of our small garrison, and the enemy's opportunity to dash to the rescue.

Here was an end to inaction, and Dyer expounded to me what had been decreed. Four hundred Hazara Pioneers, a famous corps of the Indian Army, were en route from Nushki to Robat. Dyer had been ordered to get his prisoners at all costs from Khwash to Robat, at which place they were to be handed over to the Hazaras, who would convey them back over that four hundred miles of desert to India to be kept at His Majesty's expense until the "conclusion of hostilities."

Two hundred odd miles to Robat through this desolation those precious prisoners must be taken with what escort could be spared! There was no doubt whatever that this escort would be attacked. Cats and mice were nothing to this. The mouse is usually shadowed and played with by one cat; this particular mouse had to cross a kitchen inhabited by a whole feline family.

51

I was detailed for this duty, and the maximum escort was allotted to me to carry it out. We were to march just before dawn on the following morning.

Dyer wished me good luck as I went to give my overnight orders to the escort. The "watchers" watched, Koh-i-Taftan grumbled, and the mice turned in to get what sleep they could before crossing that kitchen floor.

At the appointed time old man syce stood holding my horse, impassive as ever. He, of course, could not accompany me.

The column of camels carrying the prisoners and our rations was ready to march, the cavalry and infantry escort with them, and the advance guard had signalled all clear as far as the first ridge. Suleiman smiled and wished me good luck—which he had done before as far as this charger of mine was concerned; she was a weight-carrying polo pony, and I was mounting her then for the finals of the Quetta Senior Polo Tournament early in 1914. Poor "Strawberry"! It was a different kind of tournament now.

We had some twenty-five miles to cover before reaching our first halt, and at the pace we were tied to, that of the camels, it was sunset before we reached that water-hole. Up to then not one "cat" had showed a claw—but we had definitely left the wainscoting.

My Second-in-Command, G. and I, selected the most favourable piece of ground for our bivouac while the animals were being watered and our patrols watched the surrounding country.

Before dark we settled down. The lesser chiefs sat within a palisade of barbed wire; five infantrymen with loaded rifles and fixed bayonets guarded each fifteen-yard side of this square. Jiand Khan, his son, and his uncle—undoubtedly the biggest villains of them all—I placed in charge of the cavalry quarter-guard itself.

Pickets were posted to command possible approaches. After their food all the prisoners were bound hand and foot and warned that the first to try to get on his feet would be instantly killed.

Night fell; G. and I had our meal and sat talking, discussing our next day's trek. It was pitch dark, utterly black. A final walk around our little show to make sure that all was in order, and that the sentries clearly understood that any attempt at rising on the part of the prisoners was to be instantly dealt with by the bayonet, and any attack from outside to mean the same thing. Then we lay down to sleep. The situation could hardly be called conducive to rest, but towards early morning I dozed off.

The next thing I remember was an inferno of sounds. Shouts and yells from tribesmen, rifle shots, the frantic drumming of our cavalry horses' feet in their endeavour to break their picketing ropes and stampede, the air thick with dust and sand in the blackness.

Seizing my revolver, I stumbled through this hellish din to where I had last seen the prisoners surrounded by barbed wire and bayonets. The shock was severe. Under cover of their voluminous garments they had managed to fumble themselves quietly free of their bonds and at a prearranged sign, flinging those filthy robes on the wire, had crashed through it with their hellish shouting and screaming, having succeeded in stampeding the horses.

By now, scattered wide in that velvet darkness in ravines and watercourses of which every inch was known to them, already out of possible range of recapture, it was utterly useless to begin to organize any pursuit. Rescuing parties, hundreds strong, might cover every and any exit were they even visible.

I groped my way to the cavalry quarter-guard. There sat Jiand Khan and his son and uncle, three of my men holding lances at their throats. Thank God for that at least! I thought, feeling physically sick with disappointment and impotence. What had happened, had happened, and nothing could restore the lost prisoners. It meant failure, ghastly, dreadful failure, nothing short of that!

A picked patrol of my men were sent back to Dyer with instructions to get there by hook or by crook, and go like hell, darkness or no darkness.

It was childish and useless to see red and relieve one's feelings on those twenty fixed bayonets who had allowed such a disaster to occur. I could only await orders, as we had only three prisoners, even if the three really important ones. We might even have to rush back to Khwash fort with our now comparatively strong escort to help against an attack. Anything, I thought, as I brooded over the position, would be better than this bitter feeling of disappointment and failure.

Back, post-haste, came orders from Dyer, sent by a fresh cavalry patrol. He, Dyer, was setting out at once with a small force by a route twenty miles north of ours—we were to march at once with our remaining prisoners northwards to meet him, a small oasis being nominated as our joint camp for that following night.

The Sarhad was of course ablaze with hostility. I can remember no day in my life more heartsick than this of our northern trek. Recriminations against that prisoners' guard would never get the prisoners back. In short, I was the villain responsible for the disaster.

The Indian Army, as with others, contains every kind of soldier. There is the ambitious, intent on staff appointments, leading to the seats of the mighty. There are the picturesque and sociable, intent on gaining soft jobs by being A.D.C.s to those already mighty, and in many cases never returning to their regiments. There are the "good boys" who cling like leeches to every rule and regulation, whose life is one long, perfectly regular, horizontal line in which is no laugh, and therefore no real camaraderie or touch with the rank and file—in short, lacking deplorably that human element without which no disciplined army could exist. There are, too, the disgruntled ones, to whom life and their seniors are ever unjust. These are anathema. My mind ran on these types in my disappointment, possibly filling the hours by trying to justify my existence and find my own category. Looking back through years of peace-time service I could remember many occasions on which I had erred, and the stern admonitions of my commanding officers, while I stood trembling "on the mat." What good fellows they had all been—Damn—I liked them, and my men and my horses.

Most men, in Dyer's position, would have made my disappointment unbearable with recriminations. But he was not that kind. He simply sent his Staff Officer across to me with orders to push on as hard as I could with the remaining prisoners while he demonstrated towards the enemies' hill fastnesses with what force he could muster. This meant my escort being cut down to one troop of cavalry and some twelve infantrymen.

Dyer, with his little force, was already settled down in a perimeter (entrenched) camp. We settled down into a similar camp of our own so situated that, in case of attack, we might cover the danger zones with our crossed fire.

The night passed quietly, and before the following dawn we were again en route. We covered well over thirty miles that day, urging the camels through the defiles, and advancing by a series of moves, these consisting of a distance as far ahead as our cavalry point and a few infantrymen, taking successive positions on high ground on the flanks, could signal back to us the "all clear."

Jiand Khan and his relations rode, impassive as ever, on their camels within a ring of lances, threatened with instant death in the event of attempted escape or rescue. We were well out of range and touch with anybody. On the morrow we had to pass through a fearsome defile for at least twenty miles, for the most part with precipitous sides, narrow, in some places never reached by sunlight; silent, threatening, and reeking with danger. That night we camped near the local water, not far from the entrance; we entrenched ourselves, every man throughout the night keeping his loaded rifle on the parapet. All conceivable precautions against surprise were taken.

G. and I sat talking late, taking it in turns every hour or so to go round the defences. I found myself unable to shake off a definite premonition of disaster; it seemed impossible to fight against this abominable depression. It was exactly as if someone kept saying, "It's no good; do whatever you may, you cannot overcome the impossible. How can you, with your tempting bait, without miraculous luck, get through?"

The country-side were out, to a man, to rescue their chief and his relations. Not only the coming day, with that fearsome defile to be passed, but at least two further days to be marched after that, laid heavily on my mind.

Those dark thoughts quickly cleared, however, as the first rays of the sun saw us wending our way towards the danger-point. We would get through all right and deliver our goods to the waiting Hazaras.

Yet even that could not wipe out what had happened.

CHAPTER 7

Ambushed

The defile swallowed us up—we were so small a force, compelled to regulate our pace to that of the slipping, stumbling camels. Horsemen cannot climb the sheer walls of rock that hemmed us in. Our few infantrymen were doing their best. The tribesmen, sure-footed as goats, could make rings round us, and above us—unseen.

The high, glaring sun made the heat intense. We came to a kind of basin, an opening, in the ravine about a quarter of a mile long and over a hundred yards wide. The infantry were almost at the far end, and I was trotting ahead to investigate the route in front of us.

Suddenly this little amphitheatre became alive with yells and shots. Here and there white-clad figures darted from rock to rock. Some of my men, as they ran to cover, collapsed and lay still. Wrenching my horse round, I galloped back towards the head of the column, where the prisoners were; then came a shock, as though someone had kicked me, followed by the feeling of warmth trickling down my leg. The din was like hell let loose. In front a confused view of struggling horses and camels.

Suddenly poor Strawberry gave in—she struggled on for a few strides and over we went in a heap together.

Disentangling myself, I got to my feet half dazed. Instantly the shock of a terrific blow in the back spun me round like a top and hurled me to the ground—then darkness.

Reality returned with waves of warmth streaming down my back, which I could not see, and down my sleeve, which I could. It showed red.

I remember looking stupidly at that sleeve, which did not seem to belong to me at all. The khaki was soaking it up, this red stain, and it was running down the fingers at the end. Just above the elbow was the neatest little hole. This warm sensation was going on down my legs, too.

I recollected what had happened, and sat up to look round. A white-clad figure on the opposite slope pointed his rifle at me. . . . The bullet hit the rock inches away.

Up the slope towards me ran the gallant G. Another bullet spat from that rifle, and round he spun, falling beside me.

Again all became a blur—darkness—nothingness.

Later, back came reality; the whole world seemed one dull ache, the heat grew fiendish. What on earth had happened? I was behind a small tamarisk bush; there had been an ambush, but where were my men and why couldn't I get up? My struggle to do this brought an instantaneous crack from the opposite hillside and a bullet kicked up the sand between my legs. ... If our prisoners had been killed nothing mattered now. . . .

Thank heaven G. must have collected the survivors, and that accounted for the shots and triumphant yells and curses farther up the defile. He had vanished. These sounds died down; and then could be heard, all around, men, horses, and camels dying. A sort of dreadful sighing and groaning. ... A terrible smell, too, of blood. Soon this ceased and something came between me and the sun. ... It was poor Strawberry, standing there with her stomach ripped right across by a bullet, my saddle twisted sideways, the sword hanging hilt downwards half out of its sheath. There she stood, puzzled, a pitiful picture. A little later she staggered away in search of water, and died. This was indeed the end of the world. A violent effort to get up caused agonies of pain and a renewal of the warm sensation in my limbs; I fainted again for a time. When consciousness returned, the noise of the action continuing farther up the defile greeted me. It was evening, and I felt, as indeed I was, a mass of congealed blood. It served, at any rate, as a kind of poultice.

Once again my attentive friend across the way sent a bullet whizzing past my head. That he missed me so many times seems uncommonly lucky.

Silence again intervened; my thoughts wandered and sank to dull indifference; I might as well join that company of dead scattered round. As the sun descended a flapping noise attracted my attention. One by one vultures were arriving; one loathsome bird had actually perched on a rock quite close.

Even that did not matter. My little force must have been wiped out. I hoped to God that the prisoners were too.

Another warm trickle cheered me with the thought that dying cannot go on for ever. . . . But it might take too long. As darkness fell those tribesmen would come to mutilate the dead and torture the wounded. My right arm, unhurt, groped for my revolver which was still, luckily, in its holster. One must make every effort to keep conscious; let them come creeping up, have five shots point-blank at the nearest, and save the sixth to put oneself beyond their damned torture. . . . That is what it feels like to lie out on a hill-side with death, in the back of beyond. There is nothing heroic about it at all. What seems to be the inevitable is acceptable.

Yet it was not inevitable after all, this time.

"Sahib—Sahib! " came a voice from behind a rock on my right. I could see the face of Dafadar (Sergeant) Sheikh Haider peering at me. A superman this at tent-pegging and trick-riding—one of the finest types of Indian cavalry soldiers. "Can you get to me? " he asked.

Impossible, I indicated.

"Sahib, I have three men here. I will order them to open fire and I will come across to carry you away."

The rifles cracked rapidly; the gallant dafadar rushed across and picked me up like a feather. The next thing I remember was finding my head on his shoulder, my trickles running over him, and that bearded face laughing down at me.

He carried me to a little pocket of the hills where I found G. with a gaping wound in his neck and shoulder, my Indian officer with a bullet through his leg, a few men still untouched, and about a dozen horses. On the edge of this shelter were posted those who could use a rifle. In the middle was a pool of the foulest water I ever saw—but it was fluid.

Our little post were pushed out and covered the rest, who dragged in the dead, spending the night burying them.

At dark the yelling tribesmen closed in again, waiting for their prey; they could not get at us past those covering posts—or rather preferred to wait.

The sickening truth was revealed that of the prisoners Jiand Khan and his son, whose escort were shot dead to a man, had escaped; the third had been shot.

I have still to experience a more heart-breaking night than that. We had a little food, Indian rations, grain, and that foul water. We did our best to aid one another with first field dressings, having no doctor. Occasionally came a challenge from our posts on the sky-line, a shot, and a renewal of those yells. And thus, exactly, passed the following day and night.

By noon on the third day the horses' feed-bags were emptied—our handfuls of grain had gone. We were just about at the finish. That sickening ache and still more sickening disappointment were driving me mad. We must have been a queer-looking lot, stretched out there in the sun, covered with flies and reeking with blood.

The ever cheery G. and I consulted, and decided that as soon as it was dark we would mount the horses and go straight for the nearest post, forty miles away, where was a small fort garrisoned by levies. I was to be lifted on to a horse with a man on each side riding close to hold me up. In case we were attacked we would just go straight through, and the lucky ones would survive.

Down went the sun—I felt as if I had been lying on my back all my life. Quietly the horses were saddled. Since midday there had been comparative peace. We were out of sight in our pocket, and well under cover. The moon came up—it was time to go. The men mounted noiselessly; the gallant Sheikh Haider lifted me on to my horse. Sitting on the four wounds which a bullet must make passing through one's seating accommodation, I was not happy. Two horsemen ranged themselves alongside to hold me, then came G, then the remnants of the troop.

Off we went at a snail's pace through the end of the defile, expecting every instant a rush of the hostile tribesmen; our departure seemed to make as much noise as the "Cheltenham Flyer" going through Reading. Gradually, as the minutes passed, we realized that the enemy must have made off, fearing reinforcements.

On and on, at a crawl as it seemed, we moved, while the moonlit crags and boulders swayed and swung against a starry sky, and from time to time the troopers on my right and left closed in to push me back straight into the saddle.

Hour after hour passed, and immediate danger was over. But that terrible sense of failure haunted me. . . . How wonderful it would have been to be still escorting those prisoners, to have won through! Here was I, with this rotten sleeve holding in a cake of blood an arm which did not even seem to belong to me . . . this stupid little hole in one's back . . . everything. . . . It was the end of the world. I wished it had been the end of mine.

Centuries later the sun rose to find us still creeping on towards a water-hole where we stopped to drink. G. lay down in the sand; I stayed stuck on to my saddle, not relishing being un-gummed. G. was still asleep as we mustered to go on.

Seventeen hours from the time of leaving that ghastly defile we trailed into that levies fort. Then came string beds, clean, fresh water, friends, and the sleep of utter exhaustion.

Next morning a doctor from Robat arrived—where they had learned by means of the inexplicable desert news transmission of our plight. Followed a filthy period of removal of blood-caked clothes which did not want to come off. We had to get back to Headquarters at Kacha, just above Robat, thirty to forty miles away, and a hasty mustering of camels followed as soon as we had rested.

One camel, equipped on each side of its hump with long coffin-shaped baskets in which a man could lie, carried G. and myself; others similarly fitted carried those who could ride no longer. And so we lurched along, hanging on as best we could on those hellish rocking-horses.

Kacha, at last, the mud huts housing its little infantry garrison, was a welcome sign of civilization. High above us they stood, and we were carried up on stretchers by a party waiting in readiness. Un-gummings, probings and dressings were not made any more pleasant by the fact that medical supplies were woefully short.

What with the pain from wounds and exhaustion, and my desperate disappointment, sleep was impossible. Those tribesmen's yells rang unceasingly in one's ears. I remember my evidence being taken down, my account of the disaster. I signed it—I was in utter disgrace.

Yet there is always something bright in even the murkiest situation. During those horrible nights, every one of the hundred times that I turned to see the star-studded sky through the open door of the hut, there came a voice, "It's all right, Sahib, we are here," speaking in Hindustani. Those who were left of my men had formed a voluntary guard, taking it in turns to watch the open door of my hut, night after night. Can the reader wonder at my affection for them?

Soon came a day when at the horrible wound-dressing time that doctor, who had trekked night and day to our help, was overjoyed. My arm had come to life again; those emaciated white things that used to be fingers moved themselves. G. and I were definitely beginning to heal.

A camel convoy was being assembled to go back those four hundred miles to Nushki—over that raider-infested country. This was to be commanded by myself from one side of a camel's hump in a basket, with G. balancing me on the other side. Other camels similarly burdened with wounded, and what few rifles could be spared as an escort, completed the outfit.

We had to march entirely by night, spending the days at water-holes as best we might. It was a horrible journey, averaging twenty miles a night at the snail's pace of the camels, with cheerful and repeated rumours of a raiding-party ready to attack us.

Lying in the "coffin," heaving unevenly in time with the slouching camel, anticipating a rush of yelling tribesmen, one counted the minutes of those weeks. What earthly chance was there with the days in the sun and sand, dreading the thought of the coming night's jolting journey forcing one's wounds open again?

Yet, as ever, the bright spot arrived.

During the weeks in the doctor's hands at Kacha, a convoy had arrived from Khwash, the intervening country now being clear, and in it was the old man syce, with my second charger.

Every night of our trek to Nushki he rode alongside my camel, his little figure outlined against the sky as I looked over the edge of my basket. Nothing was too much for him to do to make the heat of the days bearable.

It seemed a lifetime, but Nushki was reached, despite rumours and alarms, without incident.

Civilization again—a railway—and good-bye to those patient but uneasy camels. To see, even to hear, an engine puffing its way up and over the mountains towards Quetta was a delightful experience.

I must confess that I felt almost done for. The last four hundred miles had been a nightmare. Everything I owned had been lost in that disastrous ambush. P. and O., Fortnum and Mason, had been engulfed.

Back again then to Quetta, G. and I in a perfectly good railway carriage, old man syce in attendance. It seemed more than two lifetimes since I had come down that tortuous mountain railway to Nushki, to the adventure of being swallowed up in the Baluchistan desert. Swallowed and thrown up again—that was what it came to. Failure is a filthy thing to bite on.

Back again to cantonments. No yelling raiders here— sympathetic medical officers decreed a return to England to fill out that arm and clear up those holes in a disappointed body, not to mention those in a disappointed mind. If only I could have got those prisoners through!

Dyer, reinforced by the four hundred Hazaras, was after the raiders through that Alan Quatermain country.

The Commanding Officer of my regiment, who was at the depôt in Quetta, sent for me just before I was leaving for England to say good-bye and to sympathize with me in the trouble into which I had got.

He was a good chap, that Commanding Officer. He told me that I was young, and that I should live it down. I couldn't help saying that I considered myself damned lucky to be alive at all.

1917

"The ball no question makes
of ayes and noes."

CHAPTER 1

Back to the War

October, 1917. Two months since leaving London; the last
lap of the journey, by train, over the Scinde desert from Karachi,
with Quetta as my destination on the morrow.

The bleak Baluchistan ranges, with their barren, jagged peaks,
towards which we were making, brought back memories. Away
to the west, hundreds of miles beyond that skyline, lay Seistan
and Persia. I was to report for orders on arrival at my Regimental Depôt. I was sure to go back and be lost in that immensity
of nothingness once more. Wondering what had happened there
since I had left in such a sorry plight, I wanted to go back. There
is a strange fascination about the desert lands, with their utter
lack of life, movement or trace of civilization. There was that first
four hundred miles due west to Robat, where Baluchistan and
Persia meet; then turning north some thousand miles, along the
western border of Afghanistan until, topping the Elburz Mountains, one looks down as far as the eye can see over Russian territory. What a long hack ride that would be! Our sphere ended
half-way, where we met the Cossacks, and I hoped to find that
my orders carried me so far, up to our northernmost post. In
due course, however, I was to do that ride, look over into Russian territory, and go farther still into that unknown region.

An Indian railway carriage, when you have it to yourself for a
one, two, or three days' journey, is like a kind of little temporary
home, and has a certain attraction, apart from its unavoidable
dirt. Its windows possess a variety of coverings—plain glass and
tinted glass, and a kind of grass screen for hot weather travel-

ling, to be sprinkled with water to cool the air. One can lie at full length on the bedding—carried rolled up in a canvas hold-all—and meals are taken either in the restaurant car of the train or at the more important stations.

We were crawling up into the hills, and the sun was setting. My convalescence in England had been marvellous. Life had seemed good, and now that adventure was over, leaving memories to brighten years, if necessary, in any wilderness.

This actual journey had been a long one, and unusual. There was a tiresome night railway trek down to Marseilles sitting in a crowded carriage. One of my greatest friends accompanied me, on his way back to Mesopotamia. Watching his tired face opposite me, as we sat jammed together like so many sardines in that struggle for sleep, I wondered how to make him laugh. And what a perfect fool I had been, slipping off, unseen by him, to the lavatory and shaving off my moustache. Yet it succeeded in cheering him up.

Ever higher our train climbed, up these Baluchistan hills. . . . Still in thought I laughed at memories of George Robey, that king of comedians—my little flat in Clarges Street—a hundred and one amusing things. I really was fit again, and life was pleasant.

Morning—and that long train drew up at Quetta; and I said good-bye to my little temporary home on wheels.

The old man syce, Suleiman, was there, collecting my kit in some magically quick way long before anybody else had even begun to move. Oh, yes, he was coming back with me to Persia if that was my destination. And it was. "To rejoin the East Persian Cordon immediately." Those were my orders.

Any British officer leaving for the Cordon at this time was instructed to take with him at least two months' tinned supplies, as the transport problem was too acute to provide more than the minimum for Indian troops and horses.

Two hectic days followed collecting this.

First, two yak-dans (leather trunks) had to be obtained, to fit on each side of a mule or camel, their inner sides concave to lie close to the animal's body. Filling these with tins of all sorts and shapes containing sausages, tongues, every conceivable thing, was an amusing business; and a necessary one, for in the inhospitable desert regions one must escape somehow, even if only once a week, from the everlasting diet of goat and rice. And certain precious bottles could not be omitted from the commissariat. As for clothing, there was a sheepskin coat and the long felt "Gilgit" thigh boots for which I was thankful many a time in future days.

The last corner was occupied by the tiniest of gramophones and a few records—there was not room for a large selection. Some were serious and classical, others the popular tunes of 1917; they were worth their weight in gold to me later on. To finish off the assortment, a mandolin, which I tortured at intervals for months, and even years.

Back again, then, down that tortuous railway went Suleiman and I with our baggage and two horses. Far below, once more we saw Nushki.

Strenuous attempts had been made to run motor transport from Nushki to Robat, but the shifting, wind-blown sand had defied all efforts. The railway, however, had been continued halfway for some two hundred miles to a spot called Dalbundin, a little cluster of tin huts and the very end of civilization. From this spot camel convoys left, instead of from Nushki, for the East Persian Cordon.

Here we said farewell to the trains and their familiar noises for a very long time.

The same old camel caravan was assembled with its little escort. That same old string of grumbling, swaying animals, snarling and shuffling along at their maddeningly slow pace; and so we wound out of sight of civilization, looking back to the last for one more view of what remained of it. . . . Soon it vanished; and for hour upon hour in the familiar treadmill way we rode onward, a distant jagged range seeming to come no nearer. Not only did the weird silence and lifelessness oppress us, but something I can only describe as malignant seemed to envelop us all.

Two hundred miles had to be covered before the Headquarters of the Cordon at Kacha, close to the Persian frontier, were reached. I had been able to gather little or no news about events while I was away. Until that time hardly anyone had heard of this adventure, or even knew that our troops were in this back of beyond. Therefore I had to wait until this ride was over before I could know what had happened. I wanted to go northward to the very end of our region. Southwards towards the Persian Gulf, the scene of my adventures with the raiders, all was quiet. General Dyer, with his garrison reinforced, had harried those villains mercilessly and driven them right out of their country, finally exacting from them what terms he chose to lay down. This time no question arose of future treachery. The raiders had learned their lesson, and to the time when our troops finally left, no hand was ever raised against us in those parts. I had no wish to return to those regions, and I never did.

The days passed without special event, riding all day alongside those camels with a biting wind driving the sand through one's very skin. That great waste always seemed to me the home of all the winds, where they made different sounds from any ordinary wind; possibly because of the absolute deathly stillness and space, where vision was clear and far in every direction, where it was no feat of imagination to consider life left behind, death a past event, and the present a gigantic ante-room where one waited for some tremendous finale. The winds whispered and chuckled and laughed and went screaming past—it seemed their very birthplace. One's unimportance seemed unpleasantly emphasized.

At that little speck of temporary civilization, Headquarters of the Cordon, a small group of mud huts with a little detachment of Indian Infantry, there would be a day's halt, perhaps two; a laugh with the O.C. Cordon and his garrison. And then on—but where? And for how long? Would one ever get back again to normal life? Ask those howling, laughing winds.

There was not much in the way of news. Since the subjection of the raiders in the south, Dyer's little force had disintegrated, and were scattered among the chain of posts wide apart in that long Cordon which stretched from Birjand in the north to Khwash in the south, the former stronghold of the raiders. Beyond convoy duties and the never-ending reconnaissances and constant searching for reported parties of German agents, there had been little to do. In fact, two squadrons, the half of my regiment, had been withdrawn to India to refit and rest, leaving only two squadrons and the Indian Infantry regiment to guard the whole length of the Cordon.

It might seem an impossibility to protect so many hundreds of miles with so few troops, especially when the enemy to be intercepted consisted only of small parties. The nature of the country, however, rendered it possible to do this with small garrisons in a chain of posts even of that great length. The answer to this apparent impossibility is that there are only routes, recognized locally, which human beings can take. Without water, which exists in that waste at points many miles apart in small hauzes, travelling for the smallest of parties cannot possibly be undertaken. A system of spies, therefore, at these hauzes ensured that news of suspicious travellers would be reported to any of our adjacent ports. The officer in command of the nearest post could then telephone north and south, and the hunt was fairly "up."

Fake alarms were many. Our spies, often from fear of losing their job, would come in with information totally imaginary, or based on rumours. Life, therefore, in those little posts meant unceasing trekking and reconnaissance. It was a lonely business, too, as few of these widely separated posts held more than a handful of men and one British officer.

A few parties had been accounted for, and our sphere had become too unpopular for more attempts to be made. Patrolling had meant thousands upon thousands of miles of travel. It almost seemed as if our force might be withdrawn and the work undertaken by levies alone, but dangerous visitors were still getting through into Afghanistan—that was a known fact—by passing through the Russian sphere north of Birjand up to the Russian frontier.

Affairs Russian were shaky in the extreme, yet that region of theirs was up to date occupied only by disgruntled troops who had lost enthusiasm. It was no difficult task for adventurous Germans to penetrate that part of the line.

My orders were to proceed to Birjand to take over the command of our squadron, relieving the one British officer there.

This was good news. Kacha had given me a very pleasant interlude, but I was glad to set out again with a small escort and camel convoy, several weeks trek ahead of me through new country. It was getting colder and colder every stage north that we went.

The slow pace of a camel caravan is maddening. Camels are queer creatures and have a habit of becoming suddenly, as it were, simply tired of living. Many times I have seen a camel stop and calmly sit down in the most unconcerned way, showing no distress whatever, and just die. Casualties like this we used to shoot, to save them from the attacks of hungry vultures who would appear as if by magic out of an apparently empty blue sky. First one dot, then another, and another—a horrible gathering of wrangling, feathered harpies.

Later, however, the order was to leave one of the camel men behind with the unfortunate animal, also a feed to give it a chance of recovering and of being brought along later in the day; and if despite all efforts it did its pathetic dying act, all the man had to do was to chop off its tail and bring it back, a guarantee of compensation. On one occasion compensation was duly paid by the officer commanding a certain convoy for the customary tail. At sunset on that day a camel came wandering into camp minus its tail! The man who claimed compensation on that day will not easily forget what he got for his abominable cruelty.

We were making for Bandan by a new route with exceedingly long marches, a great saving of time, avoiding going eastward to Nasratabad and thence across that difficult Hamun. There had been too many transport casualties in that treacherous inland sea.

One day was exactly like any other. We would start at early dawn, and darkness fell by the time the last of the camels were in. It was bitterly cold at night in one's bivouac tent, but after a meal and good hot drink we were quite ready for sleep, wrapped in our sheepskin coats.

So, eventually, we came to Bandan with its little mud fort and cluster of palm trees, the place where this story began. Beyond a small garrison of camel levies there was no living soul. Some time before it had been abandoned as a post for regular troops. Our two squadrons who had gone back to India, and who had taken turn and turn about to garrison this deservedly unpopular spot, had suffered many casualties there. Very few were ever passed fit for service again, and practically their entire strength when they did return consisted of recruits and others who were coming to Persia for the first time.

I was not sorry to see the last of it on the following morning and go stumbling and slipping through the pass to the north, out again into a farther wilderness, past the place where we used to hand over the convoys and spend the day sheltering from the sun in the fleas and sand, resting our horses before going back.

Onwards was new country; just the same emptiness, except that at distances apart of about twenty miles, roughly a day's march, lay what I had not yet seen—regular Persian villages with a certain amount of crops and a few trees, also a fixed population, small in number, of course, inhabiting them. These little oases certainly made for more comfortable travelling. There was always a mud hut inside their fortified walls; eggs were available, and sometimes a stringy fowl, also Persian bread. This unleavened substance had to be eaten, if at all, in its fresh state of doughiness before it turned to concrete.

It would not be long now before we came to the southernmost post occupied by a troop of the squadron which had its headquarters in Birjand, and which I was going to take over.

The days passed quickly enough, and the few far apart posts which boasted a British officer we found welcome halts. That tiny gramophone would be set going, and the occasion would be celebrated by what I, just back from India, could produce from my yak-dans.

There is nothing of any interest in that part of Eastern Persia—the inhabitants are just poverty stricken folk with a few head of mangy goats and sheep, whose only excitement and fear had been up to date an almost annual raid by those villains, now subdued, from the south.

Their queer mud huts, with dome-shaped roofs and a hole in the top to let out the smoke, were a great comfort after a tiring day's ride, and even the countless cats could not disturb our sleep. But no sign of Persian cat could I see—just plain old mangy tabby things, nothing more.

At last, towards the end of a long day, the Indian officer commanding the troops at Shusp came cantering out to meet me.

Then I felt that I really was back again, and the second phase, for me, of this adventure, was to begin.

CHAPTER 2

Persians & Russians

Four long stages lay ahead of me before reaching Birjand, each marked by a small village with its attendant shelter and warmth. One could sleep wrapped in a sheepskin coat, either on the mud floor of the customary domed hut or even on a camp-bed. The floor was preferable, as by no means all the smoke from the open fire in the centre escaped through the hole in the roof.

Hereabouts the inhabitants were friendly, and with good reason, as our presence meant security from raiders and the sale of whatever produce they could supply. The intervening country was just the same old lonely, lifeless waste.

It was the beginning of December, and bitterly cold. Birjand, my home to be, was my first real halt since leaving London in August, and awaiting my arrival I found my old friend G., whom I was to relieve, and who was then to return to India.

I had not seen him since our exciting days in the south, the raiders' ambush, and our appalling camel journey back to Quetta—those weeks of rocking, jolting nights in our coffin-shaped baskets with old Suleiman riding alongside. What luck to be still alive! That affair seemed such a long time ago.

At Shusp ended the camel transport. From there onwards for the odd hundred miles left of our Cordon, guarded by the squadron which I was to take over, all transport was "mule." These, numbering about two hundred, had been hired locally and were the property of two real characters, two smiling rascals by name Kerbalai Nabbi and Meshedi Ali, straight from the pages of "Ali Baba and the Forty Thieves"; Kerbalai and Meshedi being adjectives and titles due to those who had made pilgrimages to the holy cities thus named.

Not a yard of the Persian highways was unknown to these two characters and their dependants, whose normal livelihood had previously been gained by transporting various kinds of merchandise up and down the trade-routes. In our employment the reception of ample and regular pay and the minimum danger of brigandage was to them a godsend.

Even more so was it to us, in that they provided mules, drivers, saddlery and rations at a fixed rate which the Squadron Commander paid monthly—and there his responsibility ceased.

This form of transport, too, was an added comfort, since after the day's march these mules were into camp long before camels would have been, and even before our troopers had settled down for the night the muleteers would themselves be squatting round their fires after delivering their goods, discussing the next day's trek.

In these circumstances, then, the squadron was in a position to move with baggage and rations for so many days, at any moment, to any destination. Each troop, in whatever section of this hundred odd miles it happened to be, lived with its proportionate number of mules, and so came under the same conditions.

Kerbalai and Meshedi, the owners of this efficient transport, never let us down and never grumbled.

At Shusp I acquired a dog, a Saluki. (Persia and Afghanistan are the homes of these speedy hounds.) A great, long selfish one this was, and I christened him "Sandy." I also took on an orderly from the troop there.

Those last four marches were delightful with the mules coming in so soon after our arrival at the day's halt, and that satisfactory feeling of being at home again with one's own men and horses, with a new job in an unknown country.

Birjand was the first real Persian town I had seen; from there onwards the posts were garrisoned by Cossacks. Even Suleiman, old man syce, showed signs of interest. Sandy, the personification of greed and cunning, carried his tail higher.

For a mile or two before coming into Birjand the camel track became almost a road, bordered by crops, and for the last mile by poplars. It was almost a shock after so many hundreds of miles to see anything so refreshing.

At Birjand, though it is not one of the famous towns for carpets, they are made with their own peculiar pattern. Despite the primitive conditions the work turned out is marvellous. Workers, male and female, of all ages, sit in a row facing a frame over which are strung taut thousandfold threads, vertically. The actual colours are worked in and out through these threads horizontally, each coloured thread being pressed down with a comb-shaped instrument. A master director calls out the colours and technical commands. I bought one or two carpets in this place and they now form part of a collection of Persian and Turkoman rugs acquired during my wanderings in those countries. They could always be flung over the top of one's kit on a camel or a mule, and served many times as bedding when there was no shelter from the snow.

Birjand lies in a wide valley with ranges of mountains 8,000 feet and more in height to the north and south of it. Away to the west is the fringe of the formidable Lut desert, that terrible waterless waste without life or vegetation, the home of the deadly simoom, a wind laden with sand, burning or icy according to the season, which kills and buries anything living which is rash enough to risk its approach.

The town itself, on rising ground, consists of a large collection of the usual mud, domed roofed hovels with here and there one larger or better built than the rest. Into its network of narrow streets with high, blind walls we rode, and a large wooden door in one of these proved to be the entrance to my future home.

The Persian house is almost always enclosed in high, windowless walls, inside which is a courtyard with the rooms looking on to it from the four sides. Here I found G., and we spent a cheery evening together discussing old times. We decided to devote the following morning to the handing over of the little command with its accounts, dealing with the payment of mule transport, local spies, forage, and the manifold details connected with the post.

This being done, we set forth in state accompanied by a little guard of honour with fluttering lance-pennons to call on the Governor of the Province—the Shaukat-ul-Mulk, who lived about a mile outside the town within the usual high walls in a large and comfortably furnished house. He was a most attractive personage, tall and good-looking, almost fair, with the irreproachable manners common to Persians of his generation, and those before him. He spoke perfect French, which was extremely fortunate, as my command of the Persian language was more than limited. He was very friendly towards the British.

I enjoyed that visit. We sat there together for over an hour in a sort of high turret overlooking the way I had come in the day before, talking and laughing over his excellent coffee and cigarettes. One always had the feeling of being watched on these occasions by unseen eyes. What went on in this queer Aladdin's palace when that veneer of civilization was put on one side and the Eastern forgot to be Western, when his guests had gone?

A first-class bridge player was the Shaukat, a first-class shot, and well above the average at tennis. In this wild country his word was law, and in his hands lay the powers of life and death.

I was sorry to have to go, but G. was due to leave by convoy on the following morning, and the other two remaining "calls" had to be made.

Returning to the town, we visited the house of the Russian Vice-Consul, Boulatoff, who lived with his wife in penury. No more money was forthcoming from Russia although his personal escort of six Don Cossacks still stood by him. Fortunately he and his wife also spoke French, but conversation was sadly one-sided; it concerned the Revolution and what was to become of them. They produced a bottle of vodka, and became sadder than ever. They found a guitar, played and sang, and then forgot their woes in an access of optimism. Here in their little house had come the first link with white people since leaving the Indian frontier. It is hard to remember that these "white people" who looked so Western took but a second to change into Easterns; yet how fascinating they seemed! Russia had always attracted me since I could remember. Appealing names, bright stars, the wildest of music and the saddest, extremes of despair and of joy, a superficial civilization covering a kind of primitive savagery ... something not quite European, and yet not quite Eastern; amazing hospitality. A sort of blind submission to Fate, to Kismet as the Easterns have it; the Russians call it "sood bà."

The third and last visit was to the only other Englishman in the place, whose job it was to run the branch of the Imperial Bank of Persia in Birjand. He lived in a house rather like mine, but well furnished and guarded by Persian soldiery. During my stay in Birjand I dined at his house every night.

So ended a day of the most unexpected novelty and interest.

The following morning I rode out a few miles with G., and then, sitting on my horse, watched him and his little escort disappear. I could just see his hand raised in farewell as the party rounded a hill and vanished.

Old Suleiman had by now got my belongings, such as they were, in order; and I felt that since August quite enough travelling by train, boat, camel and mule had been my portion. There was a great deal to be done arranging for the forage which was purchased locally, the payment of the transport, the spies, the collecting of reports and the necessity for preparedness to move at a moment's notice all or any part of my little command, anywhere and for any length of time.

At least two days were filled by all these details, getting to know the local Persian contractors, in short, the lie of the land. Every night I would make my way to the bank manager's house to dine. The very day that G. left snow began to fall, and the ranges of hills to north and south, now picked out in black and white, seemed to come nearer and took on a new, strange beauty. The pathway to the bank became obliterated, and I sometimes found myself stumbling through the local graveyard. The graves themselves were shallow, and it was no uncommon thing to slip knee deep in one of these among the bones of the occupant. The town itself was a veritable maze of narrow, high-walled ways in which, even by day, it was easy to lose oneself.

Communication with the outer world was maintained daily on that single strand of wire.

From time to time I met in the town members of poor Boulatoff's consulate guard. It seemed queer to see white soldiers in that place. Those Don Cossacks would salute and smile, and but for those picturesque uniforms might have been taken for fine specimens of manhood from Yorkshire or Gloucestershire, and as fair in colouring; but as they approached that strange, very slightly slant-eyed look would betray the Asiatic blood, They had made great friends with our men, and many a jumping competition and play with rifle, sword and lance enlivened the general company.

As soon as I had settled down I invited them to my quarters. What they particularly adored was our plain old "bully beef," of which, fortunately, we had a good supply. The local spirit, arrack, a most formidable and potent drink, is a coarser form of the pure vodka of Russia. Faute de mieux I have often drunk this arrack, especially on cold night bivouacs; it tastes filthy, but is a marvellous proposition to heat water in the place of methylated spirits. To the minute, into my courtyard strode these six Don Cossacks, halted, faced me and saluted.

They looked magnificent, perfectly turned out, their uniforms dark blue and scarlet with gold lace, their Astrakhan hats tilted backwards at exactly the right angle. Jewelled daggers and beautifully polished, soft leather top-boots completed a striking picture. Turning as one man, they went, as is their custom, to eat apart.

The bank manager and I dined together. I wanted those splendid men to stay, but I was told it was not the custom. After about half an hour, however, they filed in, halted and saluted as before, then sat down in a semicircle. Musical instruments were produced—a kind of accordion and two guitars; and then began a most attractive entertainment. With no false modesty, they gave us song after song, sad and haunting, dance after dance on the verandah, the setting being the darkest of blue Eastern skies, a gigantic moon, and unnaturally large, glittering stars. They never tired; sometimes solos were sung, and sometimes they all stood together and sang wonderful choruses. Throughout this performance, which ended all too soon, the jars of arrack were constantly emptied and replenished; yet not the flicker of an eyelid betrayed the remotest difference in that amazing company. They revelled in their beautiful music, and in an absolutely natural way they took their turns to sing and play. It all seemed just part of them, and never a false note or step marred the thrilling effect. At the finish, they lined up, saluted exactly as they had done on their arrival, and marched away. Specimens, these, of a magnificent and proud manhood, to be swallowed soon in their country's devastating revolution.

CHAPTER 3

Infiltrations

On the following afternoon I received an urgent cipher message over that single strand of wire, all the hundreds of miles back from the Cordon Headquarters, giving the news that a small party of German officers had left Afghanistan on their return journey and was likely to pass by a route west of Birjand. I was to take immediate action to move out and try to intercept it. Reference to the map showed that their most probable route lay through a village called Chahuk, on the fringe of the Lut desert, some thirty miles west; and to this spot, where we had local spies posted, I decided to go.

Thanks to our ready mule transport, in about an hour the troop which I detailed for the job was saddled and the transport already on the way. The sun was setting and it was freezing hard as I rode off on this search for a needle in a haystack.

For these treks when the going was level and fair and not through rocky passes, a reasonable average of five miles an hour could be maintained throughout the day by riding at a walk for quarter of an hour, then at a slow, steady trot for the next quarter; the next quarter at the walk, and to finish up the hour dismount and lead. By this method great distances could be covered, and men and horses at the end of the day would be in the best of form; while those welcome, tinkling bells of the hardy muleteers which meant the arrival in camp of food and clothing would soon be heard. In bright moonlight, and over the level desert, we "got down to it."

Those night marches, bitterly cold, seemed endless. Led by a local guide, our little party crawled like an insect over this vastness. Meaningless and puny this undertaking must have seemed to that eternal, scornful, icy, chuckling wind; to that moon and those huge, brilliant stars, to whom Piccadilly, Central Asia, everywhere, meant but a glance on one side or another. Hour upon hour of this monotony breeds strange thoughts. There is a real mesmerism in it all, by night, in the rhythm of horses' feet, the occasional chink of stirrup irons, the longing for the moment when one could dismount and lead, and coax back a semblance of warmth.

Having overtaken our mule transport, our guide had reined in alongside me to point out, at last, the rising ground which marked our destination. In a few minutes we dismounted and led our horses through a gate in the fortified walls of Chahuk. The inhabitants gladly welcomed our arrival; we meant safety at least, and customers for whatever produce they had. They knew that they would be paid for this; often they were compelled to give everything for nothing by visiting patrols of Cossacks. Not our Don Cossacks; those who formed the northward part of the Cordon were of quite a different class, Siberian Cossacks, of the Semiorichenski Regiment.

Our Don Cossacks were picked men, and the few I met in Birjand were posted there solely as escort to their vice-consul, my poor, harassed friend, Boulatoff.

In an incredibly short space of time, so accustomed were we to these wanderings, men and horses were under cover in the serais, the transport came tinkling in, and we were settled for the night.

In the customary domed hut our local spies came to discuss the situation with me. They had no news of any party, German or otherwise. We decided to send out camel riders to all the water-holes within reach with orders to camp there and bring in any news of passing strangers.

The smoke was rising from the open fire in the centre of the room; I opened a tin of bully beef, and lay down on the floor where the muleteers had spread my blankets, content with this luxury after those hours of bitter cold. The smoke really was escaping through that hole in the roof; the sheepskin coat was a godsend, and beyond taking off one's boots, there was nothing to do but to wind the blankets round until some warmth began to make itself felt.

A knock on the door ... a voice. "Sahib, may I come in? " My Troop Commander, Mahomed Khan, entered.

As a regiment we consisted of four squadrons, each of a different class. Half the regiment was Hindu, that is to say, two squadrons; one composed of Jats, the other of Rajputs, of which the squadron I originally took over in that ghastly Bandan consisted. The other two squadrons were Mohammedans. One was my own original squadron, which shared that ambush with me, and the men of the other with which I now found myself were Punjabi Mussulmans, known as Awans, recruited in the Attock and Salt Range area of the Punjab.

In an Indian Cavalry regiment the full strength of British officers is only twelve: a commanding officer, adjutant, and a quartermaster; a second-in-command, four squadron commanders, and four squadron officers. The charm of that service is that from the date of joining, when barely twenty years old, instead of taking command of a troop only, the quarter of a squadron, one became at once a squadron commander, as of those twelve British officers at least a third would be away seconded on various jobs. The actual troop commanders are entirely Indian, and hold the Viceroy's commission. They live entirely apart, with their own men and horses, associating with those of their own class and religions.

Mahomed Khan was a fine type of Awan, well over six feet in height, beautifully proportioned, as all Awans are, with almost blue-black hair cut, as is their custom, like a woman's "bob." They are an exceptionally handsome race, and vain of their appearance in an Eastern way, with their turbans tied to a nicety.

"Sahib," said Mahomed Khan, "this country is all very well for us who are Mohammedans; we are all together; but you, the only British officer in the length of one hundred miles, have nobody to talk to. I have come to talk to you; it will do you good." He sat down on the floor despite my protestations that I wanted to sleep.

I shall always remember that night. We had, as a matter of fact, joined the regiment together many years before, had shared our falls in the riding-school, faced each other with padded lance and wooden sabre in skill-at-arms competitions, shared every kind of sport. The good fellow thought I might have been lonely; and his incredibly handsome profile lit by the dying embers of the fire, his perfect manners and tact, made an impression not easily forgotten. We laughed and "reminisced," and not till sleep came did he leave me. The incident may serve as an example of the spirit and comradeship which existed between British officers and their Indian ranks.

We had brought with us several Saluki hounds, coursing being the favourite sport of the Awans. That execrable Sandy was in evidence, of course. He lay watching Mahomed Khan and myself, his long, lean head with its silken, tasselled ears between his paws, the picture of devotion, with tragic eyes fixed on us two alternately. How that dog amused me. Every now and then he would swallow, and that head would go up and down as he did so; it seemed to literally flatten out in comfort. But he looked after his own comfort. Often, waking half frozen in the early hours of the dawn, I used to find that he had annexed most of my coverings. Poor old Sandy!

On the following day, still awaiting news from our spies, we organized a "course." The few hares which exist in this country are purely scavengers, and are to be found sometimes near these oases. We found one that day, and after an amazing course, Sandy succeeded in rolling him over.

We were not the first British troops to visit Chahuk on patrol, so the villagers took little interest in us beyond accepting our payment for what they could provide.

After four days with no news a patrol came from Birjand bearing a message from Headquarters that we were to return. Back we went after this typical fruitless sortie, and I was not sorry to fraternize once more with that solitary bank manager. The novelty of sharing dinner with one of one's own countrymen appealed to me. The next day came information that the hostile party, which consisted of five Austrian officers, had been caught by Persian bandits and handed over alive to the Cossacks at the next northern post, Siddeh, thirty-five miles away. I was instructed to proceed at once to take them over, bring them back to Birjand, and send them on the journey to India by the next convoy as prisoners of war.

It was snowing hard, and extremely cold, and a long and tortuous pass had to be negotiated between Birjand and Siddeh. I decided to take no transport and to go there direct, get under cover at our destination for an hour or two, and come straight back with our prisoners. Detailing my other troop for this job, I hurried myself into all the clothes I could pile on compatible with sitting on a horse. In an hour's time we were off.

I had learned my lesson, the reader will remember, in the matter of escorting prisoners, and not a moment's peace should I know until these five Austrians were safely in Birjand under my guard.

Nobody knew the exact situation in the Russian sphere which we here entered for the first time, and leaving Birjand at about 5 p.m. with five led horses for the Austrians, thirty-five miles to go and the same distance back, we expected to get to Siddeh by midnight. The snow luckily ceased falling after about an hour, as we entered the pass. No Christmas card of the old days could suggest the amazing brightness of the moon and stars, the incredible beauty of the jagged, snow-covered hills; but, to compensate for this loveliness, the icy wind rushing through the pass and booming out again over the desert had an edge keen as any north-easter, and I doubt if Kingsley would have hymned it.

Five minutes halt after each hour, and the cheery assurance of the Troop Commander that all was well. . . . "Mount" again and push on, ever turning corners in this fairyland ravine; eventually through the pass and back to the flat desert, frozen stiff, yet with discomfort overcome by the fascination of moving in some magical, silent, huge, and lifeless world of the night.

Soon after midnight we reached Siddeh, and answering the challenge of the Cossacks at the gate, filed into the narrow village streets.

While my men found shelter for ourselves and the animals, I went with my Troop Commander to see the prisoners. The

Cossack post there, a very small one, consisted of about twenty men—a detachment of the Semiorichenski Regiment, and a strange, wild lot, resembling not at all my Don friends in Birjand, but clad in ill-assorted uniforms of sheepskins and leather, badly turned out, rather undersized and extremely excitable. Most of them Mongolian in type, they were fair-skinned, and nearly all Mohammedans. They had been expecting us, said the kind of non-commissioned officer in charge, whose only method of communication with us was in Persian. Their faces illumined by the great fire, this circle of slant-eyed villains eyed us with intense curiosity.

The prisoners, those unfortunate five Austrians, were standing against a wall, their hands tied behind their backs, blue with cold and terror, and, as I afterwards discovered, exhausted by hunger, poor devils! I gave orders to begin the march back at 5 a.m., released these unfortunates, and removed them to our bivouac, where we covered them with spare horse rugs, gave them a drop of arrack, and detailed a guard over them.

Just before dawn we moved off again with our wretched Austrians perched on the spare horses. They retained their so-called disguise as Afghans, the only kit they had; but never have I seen such sorry Afghans, before or since. Clear of the village I halted the squadron, dismounted, and ordered my men to charge their magazines. The unfortunates thought that they were going to be killed out of hand, but I reassured them; it merely meant that they would instantly be shot if they tried to escape or if any attempt at rescue was made. They were not horsemen, and I felt as sorry for the spare horses as for their wretched riders.

Half-way back one gave in, his face green, and asked to be left behind. Examining my medicine-case, after considerable deliberation I administered two tablets of bismuth. I think bismuth was the label; at any rate it had a good sound about it, and I hoped for the best. For the remainder of that icy ride I had him beside me, leading his horse, and at any sign of shakiness all I had to do was to rattle that tin box of drugs.

After all, they were sportsmen, those chaps; they had crossed the Lut, penetrated to Afghanistan, and had been through hell in those Arctic regions at the hands of their captors, the Persian bandits, not to mention those shifty-eyed little Semiorichenski gentlemen.

Back at last after seventy miles of it, the five Austrian "Afghans" were ushered into my courtyard in Birjand, where a room had been prepared with a large charcoal stove; a sheep had been roasted, and plenty of hot tea was ready. On the only door to this room a permanent guard was placed.

How those poor devils slept under piles of spare horse-blankets! For all of us it had been a pretty tough twenty-four hours; but the job was done, and I was glad to sleep as well.

The next day I arranged for them to go to the local Turkish baths. Nearly all Persian towns have these in specially constructed underground buildings; rough and ready, but efficacious. Meanwhile, we ransacked stores, and found for each man thick underclothing and a grey "Tommy's" shirt and grey socks. By evening our prisoners, clean, warmed, and fed reasonably well, had reached the smiling stage. They did their own cooking on the stove, and had a plentiful supply of the Russian cigarettes obtainable in the town.

My men took it in turns to guard them as the prisoner "sahibs," and attend to them. For exercise they could walk round my inner courtyard, where I greeted them each morning, looking very different from that terror-stricken, frozen, hungry group which I had taken on at Siddeh.

CHAPTER 4

Cossacks

After my two absences from Headquarters I was very busy with my squadron accounts. Old man syce had become a great favourite with the Austrians, to whom he took from time to time, what little extras could be spared.

Visiting again the unfortunate Boulatoffs, I found that their Don Cossacks had left, part and parcel of the revolution, and were en route for Meshed, some four hundred miles north, the famous holy city and the one large centre of all Eastern Persia. My friends seemed desperately downcast and, of course, had no further voice in affairs, there not being a single Russian subject except themselves left in Birjand. The usual bottle of vodka was produced, followed by music on the guitar, and their pessimism was soon replaced by a kind of spurious optimism and hope, though what hope they had at that time it was difficult to conceive. Christmas was drawing near, and my invitation to the party which the bank manager and I intended to give may have helped to cheer them up. Obviously it could only be a short time before they must pack up and leave for Meshed, whither all in the Russian sphere seemed to be bound. Already there was for them no hope, no pay, no occupation, nothing.

I enjoyed those few days after my return with the Austrians. The prospect of our forthcoming party, with the Boulatoffs, the Persian Governor, and one or two lesser lights present, was pleasant. Meanwhile a convoy was due to go south, taking with it my prisoners, bound for India and civilization.

The bank manager very kindly gave me a few bottles of wine. Old man syce excelled himself and made a gigantic cake. I added a few tinned efforts from my stores.

I wonder if any of those Austrian officers are still alive and if they remember the night before their departure—how they sang, and how well, in that room of theirs? They were sportsmen and I admired their pluck; they had lost in any case, but were good losers. They wound out of sight in the morning, out of Birjand, and certainly out of my life. Good luck to them!

And then an astounding thing happened. From the south, out of the blue, a motor-car appeared! In it sat the owner, an elderly Sikh, and his driver. This was a great effort. Dyer, of course, had manoeuvred a car all the way south to Khwash. Our friend with his old Ford had come out, with a view to trade, leisurely trundling all these hundreds of miles from post to post, manhandling it over the passes, finding a sure way across the deserts by means of stores of petrol accumulated by passing convoys against the day when a regular car track should be made, if necessary, along this scattered Cordon.

It was like a fairy story, with that silver-bearded, extremely handsome and genial old Sikh as the "genie" who appeared at the rubbing of the magic lamp. He had run constant risk of being looted by brigands, but here he was, at the end of the British sphere, in the first so-called town of east Persia, talking to me like a grandfather in my own little courtyard: a splendid old man, who proved very shortly to be a most useful visitor. He had two nephews in the 20th Royal Deccan Horse, and was interested to learn that I had at one time actually been in command of that Sikh squadron in France.

With Christmas Eve came real Christmas weather, typical of that part of the world, on the threshold of Russia. Four hundred miles only separated it from that country; but what was four hundred miles to us? Just a few hack rides—in fact Nichevo, nothing.

The bank manager and I, busy with our preparations for the following night, planned a real party, and those poor Boulatoffs were not going to be allowed to forget it. What luck to be here in Birjand. As far as letters and post were concerned one simply was thankful if one ever enjoyed the privileges of getting any. Whatever there happened to be for us on that Cordon left India once a fortnight and came along with the supply convoys. But it was great fun when one did get one's post. Sometimes two or three fortnightly posts at a time, especially in my case, when I had spent nearly all my time on the move. I was lucky enough to get one on that day which made everything more cheery for me.

What with reading all those letters and answering as many as I could, the day passed pleasantly enough, my squadron work too being well up to date, and I was looking forward to a quiet evening with the bank manager and to discussing the final details for the morrow's party.

I had by now found a way which did not entail crossing that cemetery and finding oneself knee deep in some unfortunate grave.

Hardly had I been ten minutes in his house when an orderly from my squadron came in with a long cipher message for me. Each squadron has a "squadron writer," a kind of confidential clerk to the commander and probably the only member of the squadron who can talk, or write, English, whose duty it is to receive the nightly messages which came by 'phone. I had the cipher key in my pocket. I was to proceed instantly with my force to a post seventy-five miles north, Kain, hitherto occupied by Cossacks, who were understood to be preparing to leave for the north.

I went to the telephone and got on to my two troop leaders posted south of Birjand, ordering them to march on the following morning complete with their mule transport through Birjand and on to Kain, where they would find me. My other two troops, in Birjand, were instructed to march straight to Kain on the next morning with as much rations and forage as could be taken on their share of our ever-ready mule transport. That meant for them a two days' trek, so that on the day after the morrow my first detachment would reach its destination. The two troops from the south would follow them at only a day's interval. I must say that those two members of the "forty thieves," Messrs. Kerbalai Nabbi and Meshedi Ali, played up like men with their mules, and both these detachments got going like clockwork. This having been put through, I went to find my old Sikh friend and consulted with him. My scheme was that he should try to get through with me, in his Ford, so that we should be a day ahead of the Birjand half squadron and be able to investigate affairs; and he was quite in favour of the idea.

No Christmas party now! The bank manager agreed to have several sacks of Persian silver coin at my house by an early hour; for I did not quite see the fun of arriving in the Russian sphere with no wherewithal to pay our expensive way.

At dawn that ancient motor-car came for me and was loaded with these sacks of money, one or two spare carpets I had bought, a little food and drink, the old Sikh, his driver, Sandy the dog, and myself. Old man syce was to come along with my horses, and the transport and my kit with the Birjand detachment.

The Sikh was delighted to come with us, and proved invaluable. We had seventy-five miles to go, and I hoped to reach Kain, our destination, with luck that night. We made a good start and went grinding and creeping up the pass towards Siddeh. The desert part was easy enough on the hard frozen ground, but that pass was ghastly. Time and again we had to stop and cool the engine, and then push behind to get the car over some especially awkward place. We reached the top somehow, then descended slowly and carefully over the desert to Siddeh. Another pass had to be overcome up to a little post called Rum, whence the track went down into desert again and on to Kain.

The sun was sinking as we left Siddeh, but we determined to chance our luck through the Rum pass. The gallant Ford got us over the highest point, and we were congratulating ourselves on being the first motorists to do the Birjand—Kain seventy-five miles of roadless nothingness when we ran into a snowdrift and stuck. Our combined efforts failed to move the car, and night was near. There was nothing for it but to bivouac as best we might and await the two troops who would be due in the morning. To add to the general cheer snow began to fall. About twenty miles on to Kain was an impossible distance in darkness on foot.

Fortunately the gallant Ford, if immovable, still stood upright, so, sharing what food and drink we had, not forgetting poor old Sandy, we scrambled under the car with every bit of covering we had with us, and on us, including my carpets, and managed to pass the night in comparative warmth while the snow blanketed the seats above us and the ground outside our oily shelter.

So passed the night of Christmas, 1917, as far as I was concerned. In any case, the squadron was on its way to its appointed destination, and whatever happened I was bound to be picked up by the first detachment on the morrow and get to Kain with them.

"Things might indeed be worse," said old Grandfather Sikh.

We were all dead tired, and in these strange surroundings and the warmth of sheepskin and Persian rugs slept undismayed.

The next morning looked a bit grim as we crawled out from under the car, but after strenuous efforts we managed to get a fire going with bits of scrub and splinters of wood from a small store-box. The weather changed to a glorious, cloudless day, with the sun bringing dazzling reflections from the pure whiteness of the snow. While these preparations were afoot, Sandy remained in that tumbled heap of carpets and sheepskins watching us with attentive eye. Soon tea was brewing, with melted snow and an old tin pot owned by the Sikh—who, amazing old man, seemed none the worse for his Christmas night bivouac. Even that beautifully groomed silver beard was in order!

The two troops from Birjand were due to overtake us shortly, but the old man wanted to wait for the mule transport that followed them up. We were on the Kain side and almost at the end of the Rum pass, in the foothills which gave way, as one could see, to the open desert again a few miles farther ahead. When our troops came in sight they made a fine picture upon that snowy background. My Indian officers had, as usual, risen to the occasion, and despite the conditions had done their very best as regards turn-out. The men had their turbans tied neatly; the light breeze floated out their lance-pennons, red and white against the snow. Even the fit and well-groomed horses seemed to sense the occasion. In fact, our Awan squadron evidently intended to show the Cossacks that Indian Cavalry were not to be despised. Not often, in history, have Indian Lancers and Cossacks met. Easterns both, but with the difference that Cossacks have white faces.

Dismounting, the men had our car out of that snowdrift in a moment. Its owner insisted on waiting for the mule convoy, so we started his engine for him and let it warm up. It was more or less level going as far as Kain, and the little snow that remained would not worry him.

From the rear of my detachment came the old man syce riding and leading my horse alongside, saddlery beautifully clean, almost as if it were a parade for General's inspection. I hurried behind a rock to tie my turban up to this standard and do what I could to live up to it in spite of the handicap of spending the night under a Ford car!

Soon we were wending our way down the last slopes of this pass and on to the great Kain plain. Sandy trotted alongside with several others of his ilk, the property of the two troops.

After a few more miles Kain itself appeared in the distance. A fair-sized townlet, it was completely surrounded by a high fortified wall of mud with huge wooden gates, closed at sundown, giving egress to the south, the direction from which we were coming, the north, and the west. The approach seemed never-ending, and we alternately trotted and walked in the same old treadmill; but at last we topped the final undulation about half a mile from the walls and saw a body of horsemen cantering to meet us.

I formed my men in line, halted, and waited.

Their officer, a youngish Russian, came up to me, shook hands, and in perfect French asked me what was the particular honour which the British troops were doing him in paying this visit—in short, what on earth were we doing there at all. I told him that I had come to take over the Kain section of the Cordon as I understood that the Cossacks were leaving.

"Yes," he said, "we are leaving, but we had no news of your possible arrival. I suppose this is the end for us."

And there we sat on our horses, this young officer and his Cossacks eyeing us as interestedly as we eyed them. He was dressed entirely in leather, to keep out the cold; his men wore a variety of uniforms of Cossack type made of leather or sheepskin, but all with the same jaunty Cossack Astrakhan cap and the letter "C" on their shoulders, signifying Semiorichenski, the "C" in Russian corresponding to our "S."

They were a mixed crowd, white, of course, but nearly all Mohammedans, recruited in the Vyerni district north of Tashkent, and mounted on stout little cobs. With their carbines over their shoulders, and two crossed bandoliers of ammunition, a sword, and daggers in their waistbands, they presented a most picturesque appearance. Wheeling about, they fell in behind my men and we trotted on together to the great southern gate of Kain where I pulled up my horse and watched my men filing in.

A fairly large attendance of the inhabitants presented a by no means friendly attitude to us newcomers. Subsequently I learnt that they had every reason to fear and loathe the presence of troops, but this was their first sight of a British force, and, in the circumstances, the more imposing such visitors were, the more they thought they had to fear.

My men quickly found a large empty serai with a big courtyard, unsaddled, and settled down to work. The horses were watered, picketed and fed, and the rooms opening on to the courtyard were being vigorously cleaned out to make, before night, really comfortable quarters. I agreed to take on a little mud house in the middle of this townlet which had been occupied up to date by the Russian officer. He took me there between a maze of high, narrow walls.

We came suddenly to a small opening into a small courtyard in which lay a dead donkey, frozen stiff. Up from there led a little winding stairway, and then a landing. On one side was a tiny room, in the middle a sort of kitchen, and on the other a narrow apartment perhaps twelve feet wide and twenty feet long. Above this little "flat" a level roof could be reached by a short flight of steps.

The Russian had already packed up his effects.

"I have been here a year," he said. "There is the sky, the earth, the sun, and the moon. I only hope you don't go mad in this place, because there is certainly nothing else."

He left then, as we both had our work to do, but promised to come and dine with me, or let us rather say feed with me that evening.

CHAPTER 5

Farewells

The first thing was to remove that frozen dead donkey. This was done at once, and old man Suleiman got busy with my kit and belongings while I went to see how my men were getting on. The good big serai, in which they had established themselves already, had taken on an air almost of comfort. The horses were neatly picketed, and everything was going like clockwork. We had two days' rations and forage in hand, and so had the two troops who were due on the next morning.

But not a living soul was to be seen of the inhabitants of Kain. They had just locked themselves into their dwellings, terrified at the arrival of those great, big, hearty Awans with their lances and horses and soldierly, efficient air.

The next event was the arrival of the Ford car. Imagine the hidden eyes which were watching that monster, a thing they had never seen before, as it chugged its way into the serai and parked alongside the guardroom! Then followed the mules carrying forage and spare ammunition, all to be neatly packed away in our new quarters.

There was plenty of room for the entire squadron, so I decided on a two-day halt in Kain. Taking my squadron writer with me, I next went to the Persian telephone office, and after long delay made connection right back to Headquarters, informing them of our arrival and appointing a daily hour at which to get into communication. The local operator seemed very disinclined to help us.

Finding my way back with difficulty through the maze of narrow streets to my new quarters, I was astounded at the change. The floor of that long, narrow room had been covered with beautiful carpets, a large Russian stove stood in one corner, my camp-bed was up, also decorated with a carpet, and my yak-dans had been arranged in the corners against the walls as seats. Opposite the little window a stool stood in front of a rough table. Old man syce was beaming and had lit the stove which was filled with logs.

Our Sikh had achieved this; exactly how he did it all is a mystery. I had certainly not rubbed the magic ring; miracles seemed to happen without that.

I made the best preparations possible for my Russian guest. Fortunately a few bottles of wine were in my kit, a parting present from my banking friend of Birjand.

In due course my guest arrived. The walls of this room, incidentally, he had covered with crayon drawings and sketches, and very clever they were. This was the place I was to go mad in, he said. I can see now the red of the stove, the hurricane lamp which hung from the ceiling. Sandy was lying on my bed gazing at us with a preternaturally grave expression. It did not seem terribly depressing after all.

The Cossacks were to leave to-morrow for Meshed, he told me; he would accompany them. What else could they do? There was no pay coming; their own country was in a turmoil. This officer was obviously in a bad way after a year's solitude in these surroundings. He went on talking of the war, of his upbringing, of those wild Cossacks whom he commanded, of his future which held nothing: a picturesque figure and extremely interesting. Catching sight of my mandolin, he began to play, singing sad Russian songs in an unaffected way, as if he thoroughly enjoyed it. I did—it was a charming entertainment for me. I produced the little gramophone, which sent him into ecstasies, though it is difficult to imagine anyone ecstatic over an indifferent gramophone! My records were not high-brow; merely the more well-known and beautiful melodies of Chopin, Liszt, Beethoven, and the 1917 popular tunes of London. But the circumstances, the situation, and the surroundings were enough to move even an ordinary soldier like myself.

As the music went on the far end of the room quietly filled with Cossack N.C.O.s, who sat on the floor and listened in silence, absolutely motionless. I chose the very best records, and played them one after another.

Leaning back in the shadows, I looked at all those faces, the white Easterns with their eyes aslant and hard mouths, ever and again staring at me with curiosity, the first British officer they had ever seen. I passed round the Persian cigarettes, the remains of my bottles of wine, which were not appreciated, and the jug of arrack thoughtfully provided by the Sikh, which was.

They clamoured again and again for the gramophone. The atmosphere became a swaying smoke cloud through which gleamed those curious eyes. It was a charming interlude.

As with their brothers in arms, the Don Cossacks, there was no sign of drunkenness, of noise. Those hard faces simply became harder. Finally, at my invitation, they sang Russian songs in perfect tune and time. Those Russians adore music, and there is no false modesty about them. Even those hardened Cossacks seemed to become in an instant almost babies, and were carried away by the rhythm and beauty of the very music which they created—chiefly old folk-songs, exquisitely rendered.

For the second time since being charmed with Cossack singing, it seemed all too soon when they rose to their feet like one man, saluted, and filed out of sight down that stairway. Their officer stayed behind to thank me for what he was pleased to call my hospitality. I could not sufficiently thank him and his men for their marvellous entertainment. They were due to leave for the north in the morning, and I made certain of the time of their departure in order to be there to wish them bon voyage. Assuring me that I should quite certainly go mad in this God-forsaken Kain, he disappeared down that quaint little mud stairway and clanked off into the darkness.

Next morning I found our Semiorichenski Cossacks drawn up in line ready for departure. Their form of transport consisted of wagons, four-wheeled, drawn by three horses abreast, the usual troika. Long and low and extremely strongly made, they cover surprising distances in a day. The Cossacks themselves on their sturdy little horses seem to travel always at the same pace, a kind of "triple." I was just in time to shake hands with the officer before they moved off, and so once again I watched into the distance those whom I had relieved.

Not long afterwards my next two troops came in and settled down in our serai. In any case there would be a halt for the whole squadron for the next day.

The forage problem presented little difficulty, for Kain was a large oasis and contained exactly what we wanted for our horses, and the necessities of life for our men. The old Sikh had produced a local notable whom I was to know very well later, and whom I always called "Hadji."

Hadji, however, was not very helpful. "The villagers are terrified of your men," he said. "They refuse to produce anything."

Kain possessed a Governor, and the obvious thing to do was to call on him at once.

Hadji went in person to convey my greetings and to inquire what time would be convenient for me to pay my respects. In due course, then, with a picked escort of my men, and turned out as well as we possibly could, I threaded my way through those narrow, empty passages to the Governor's house. Not a soul did we meet, but we felt that eyes were watching our progress, our horses daintily picking their way, and the red and white pennons fluttering in the breeze.

There was a small guard of ragged Persian Infantry at the stout wooden gate of the great man's dwelling. We halted and dismounted, and I was ushered in by those comic opera braves. After what seemed an age, through twisting, narrow corridors, up and down short flights of stairs, past curtained doorways, I was shown into a long, narrow room, the walls of which were hung with beautiful silk carpets and the floor also covered with them. One little table was in the centre, and two chairs; beyond that, nothing. The door opened to admit the living image of my mental conception of Omar Khayyám.

I had already picked up enough Persian to be able to respond as I should to the long, flowery greetings peculiar to that country. Then, in French, this charmingly mannered and handsome old gentleman asked me to be seated; a servant entered with delicious coffee and Russian cigarettes, and we were left alone.

Three cups of coffee had to be drunk, as I knew, according to Persian etiquette, while we discussed the weather or trivial matters, and I was aware that the Governor was summing me up. The picture that he made fascinated me, from his silken turban down to his soft, red leather shoes with their backward curve at the toe; his well-bred face, its white and beautifully groomed beard, impressed me favourably. The return of the servant to take away the coffee and bring tea in a samovar meant that the business in hand could be approached. There had been a humorous twinkle in those keen eyes for some time, and their owner wasted no time in telling me that he knew exactly why I had come. He told me of the Cossacks.

They had apparently taken what forage they required for their horses, what rations were available for their men, they had used force, and had paid for nothing; they had raped women; everything had been done at the point of the sword.

"And now you come here, Sahib, with your troops, to a neutral country, where you have never been before. Frankly, the people here are terrified of an occupation even worse than that of the Cossacks."

I assured him that every single thing would be paid for, transport or forage or whatever it might be, and that there was no question of any of his people, man, woman or child, being molested; also, that during our occupation they would be protected against raiders from over the Afghan border.

"And what guarantee have I for this, Sahib?"

I could hardly help laughing as I told him that he had only my word. After all, it was merely a question of gaining the confidence of these people. We had the wherewithal and the will to pay. As regards the discipline of the Indian Cavalry—that went without saying.

That humorous twinkle developed into a smile as he granted my request, according to custom, to be permitted to take my departure.

This interview had apparently put matters right, for Hadji

came to see me that evening and guaranteed to produce supplies, transport, everything needful.

So far, so good; I could now proceed with taking over this Cordon another fifty miles to Rui Khaf, that meaning a hundred and twenty-five miles from Birjand to Rui Khaf, included, to be guarded by my squadron. I told old Hadji what was wanted, and gave him a free hand to collect as much forage as he could lay hands on, in addition to any foodstuffs he could get for my men.

I was glad to get back "home," but when I sat down in that long room, thanking God for the stove, and the light, I really began to feel what it was to be alone with not a soul near with whom it was possible to speak one's own language. I imagined that Russian officer spending a year here and drawing those exceedingly clever sketches on the walls, remembered his opinion that this was a place to go mad in. It had been an interesting day, and I had thoroughly enjoyed my interview with the Governor. The results, at any rate, were good, and I could get on with my job the next day.

Meanwhile, Sandy and I shared my customary stewed goat, George Robey entertained us on the gramophone, and a jug of arrack stood handy. Teetotallers do not thrive in the East. I can assert that on the strength of twenty-three years' existence on the far side of Suez; also that overdoing it is the shortest way to the grave. An Indian Cavalry soldier's life leads him through the most unpleasant climatic situations imaginable. There is no "going to the hills" in the hot weather except on leave. Three-quarters of one's time is spent in frontier outposts and their ghastly climate. In short, where one's men can go, and where British regiments cannot. A good life, too.

The situation was interesting in the extreme; let the future take care of itself! There was my camp-bed, we were under cover, and a comforting red glow came from the stove. That fearful Sandy would crawl up, and the last thing I remembered at night was that long, lean head with its great grave eyes on the makeshift pillow, and so we slept together as we did every night of my residence in that place. I am, and always shall be, a dog lover.

I had a home, and was likely to remain alone in it for some time; the first since leaving a flat in Clarges Street! It was delightful, the comfort of that room, as, with the knowledge that my men and horses were all under cover, I fell asleep with that grave dog's face next to mine and dreamed of people from the fairytale books, djinns and magicians such as are portrayed by that king of imagination, Rackham. I had seen one of them that day.

Walking down next morning to my horse lines I found that Kain had taken on a completely new aspect. It was obvious that the edict had gone forth after my visit to the Governor that we newcomers were not to be feared. The inhabitants were once again leading their normal lives. The men, wearing the usual dome-shaped brimless hats with long coats and voluminous baggy trousers and kamarbands round their waists, eyed me as if I were something which had escaped from a zoo. The women, with their blue skirts and black yashmaks, which only allowed their eyes to be seen, turned their faces to the wall as the "unbeliever" passed by.

Half of the squadron, two troops, had to march on the following day for Rui Khaf, a post fifty miles north-east within sight of the Afghan western border. These two troops I detailed to proceed by separate routes, thereby passing through villages on either side of the main caravan way, halting for the night in different places. My idea was to bring these isolated and frequently raided fortified posts into touch with us new-comers, to get them to realize that we meant protection from raiders, also cash-paying customers, not only for forage and rations, but also for any information they could send of the presence of German parties in their neighbourhood.

These two troops carried out their march most successfully. True, their arrival near any of these places for the first time meant the instant closing of the gates, the manning of the walls by armed men, and all preparations to keep them off. They converged, however, on Rui Khaf eventually, having won the confidence of the intervening villages.

We were in touch with these two troops by the same telephone wire, and reports came in daily as to the situation. Meanwhile there was in Kain no lack of applicants for the jobs of spies in inhabited places and water-holes for the whole length of my new portion of the Cordon. These were duly appointed, and left for their various destinations. We were fairly settled down in this sphere of former Russian occupation, and the inhabitants had ceased to stare at me in my goings and comings. In fact, I was beginning to know some of them by sight, and a morning "Salaam, Aleikum" was frequently exchanged.

And so this was the place where I should go mad with boredom. I wonder if that Russian officer is still alive.

CHAPTER 6

The Wild Frontier

The British sphere by this time had been definitely extended as far as Rui Khaf. What was happening northwards between that post and the Russian frontier was uncertain to a degree. Naturally any enterprising hostile party would choose that sector to penetrate, considering the state of the Russian troops who occupied it. It was from Kain roughly three hundred miles to the first town on the Russian border, Askhabad. My business was now the sector Birjand to Rui Khaf. The situation was satisfactory enough as regards the inhabitants of that sphere, so the thing to do was to make ourselves known throughout as soon as possible. I had appointed, and sent, agents to all points, especially to the west, through which a hostile party might come; few enough those points were in this desolate country.

I decided to go up to Rui Khaf to see how my troops were getting on there. Having detailed small patrols to visit the places where I had appointed agents, to get on friendly terms with the inhabitants, and leaving my senior Indian officer in charge at Kain, I set off with a small escort northwards.

The journey was only about fifty miles, and the weather was kind. Snow lay throughout but only to a depth of a few inches; the sky was clear with a brilliant sun. Halfway we halted for the night at a water-hole with its mud shelter, sharing it with a small camel caravan coming south, whose people were very interested in us and fraternised with my Mohammedan escort. By great fires of brushwood they cooked their food and baked the bread. A Mongolian type, these, from Turkestan, with carpets and silks, the women-folk fair and extremely handsome, their national head-dresses strung with coins. A huge bonfire of scrub was lit in the dirty courtyard of the serai, and there we men sat drinking tea and eating their bread.

There was exceptional charm about nights such as this, with the flames of the fire leaping high and lighting up those handsome Asiatic faces, curious at their first glimpse of an Englishman. "Why does this sahib of yours wear a turban?" they asked. I knew enough Persian to understand most of their questions. The perfect manners of this people appealed to me, their hospitality, their picturesque appearance, inhabitants as they were of a country little changed since the days of the Bible.

They all possessed some kind of firearm and wore bandoliers of cartridges. Long daggers they carried pushed through their kamarbands. Probably they were murderers to a man, but they had a dignity, and a manliness too, which one would have to go far to find in the civilization of the West.

Early in the morning we were on the move again with only twenty-five miles to Rui Khaf. The route was, as ever, a wild waste of nothingness; the pace, as always, that quiet five miles an hour, walk, trot, lead and walk again, so that shortly after midday we saw, from a slight rise in the ground, an oasis the like of which we had never seen before. We stared at row upon row of tall poplars, behind which stood the usual mud fortified walls which enclosed the fruit gardens and houses of Rui Khaf and protected them from the almost constant and devastating wind. It came as a shock to see such things as trees again. The very green of them was a delight to the eye.

The Indian officer in charge of the two troops there came cantering out to meet us. All was well and he bore a message from the head man of the place asking me to stay the night in his house.

As we reached the main fortified gate I noticed something suspended from the middle of the arch and asked the officer what it might be.

"They hanged a man here yesterday," he said.

There swung the corpse, and it was difficult to get through

on horseback without touching it. The hands were tied behind the back, and on the earth underneath were marks indicating dried pools of blood. The neck had stretched to an unnatural length with the tortured face sideways, the feet were close together and turned inwards.

This had been an Afghan raider from Herat, not so very far eastwards, and in fact almost within the range of vision on a clear day. He had been captured during an attempted raid on the village and sentenced to death by shooting. Three or four Persian soldiers were detailed, but their volley only succeeded in wounding the unfortunate Afghan in both arms and through the shoulder. A rope had then been tied round his neck and attached to a horse with a rider, who dragged his victim through the town to the gate, where he was swung aloft to choke out what life was left in him amidst the execrations and curses of the crowd. To and fro in the wind swung this horrible body.

Death is not easy in that part of the world to a criminal. There seemed no method of handing out a sudden merciful end, and whatever method was chosen, it was carried out in the presence of the multitude. A band of sorts would play, and the day would seem to be a public festivity for all except the wretch who provided the central attraction. The victims in almost every case were raiders, and doubtless the punishment fitted the crime, or rather crimes, for which they were responsible. In Meshed, up north, where they had a certain number of what we might call "pieces" of artillery, the condemned were sometimes blown to bits, strapped to the muzzles of the cannon. One peculiarly horrible form of execution was the "throat-cutting." With his hands tied behind his back the victim was forced to kneel down, while the executioner with a razor-edged knife approached from behind, tilted up the chin with one hand and slit the wretched man's throat from ear to ear with the other.

Over in Afghanistan the most dreadful tortures were enforced. Stoning to death was common—a hideous death, too—and one which it has fortunately never been my lot to witness. Burying a man up to his neck in the ground was also a favourite practice.

I believe that some victims of this torture lived for incredible times in agony, especially when the ceremony took place near some ant-heap and a trail of sugar was led to the head of the buried one.

I found my detachment in great form and comfortably housed. The mere fact that they paid for what they received, and were not a menace to this queer place, had worked wonders. The Indian officer in command had done his job well, in short he acted as the king of Rui Khaf. As I had arranged, patrols took it in turns to visit every water-hole or dwelling-place in reach of either side of the Cordon, so that every man soon came to know the lie of the country, and what was more important, the country-side soon knew them. The result was a complete cessation of raiding parties from over the Afghan border and a cordial welcome wherever we went. The fortified gates no longer closed, the walls were not lined with hostile riflemen. Rui Khaf did not boast a governor, but there was a kind of "elder" to whose house I went to spend the night.

An astonishing array of good things awaited me in my scrupulously clean mud room. There was a gigantic tray containing chickens and eggs and all kinds of Persian dishes unknown to me, little skewered rolls of meat enclosing a plum or some kind of fruit, in brief, enough for at least six people. Great flagons of Persian wine, white and red, flanked this amazing feast which I was left alone to compete with. What a time Sandy would have had! That rascal I had left behind in Kain.

After I had done what execution I could, my host, a merry man, appeared to take coffee with me. We sat together far into the night while he told me of his life in that place, of life in far-off civilized Teheran, of a thousand interesting matters. He also said that they had been dreading the occupation of their town by us. It was naturally a delicate situation for troops of any kind to occupy a section of a neutral country, and doubly so when they occupied a part recently abandoned by the army of another country where revolution was now rife.

I left almost at dawn on the following morning, and rode hack to Kain with my little escort by a roundabout way. From Rui

Khaf we struck due east till almost mi the Afghan frontier. Herat itself was visible. We were not, of course, allowed to set foot in that country—woe betide us if we did, and were marked down.

Three days were spent on the return journey, the two nights in the security of the high walls of outlying Persian villages.

It was bitterly cold again, and I was glad when Kain, which I had already begun to look upon as my home, came in sight. Back again in that long, narrow room, with Sandy wagging his tail, the stove burning merrily, and an "all well" report from my Indian officer whom I had left in charge, I felt "at home" once more.

There was a great deal to be done settling the forage and transport accounts. Our bank was still represented by those sacks of Persian silver coinage which we had brought from Birjand. Here, as at Rui Khaf, I arranged for continuous patrols to scour the country both east and west, their distribution and numbers ensuring a sufficient number of men always being at Headquarters at Kain ready to move out at a moment's notice, and strong enough to deal with raiders or chase a German party.

The raiders did not raid, however. They had been accustomed to the Cossack régime, which had become more and more slack as the disturbing revolutionary news found its way to them. They did not seem inclined to come to conclusions with my Awan Lancers, who were constantly on the trek in their once easy playgrounds.

The German parties were rapidly becoming a myth. Why should they try to get through to Afghanistan via the British sector when they had those three hundred odd miles north of us occupied only by disgruntled Russian troops who hardly cared whether they passed or not, and who certainly would not dream of turning out to chase them in the Arctic cold? At the end of January a month had passed, and our sector was an open book to us all. I do not think that any stranger could have passed through without having us after him long before he could reach the Afghan frontier.

A time came when one felt that there was nothing more to be done. Everything was satisfactory enough; our sector went well. But nothing happened. That narrow room and the ice-bound Kain were taking on the aspect of a prison. I hated those clever wall drawings. I found myself sitting there, and hours afterwards still sitting, looking at nothing and thinking of less. This would not do at all. It was a kind of "cafard" bred of nothing else than a lack of energy to cope with an unusual situation; a situation that had to be dealt with at once. The day must be properly parcelled out and scheduled so that there should be an end to this sitting about and thinking of nothing.

Once a fortnight a pair of camels arrived from the south bringing letters or post from India. This was an outstanding event, and one to be honoured. I remember making a series of sketches of this longed-for day and sending them back to the Cordon Headquarters; it amused me to do this, and I heard later that it also amused the recipients. No. 1, waking up on that day knowing that something outstanding was afoot. No. 2, going out for a good ride on the plain followed by Sandy. No. 3, coming back and spending an hour at "stables" with my two troops. No. 4, the selection of one of my last tins, preferably a tongue, to celebrate the occasion. No. 5, ascending to my roof with field-glasses to watch for the dust of those mail-laden camels. No. 6, the squadron writer entering my long room with the letters. No. 7, a copy of my only letter, from Cordon Headquarters. "Reference your No. Kain 555 dated the so-and-so, please furnish details of your expenditure of—thousand krans (Persian coinage) on the 12th instant, enclosing receipts for the same—". Somebody then had the honour to be "Sir, your obedient servant," and we all had to wait another fortnight for this exciting day.

I had sent all the way to India for a miniature library of the newest books, also for the famous booklet of Monsieur Müller, the physical-training expert. In two and a half months they might be expected to arrive, with that railway creeping to the Persian frontier from Nushki and the motor track being continued thence northwards.

Meanwhile there was the morning gallop over the plain with Sandy in attendance; the hour of "stables" with my detachment. Back to the long room then for office work, paying for transport and forage, and keeping up the weekly report and diary.

In the afternoons I organized games for my men. We had

a football in the stores, and I used to thoroughly enjoy being downed by those cheery Awans. Some days we arranged a course and out into the plain we would go with the squadron long dogs, Sandy to the fore. Hares were very few and far between, but we had excellent sport on some occasions.

This was always on foot, as we could not be far away from our post in case of the sudden call to chase men instead of hares. At the back of Kain to the east there was a range of bleak hills several thousand feet high, where I had discovered an old disused mosque, or rather a small temple, about a thousand feet up. It had a small courtyard and a stunted tree; from its shelter one could look over mile upon mile of nothingness, with the ever-changing light playing fantastic tricks with the imagination. Sometimes on mail days I watched from this vantage-point for the two dots on the horizon which did move, to pass the other tiny dots which were camel scrub.

Meanwhile I had become a familiar figure to the inhabitants of the "town." Every day my wanderings took me through intricate and absurdly theatrical by-ways leading from my house to the gates opening on to the desert. There was no more hostility; the men would exchange a salaam, the women no longer turned to the wall in disgust at the unbeliever. Most of the women were, in their uncivilized way, extremely beautiful. Like all Eastern women they walked and moved with a peculiarly graceful carriage, but it was seldom that one could obtain a glimpse of their faces, veiled as they were to the eyes with their yashmaks. I suppose they must have been curious about this British officer who lived in their midst. As the time went on, and I was anxiously awaiting my "library" from India, and becoming more and more accustomed to this queer life, I began to recognize certain of those veiled figures that I met during my regular routine movements through that maze. The yashmak would drop sometimes, and as we passed I would see briefly the most attractive Eastern beauty, the most wonderful large, dark eyes set in a perfect oval of delicate, fair colouring crowned with glossy, dark hair. A smile came, and a whispered greeting in that beautiful language of theirs, the Italian of the East.

It all inspired the feeling, as the time passed, that one wanted less and less ever to go back to one's own life and people. I loved my hill-side temple, my rides over the plain. What matter if one did sit motionless for hours and hours? My men were contented, and as far as this sector was concerned, we had only to ask to get whatever we wanted. No one interfered.

Meanwhile all the way up from rail-head, up the Cordon, the garrisons of the far-separated posts had been busy making the difficult bits of the desert and the passes as suitable as they could for motor transport. Where that sporting old Sikh had gone in his battered Ford was hardly impracticable for Government Transport. The Headquarters of the Cordon had moved up, by car, to Birjand.

The next excitement was the arrival of the O.C. Cordon who was coming up to Kain to see how we were faring. I did not want to see him, or anyone else, in the least. I looked upon Kain as my own home. It was in this uncharitable and most unsoldierlike frame of mind that I rode out to a small, sandy hill in the desert to sit and scan the horizon through field-glasses for the moving dot which would be the G.O.C.'s car. My squadron and I had made this out-of-the-way tract our home; its people were now our friends, its ways our ways. What did it matter if one was content to sit quite still in hill-side temples for hours? . . . What did it matter if one never even spoke one's own language again? We had done, and were doing, our job. I didn't want to see any General. I didn't care whether that consignment of books arrived or not. That is how things were going with me. My men and horses were fit, and we had scoured that odd hundred-mile sector together. Trekking, always trekking, then back again to that funny, long room, in and out of those tortuous, narrow, high-walled ways of the little town. My Persian friends, their hospitality . . . but I could focus a tiny, moving dot. No camel this, but something with a trail of dust behind it, zigzagging to pick the best way through the thorn bushes. The car was soon well in sight, so I handed my horse to my orderly to lead back, and walked to meet the visitors. The car contained the G.O.C., his Staff Officer and driver.

When I shook hands with these cheery people, I felt thoroughly ashamed of myself and my moods and thoughts. Climbing up behind to show them the best way in, I realized that it wouldn't "do."

Later, after the inspection was over, I am glad to say satisfactorily, the three of us sat down to what fare I had been able to provide in my long room, and the interesting situation which had arisen in this corner of Asia was explained to me.

CHAPTER 7

Holding the Line

We were in a neutral country, of course, but the trend of events was making it increasingly difficult, not only for the Central Government in Teheran, but also for the provincial governors of Persia, to maintain this strict neutrality. Various happenings had caused affairs in this country to change.

Turkish successes had badly undermined British prestige, and in many quarters the Russian Revolution was looked upon as the prelude to a complete victory for Germany. Persia contained many Europeans whose sympathies lay with Germany. In Meshed, the only real town in the whole of the eastern part of Persia, anti-British propaganda was being vigorously carried on. To this town, which is one of the holy cities of Islam, comes an unending stream of pilgrims, rendering the detection of hostile spies and agents a most difficult matter. In Meshed itself there were many European residents, British, American, Belgian, Italian and others, connected with business or employed in one way or another by the Persian Government. Up to this time the presence of Russian troops there had been a safeguard for this European contingent, but now these troops were leaving their officers and flocking northwards to their own country.

The situation was critical, as the massacre of those Russian officers and their families, or even of all the European residents, was by no means an impossibility. It had become imperative for the British to act at once.

Part of the Punjab Infantry regiment on the Cordon was already marching northwards to Meshed. The two squadrons of

my regiment, which had been back in India, were now returning, also bound for Meshed. The Cordon which we had previously shared with the Russians was to be taken over entirely
by us. And what was going to be done by those Russians? The
Turks had made a great advance in Caucasia and had occupied
Baku. This, more than anything else, had compromised heavily
our position in Persia. In fact the whole situation was fraught
with interest and possibilities.

Meanwhile the Cordon southwards was to be strengthened;
all was quiet there, and every effort would be made to convert
those hundreds of miles into a reasonably passable line of communications.

I was to remain in charge of my present sector and at the
same time map out northwards the best route I could find for
motor transport. This route lay due north in the direction of
Meshed, not to Rui Khaf, which lay north-east, closer to the
Afghan frontier.

It did me a world of good, this visit of the G.O.C. Things
were beginning to move, and life seemed no longer mere stagnation. When my guests had departed, and their zigzagging,
distant, dust-followed pin-point of a car had vanished over the
horizon, my Indian officers and I had a consultation concerning this new road-marking venture. On the following day we
moved off, a small village fifty miles to the north our destination,
aiming to get there on the second day and work our way slowly
back, making landmarks as we went.

We reached our goal after a most enjoyable march, riding
quietly along. On arrival our local spy came out in great excitement to tell me that two Europeans had spent the night in a
little village some ten miles away. Off we went to investigate.

There were certainly two white people in one of the village
huts, but no German agents this time. Two Russians these, a man
and a woman. He was an officer of a Russian regiment which
had deserted from Meshed northwards en masse, and murdered
the few officers who had elected to go with it. They had fled
and were making their way south as best they might, but the
little transport they had in the form of camels had disappeared

the night before with the drivers and every single belonging of theirs with the exception of what they stood up in. They were practically starving, poor devils, and overjoyed to see me. I lent them a few mules of our transport and sent them back to Kain with a small escort to my "home" there, to be looked after by the old man Suleiman.

Several tedious days followed, marking out a possible route over the desert with shingle heaps, mounds of sand, any conceivable method which we could invent. This was later to become the main way northwards for our transport and lines of communications.

Returning to Kain, I was delighted to find my Russian friends in possession of my long room. They were in good spirits now and filled with that amazing optimism which only Russians can attain. It was strange to find them there; strange, too, to see a woman in that place.

However, I could send them along with the next empty, south-bound convoy on the way to India and safety. I was indeed sorry when the time came to say good-bye. They had been marvellous company, had entertained me with their experiences. We had sat up late at night playing my little gramophone, and they had given me song after song.

They very kindly left behind two little ikons as souvenirs, which I still treasure.

What with the visit of the G.O.C., and this unexpected Russian interlude, I felt the loneliness very badly when it was all over. I used to think of that young Russian officer whom I had found when I arrived, and look at those clever drawings of his on the walls. Had he been murdered, too, with the rest? He was right about this place when he said it was enough to drive anyone mad.

Yet it had a queer fascination for me all the same.

The weeks went by, and we took it in turns to go out and make what improvement we could to this northward motor track to be. All was quiet along the Cordon. It seemed that this "interlude" would last for ever, this life of nothingness; although strange rumours came of turmoil and chaos from beyond the Russian frontier.

Then, to my joy, came the two squadrons on their way to the holy city of Meshed.

Winter had paid us one last visit, and it was an icy one, with howling snow-storms by day and hard frost at night. The squadrons had suffered a bad time and were glad to reach the shelter of Kain; but hardly more pleased than I was to have the company of my old friends once more.

After their one-day halt, I rode out with them on their northward trek and wished that it had been my squadron's job to accompany them, to go up to Meshed, the first civilization since leaving Quetta all those hundreds of miles south, in India.

All that was to come later; but I felt abominably depressed as I rode back alone after seeing the last horseman disappear from sight round a spur in the hills through the winding northward pass; in fact, by way of our "motor road."

There was plenty to do, of course, in my sector. There were hundreds of miles to be ridden, there was constant work on our "motor road." Horses' forage and transport had to be looked after, and the unending accounts, which were a mental torture to me in this Persian silver coinage. There were the spies' reports to be diaried and sent back to Cordon Headquarters.

After a few weeks that settled feeling returned—Kain was "my" home, and I was quite content. Each hour of the day had its duties—ride, office work, stables, afternoon climb to my little temple, an occasional visit to some outlying village to see that my "agents" were doing their job.

The inhabitants were no longer curious. I went my way among them unnoticed, in and out and through their fortified mud walls and wooden gates. The Governor would come and have tea with me sometimes, and so would some of the village elders whom I had got to know through my Indian officers. I was able to carry on a conversation in their own language, a language after all not so very different from the "Urdu," the dialect which one uses in all work and dealings and talk with one's own men in the Indian Army. The "library" had arrived from India. I didn't want it, with the exception of Müller's physical exercise book. I worked this all out with my men, and we never missed our daily hour. They were quite content living here among their co-religionists, busy patrolling, escorting convoys, road making. In the evenings those who were in would organize a course, or games. The horses were marvellously fit. May came, and the climate was glorious; but we seemed to have spent a lifetime in this monotony.

Kain itself in its oasis of crops, now green and flourishing, with here and there patches planted with poppies, red and white, for opium making, assumed an appearance very different from its shut-in, high-walled, winter gloom.

From time to time the old Governor or one of the elders would invite me and my Indian officers to dine. Then I realized what was contained behind those sinister-looking, uniform high mud walls.

Well, there it all was, once one was admitted through the high, narrow gate, all that I had ever imagined when reading Omar Khayyám. It was fascinating.

A bright moonlight night; a sky cloudless, almost dark blue, with huge glittering stars that looked absurdly like lamps hanging from it. Rose trees, vines, apricot trees. A rippling streamlet bubbling through; in the middle perhaps a little fountain—nightingales. In the centre, from which paths led outwards, a square of well-tended grass. One's host . . . his perfect, quiet manners, and his greeting. . . . The marvellously handsome dignity of those village elders, with their picturesque, perfectly tied snow-white turbans and long, loose, silken clothes. It was difficult not to stare and stare at those delightful old gentlemen, and on some of those nights difficult to imagine that one was not dreaming. It was for all the world like walking straight into a fairyland.

We would sit in a circle on beautiful carpets. Persian wine was brought, white and red; and Persian wine can be delicious. . . .An amazing variety of perfectly cooked food, eaten, according to custom, with one's fingers. Bowls of rose water were passed round between the courses for the hands. It all seemed so natural. The conversation went easily, and not by the flicker of an eyelid did my host ever betray the amusement which my incorrect Persian must have frequently excited. All too soon we would go back, out of these walled fairylands and away from their fairy-tale owners, back through those high, narrow, twisting ways, to that queer long room where the dog Sandy, who had annexed my camp-bed, would thump a greeting with his tail and beg me to let him stay there. That great, long-legged, silky-eared Saluki dog was a godsend to me. Such a grave face, I love animals' grave faces. Such a long, lean, flat head which when he was really pleased seemed to go all "flatter" than ever.

I suppose the only thing to complete these romantic Persian nights would have been the appearance of some beautiful houris, dancing against the shadow of those roses and apricot trees. But these were not for the eyes of the unbeliever. Exist they did, and marvellously beautiful they were. I did not live, as one of themselves, alone in that fascinating place without having a glimpse every now and then of the most beautiful Eastern types. Some of them I knew well by sight, and the yashmak (veil) would chance to fall as we passed. It was not the fact that east is east and west is west, or even the chance of a jealous knife between the ribs, that made my acquaintance-ship end with the male population. Never once did I have a complaint even against my men in all their comings and goings in that land. Things, alas, as usual, are not what they seem. That part of the world is infected, to as large an extent as ninety per cent, and such a degree, and for so long, as to be immune itself, with disease. What else can you expect when any camel driver or muleteer for his one night's halt in some such place as Kain, where his caravan stops, can be officially married, and is again in the next stop a hundred miles away?

The weeks went on and summer came; no devastatingly hot Indian summer but a delightful climate. The summer far away south in Quetta is a marvellous one, but up here it was gorgeous.

That same feeling had long ago come back that one didn't mind if one spent the rest of one's life in this Chu Chin Chow atmosphere—one's own language nearly forgotten. In the evenings I used to climb up to my roof and sit there for hours, sometimes alone, sometimes with my Indian officers or Persian guests. A glorious view over the desert to the south was the reward as the sun went down behind the distant hills, then came the rising of a gigantic moon and the fresh coolness of the night. On the other side one looked down into the courtyard of the Mosque, heard the evening call to prayer.

I had already been honoured with an invitation to visit the Mosque and had even been permitted to lay therein a carpet, my humble gift.

Taking off my boots I had been escorted within and shown all there was to see. Little enough that was; but to them, to the people of Kain, everything. I had made a new friend there, the high priest, who conducted me on that evening. The sincerity, the fervour, the earnestness of it all somehow filled me with shame for my very unimportant, ignorant and indifferent outlook upon the vital beliefs of others.

Yes, the fool of the family even could be carried away on those summer evenings in imagination and filled with a great respect for this Biblical people and a real liking too. Torture, tragedy, hideous cruelty, exist in those backs of beyond, and an incredible indifference to human suffering and life and death. After all, who is to say that our own Biblical characters did not lead just such a life, our religious historical heroes. Yet, they were real men. They and their deeds and their history are read aloud in thousands of little centuries old English churches, of how they too tortured, stoned, fought, and massacred, clamoured, cried, and were themselves murdered and mutilated—read aloud by gentle-toned, earnest and sincere clergymen to congregations of reverent, civilized folk in whose lives, fortunately for them, no such horrors occur.

Then the train of thought would change to just eighteen months ago—to London of 1917—to the little flat in Clarges Street—to laugh upon laugh—to the inimitable George Robey—to the well-being of it all—possibly to the sudden unexpected turn of the profile of a face hitherto unattractive which caused it to become beautiful —to the welcoming smile of the cloak-room attendant at the Savoy, who is incidentally still there. In short, through a maze of disconnected thoughts and mind pictures until another night brought sleep. Now, this for any length of time is definitely not good for anybody, and time was passing. It was August now and I had been nearly eight months in that place.

I was going too often to sit in that old temple courtyard up the side of the mountain, and it was becoming a habit to fix one's eyes on some object miles away, and forget, and just stay there.

I had taken to visiting the outposts, even distant Rui Khaf, by camel. A Persian friend lent me two beautiful riding camels, and sometimes I set out on a round of visits and inspections lasting for a week. Away to the Afghan frontier and back west of my sector, day after day, my orderly and I shuffled along on these creatures. We would trot for half an hour and walk half an hour through the early mornings, then dismount, tie our animals' nose-strings round their forelegs as they sat down, and sleep the hot midday hours in their shade; then on again.

I used to amuse myself studying a Persian Grammar, part of my disused library, while we walked.

Hundreds and hundreds of miles must have been scored trekking during those months in Kain. Day after day in the open desert, a bivouac within the walls of some village and the night's sleep. Raiders were definitely not known in this constantly patrolled sector. The inhabitants of those far apart hamlets were definitely grateful and wonderfully hospitable.

At last came a message to the effect that an officer of the rank of Major-General, with two Staff Officers, was coming north, bound for Meshed, and would I look after these visitors on their way through Kain.

The "interlude" was at last to be broken. All this time news had been trickling through from the north that the arrival of our troops in Meshed had calmed things down there, but what chaos was afoot over the Russian frontier, and how it would affect us, was an unknown quantity.

The Major-General came and passed a sphinx-like night in Kain. I had quite forgotten that Generals existed. He passed on, and later I heard that his first remark to the CO. of my regiment in Meshed was, "Are you mad, too?" He drove along my "motor road" in his car to where the caravan track became one hundred miles north more and more suitable for wheeled transport as it led into the holy city of Meshed.

A message came from the O.C Cordon asking if I would like a month's leave in India. No, I didn't want leave anywhere. Another message arrived: "I am sending a Ford lorry in which you will leave for India on the—th inst."

Good-bye to Sandy—to the squadron—to the officer sent by that car to relieve me. Suleiman and I bumped our way southwards.

1918

"Unborn tomorrow and dead yesterday,
Why fret about them if today be sweet."

Chapter 1

Turks & Bolsheviks

On this southward journey down the Cordon to rail-head, which was now practically on the Persian frontier, south of Robat, signs of activity, change, bustle, were evident; chief among these was the preparation of a passable route for motor transport. The Seistan Levy Corps had been greatly augmented and were busily engaged in this task, and that meant more British officers.

There was talk of more Indian troops to come out from India—motor transport units—stronger garrisons for this little span of posts which had ceased to be an attractive hunting-ground for hostile propagandists on their way to Afghanistan. We now occupied the whole stretch of that country right up to Meshed, and to the Russian border. In short, it seemed that the Cordon was to be transformed into a line of communications.

What had begun years before as a little unknown mission when my own regiment and the Punjab Infantry had gone "into the blue" to search for needles in a haystack and fight Biblical battles with tribesmen, seemed to be growing into a much greater significance. The trend of events in Bolshevik Russia was responsible for this and for many dangers threatening us.

Our Ford lorry made wonderful records over this beginning of a motor road on our journey south, though some of the passes certainly gave us a lot of trouble. There seemed to be a British officer in nearly every little post where we halted for the night, and it was not long before Kain and its solitude seemed to fade into a kind of impossible dream—yet a dream which for me has never lost its fascination—and I looked forward to a month of normal and cheery life in India.

At last one evening after a long day we arrived almost at nightfall with engine nearly red hot, crawling into that most grim of all places, Robat, over the point where Afghanistan, Persia, and Baluchistan meet: the corner of the Black Mountain, Koh-i-Malik-Siah. A short struggle on the morrow would get us into rail-head.

There was the old mud rest-house and the serai for the little infantry garrison to remind me of the first time I saw the place—1916 seemed long ago!—and of that dreary wind-swept ride from far-off Nushki.

I saw a light in the rest-house, which we had approached from behind, and hastened up the rise towards it intent on greeting the British officer in command, looking forward to a night there with him, to hearing the latest news from India, to a civilized and cheery time. It was still a change to me to talk to my own kind again. Through the window I could see him in the light of his lamp, in bed; he appeared to be sleeping. There was no answer to my shout, and ignoring the sentry's warning, I entered the room laughing. The next moment I knew that I was standing at the bedside of a dead friend.

In the little apology for a mess I found his subaltern, in officer of the Indian Medical Service, and two British N.C.O.s, the forerunners of a coming Motor Transport Company. From them I heard the sad news that the CO. had died that afternoon from pneumonia.

That Dante's Inferno of rocky gully took on an even more malevolent and sinister aspect on the morrow as we buried the poor chap, and the words of the burial service seemed to be carried on the wind to echo against its jagged, precipitous, merciless walls.

It didn't seem like a month to me before I was back again in Nushki, but this time those dreadful four hundred miles to the Persian border were accomplished by train. Coming down that sinister gorge from Quetta for the third time, the view of that back of beyond shrouded in one of its frequent sand-storms made me wonder whether I should ever return. It was now early September, 1918.

It had been a merry time, that month's leave, and the prospect seemed for all the world, or may I say that the outlook over that apparently endless nothingness gave me the same feeling that I remembered as a child when confronted with a dose of castor oil—the inevitable. If old Suleiman felt troubled he certainly did not show it. All was bustle on that railway; we were nobody's children, and had to find our way as best we might to get back to Headquarters of the Cordon at Birjand, where I expected to receive orders.

Leaving the farther end of the railway, stage by stage and from post to post we travelled, sometimes by lorry when we were lucky enough to get a lift, and at times by camel convoy, journeying at night and walking hour after hour alongside our old grunting, grousing, gurgling transport. Beyond the fact that each widely separated post was now connected with a fair motor track and was inhabited by a slightly larger garrison, there was little difference, but all pointed to preparations—to expansion.

One thing was evident: the old Cordon was being changed as rapidly as possible into a line of communications. Whither, and why? A brief explanation of what was happening in that corner of the world may help.

Why had that sphinx-like Major-General and Staff come through Kain? Why, again, was a General Officer appointed in command of this thousand-mile line which was being made into military lines of communication? Why all this motor transport, depôts, garrisoning of outposts?

In the beginning the cause may be traced to the fear of enemy action and propaganda in Afghanistan, and the resulting threat to India, which had first led to the dispatch of troops to Eastern Persia. Until 1917, the year of the Russian Revolution, the only road open to enemy agents into Afghanistan had been across Persia, where they had to run the gauntlet of what was then the Eastern Persian Cordon in the shape of the Russians or ourselves. The Russians had left, and the Cordon had been taken over by us up to Meshed and a hundred miles on to the Russian border.

Over that lay Transcaspia, Russian Turkestan. The advent of

the Bolshevik régime had opened an easy route for the enemy agents along the Central Asian railway from Krasnovodsk, the port on the Caspian Sea, following the north Persian border for some four hundred miles, through Askhabad and on towards Merv, branching southwards down to Khushk on the Afghan border itself.

General Dunsterville, by his occupation of Baku, had for a time closed the road.

With the fall of Baku (which was only seventeen hours steaming from Krasnovodsk on the eastern shores of the Caspian) and its occupation by the Turks, the menace to India through Afghanistan reappeared.

This meant that the occupation of the Krasnovodsk-Merv railway would have given Germany the alternative approach to the East which she sought after the Baghdad railway had been closed to her.

By the summer of 1918 they had definitely schemed and filed this Berlin, Batum, Baku, Bokhara plan. Had this succeeded, the Germans would have been a great deal nearer the Indian frontier than Baghdad. The danger of a German strategical railway here could not be over-estimated, not so much from the point of view of an armed invasion, but as a menace of political propaganda, agitation, and general trouble on our border. Thus enemy agents were free to pass into Afghanistan along the Central Asian railway, also, possibly, bodies of Turkish troops. It was absolutely essential that measures should be taken to oppose the Turks, including, if necessary, the destruction of the railway itself.

There was, too, ample evidence that the Bolsheviks had already entered into negotiations with the Turks with a view to allowing them the use of the Central Asian railway to convey their troops to Afghanistan. In fact, the plot thickened; the smallest events were fraught with interest; and it was from this corner of Russia that we might have expected most trouble in this extremely critical period.

Yet, as ever, there was another side to this question, and one in our favour.

Russian Turkestan had become a Bolshevik state, so called.

126

Askhabad, the capital, was the centre of interest of Transcaspia, itself to all intents a Russian colony. The bulk of the Russian population consisted of employees of the Central Asian railway, which ran throughout the length of the province; they were augmented by ex-officials, military and civil, of the old Imperial Government, with a few traders and professional men. Here, as in all towns, a sprinkling of Armenians and Caucasians could be found.

The indigenous inhabitants, the Turkomans, are a sensible people, and Transcaspia was proving the most unfruitful soil for Bolshevism. The Turkoman is accustomed to do what his chief tells him, and the idea of the division of property is the last thing to appeal to the head of a tribe. Therefore Turkoman and Russian, whose relations have never been too cordial, became united by the common fear of the extreme Bolshevist and of the retribution that would descend upon them if the Tashkent Army were to come down on Askhabad.

There were degrees of Bolshevism in Russia, varying in colour from palest pink to darkest red. In Transcaspia, pale pink might be termed the prevalent hue. The darkest red pundits in Tashkent were certainly dissatisfied with the quality of Bolshevism there; in fact, they looked upon Transcaspia almost as the centre of a counter-revolutionary movement. They had therefore sent an emissary to instil true "political" ideas among the disaffected. From him and his excesses Transcaspia began to learn exactly what Bolshevism meant.

These Transcaspians styled themselves Mensheviks, as opposed to Bolsheviks. In the Russian language the prefix "Bolsh-" means more, greater, the bigger, the larger; "Mensh-" means the less, the smaller. I think that sums it up.

Things came to a head when this emissary, Froloff, a handsome savage with a lust for persecution, was approached by a peaceful delegation of railwaymen with a petition. He shot the whole lot with his revolver. Railway workmen instantly attacked him and his wife and killed them both.

This brought what might be termed the breaking-point.

A culmination of serious developments in Central Asia had

long been foreseen, hence the presence in Meshed of the sphinx-like one and his staff; and a deservedly popular sphinx and staff they were!

The British object was to prevent a Turkish advance from Baku through Krasnovodsk towards Afghanistan. The aims of both parties, the Mensheviks and the British, were united in a desire for the removal of the Bolsheviks from Transcaspia. The Mensheviks had now agreed, once they were, with our assistance, "top-dogs" in Transcaspia, to do their utmost in preventing the Turks from entering their country, and in intercepting enemy agents who were trying to work their way eastwards.

Incidentally, we agreed that in addition to rendering monetary assistance, British support in the form of troops should be concentrated on the Russian border for moral effect, and for this purpose a small detachment of the Punjab Infantry with machine-guns had been sent to Artik on the frontier.

When Suleiman and I reached Birjand, my own orders were disappointing. The Awan squadron, complete with Sandy, had gone on north from Kain, and the squadron with whom I had shared that disastrous ambush in 1916 had moved up to Turbat-i-Haidari, half-way between Kain and Meshed. I was to take over command of that squadron and of the post itself.

Off again, then, over the same route which we had travelled in the Ford car with that amazing old Sikh a year before. My friend the bank manager had been absorbed into the force as the Field Treasury Cash Officer, and was in Birjand busily dealing with the problems and accounts of all engaged in this picnic from Nushki to Russia.

We passed through Kain by night with a camel convoy. Somehow I felt glad not to see again that particular place in other hands; it had been so very much my home.

The route lay a mile or so to the west, and Suleiman and I kept looking back to that line of jagged hills outlined against the moon.

"We were happy there, weren't we, Suleiman?"

"Yes, Sahib."

That was all in the way of comment that I could ever get

out of that amazing old man. And so on we crept from day to day, over one pass, on to another desert stretch, again a pass, and through it until we reached the last halting-place for the night, with but a ride of twenty miles on the morrow to Turbat, where I was to take over command. Here I was delighted to find a small escort under an N.C.O. with one or two spare horses to meet us and accompany us the next morning.

These men were from my own original squadron, the Dekhanis, Mohammedans who had shared that nightmare ambush with me in the far-away south raiders' country, and whom I had not seen since. There is nothing of interest on that route from Birjand to Turbat. The nights were spent in small villages. One arrived dead tired after the day's monotonous and dreary crawl with the camel convoy, and no sooner had sleep come than it seemed that the early-morning bustle and loading began again. Suleiman brought tea, utterly unmoved by all the bustle and clamour, and woe betide the camel driver who dared to lay hands on anything that he did not consider ready.

Here again this little old man seemed always able to get his own way. He would curse with terrific vigour and invective the biggest and most truculent camel men; they simply gave in and did what he told them. Why, I could never fathom. The old man remained a mystery to me to the time of his death, years later, when we were again on active service in Waziristan on the north-west frontier, engaged in a civilized warfare compared with these years of ant-like wanderings so very much farther afield. What I owe to that faithful little Sinbad man is incalculable; I am quite sure that he shared, at this time, my disappointment in not being ordered to go farther north up to the Russian frontier.

It was heartening, the next morning, to trot out of that last halting-place with our little escort on our twenty-mile hack to squadron headquarters. We left the camel convoy behind and felt that we were back once more with our "family," no longer nobody's children, begging our way from post to post, now in a Ford lorry, now by camel, and even by foot, so busy had this line become. The Kain that I had known no longer existed, and that seemed a comfort to me. Nobody else could have those eight months of what I had actually enjoyed.

Riding quietly along, chatting with the N.C.O., and looking forward to being once more with my squadron, I felt how good it would be to have a definite job again. It was beginning to get very cold, with a wonderful crisp atmosphere, and the farther north we went the colder it became. But that day a bright sun shone in a cloudless sky after a night's hard frost. Towards the end, after slowly mounting a long slope of several miles, we looked down on Turbat, the first town of any size I had seen in Eastern Persia, standing in a valley dotted with tiny hamlets and orchards; in fact a large oasis. Through the orchards, bordered by mud walls, we approached the place itself. To see growth again, even if leafless, was cheering. The town consisted of the usual mud-domed, high-walled dwellings along a narrow way which soon entered a covered bazaar. Through this the road widened, and for almost half a mile we followed it before turning out to the quarters occupied by the British officers of the post.

A charming picture this bazaar presented. It was filled with people; with the inhabitants, with traders and camel men from Turkestan, Tashkent and Bokhara, with many bearing a distinctly Chinese or Mongolian appearance. Shafts of sunlight through ventilating holes and cracks in the vaulted roof played upon this throng of picturesque Asians in their many-coloured garments. The noise was deafening. Here and there sat camels, impervious to the din, their proud, disdainful heads turning lazily now here, now there. Strings of mules were wending their way along this thoroughfare driven by clamorous and excited muleteers. Through all the clamour seemed to run a continuous clicking, clanging noise—the sound made by sellers of sweetmeats, cutting off lengths from long strips of sugar with huge scissors. I always associated Turbat afterwards with that queer noise.

Graceful figures of women flitted past, veiled to the eyes by flowing, dark blue yashmaks. A posse of Persian Cossacks galloped through the mob with cracking of whips and toss of white Astrakhan caps. Aged and ragged beggars clamoured for alms from the passers-by. Merchants of all kinds of wares and foods were presiding over their stalls, and trade seemed good.

This wide, domed way lit by shafts of sunlight, this panorama of figures and faces, now humble as of the Persian villager, now fierce, handsome and lawless as of the Turkoman and Mongolian trader, raider, camel-man or muleteer, left an impression on me which will not easily fade. Here was a world, a picture of romance, through which I rode as in a dream. Never had I seen such a panorama of picturesque villains, though not shifty-eyed villains. They looked what they were—they cared not a damn for anyone.

My N.C.O. rode alongside to show me where we wheeled to the left down a narrow by-way, ending in a cul-de-sac. A door swung open as we dismounted.

"Hullo, Jimmy! Thank God you've come," said the officer whom I had come to relieve. He had been having a bad time with malaria and had been ordered back to India. Through this door I entered into my new domain —the usual courtyard and so-called garden, with a building whose rooms looked out upon it. A sense of great content overcame me; somehow I felt "at home" again.

CHAPTER 2

Friends

The handing over of business was soon completed—merely a matter of signing receipts for so much money, ammunition, so many secret documents, etc.—in fact the customary prosaic procedure.

The garrison consisted of a whole company of Indian Infantry, newcomers scattered from Turbat southwards in the various posts to take the place of the Punjab Infantry with whom, in 1916, we had set forth upon our original mission. The Punjab Infantry were already ahead, in Meshed, the holy city, and on the Russian border. Here, too, I found my own Dekhani squadron. That made a total of four British officers—three with the infantry and myself with the squadron.

In addition to these there was a Sapper Officer in charge of all road-making operations, for which he used local hired labour, and a young Indian officer of the Indian Medical Service.

A large supply depôt was being formed. This was in charge of two British N.C.O.s of the Supply and Transport Service.

Last, but not least, came the British Corporal in charge of all telegraphic communication via that same old friend, the single strand of wire which joined Russia with India. In him I immediately noted a character. He was a tiny little man, a Cockney of the very best type, and a grand type, as all who have served with such men will agree. He had his own quarters, close to mine, complete with the instruments of his calling. Well over middle age, he instantly constituted himself a sort of father advisor to me. He it was who brought in the daily mass of messages in the morning, and duly tapped the replies in the evening.

Few were the evenings during my short stay that I did not find my way into the little man's sanctum to discuss the day's doings and listen to his humorous and wise words. A pre-war soldier, he had been wounded in France while one of the original members of the British Expeditionary Force.

The sun was well down and the biting cold had set in for the night when, these introductions over, we gathered in the little mess, one of the rooms looking inwards on the usual courtyard. Old Suleiman had arranged my kit and gone off to the squadron lines.

This was indeed a change, this cheery gathering. And a good lot they were. We celebrated the occasion in fitting manner. It was not arrack any longer; here really good Persian wine, white and red, was available, and even such civilized products as whisky at times. Happily I could produce this from the remains of the stores which I had brought out from India.

I thought of the loneliness of Kain, of the hill-side temple, of all the uncertainty and attraction of that life; saw again that long room with its stove glowing red; I could almost hear poor Sandy's tail beating a welcome on my bed. Sandy had gone on with the Awans and their pack of Salukis to Meshed. Through my head ran the words of the Persian poet:

The ball no question makes of ayes or noes,
But right or left as strikes the player goes.

Through the haze of cigarette smoke and the cheerful noise of laughing voices my host, whom I was to relieve on the morrow, brought me back from my dreams.

"Come on, Jimmy, I must take you to meet the Russian Consul."

And so out into the icy night we went.

Our way ran down the narrow alley by which I had come in, and which led to the entrance of our quarters from that bazaar. Not a soul could be seen, and in that intense cold I was glad of my sheepskin poshteen coat. In the clear light of the full moon the bazaar itself took on a kind of romantic, mysterious radiance, with sharp contrasts of inky darkness pierced by

133

shafts of light through the holes and gaps in its roof. Turning to the left we reached a large open space, the public square, as it were, of the town.

In one corner a group of squatting camels, facing inward to a wood fire round which sat the huddled figures of their drivers, moved their lazy, curious heads at the sound of our footsteps. In the centre of the square the moonlight was strong enough to show up what appeared to be a tall pole, the straightness and symmetry of which attracted my curiosity in these typically Oriental and un-symmetrical surroundings. On closer inspection I found it to be made of iron, fifteen to twenty feet high; from the top projected a length of about four feet at right angles. At the end of the projection could be just discerned a small pulley-wheel.

I realized that I was standing under the public gallows—a gruesome thought in this icy moonlit stillness. Not half so gruesome as the actuality that I witnessed later when this sinister iron tree was appeased by a victim of Persian justice.

"Who are these Russians we are going to visit?" I asked my companion. "I understood that they had all left this sphere long ago for Meshed and the border."

These, I was told, consisted of one Ivanoff who still clung to his post and termed himself Russian Consul, his stepdaughter who had recently escaped from Russian territory via the Caucasus, and Borodin who termed himself Vice-Consul, with his wife.

In due course we came to a large wooden gate in the high mud wall enclosing the Russian Consulate and garden. This was swung open to our knock by the Cossack sentry on duty, who saluted and let us in.

I noticed about five others of his type, in a small, adjacent guard-room. These were men of the Persian Cossack Brigade, a corps recruited in Persia and officered by Russians with a nucleus of Russian N.C.O. instructors. They were then the best troops excepting artillery which Persia produced, though there could be no comparison between them and the real thing. In their white Astrakhan hats and plum-coloured long coats with white facings, daggers aslant at the waist, and soft leather top-boots, they presented a most picturesque appearance. Swash-bucklers—but this was a land of swashbucklers.

We were ushered into a large room, brightly lit and warmed with the usual Russian stove. On the walls hung beautiful silk tapestries, and against the three inner sides were comfortable divans. On a round table in the centre stood the samovar and glasses for tea. Small framed ikons in the corners where ceiling joined walls, heavy curtains shutting out the night, all gave an impression of warmth, comfort, and even luxury.

I was presented to Ivanoff, to Sonia his stepdaughter, and the Borodins.

Ivanoff was a giant of a man, clean-shaven, with a typical Russian face, high cheek-boned. He wore magnifying spectacles which gave his eyes a queer, glittering aspect. His greeting was almost effusively cordial. Borodin, a fat little nonentity, could be summed up at once as being extremely fond of himself. These two wore undress Russian uniform with the customary soft leather boots. Borodin's wife was very silent, a dull-looking type of what I had rather imagined the peasant class to be. However, as she was only able to speak her own language she had perforce to say little. Sonia had taken no notice whatever of our entry, but seeming suddenly aware that strangers had arrived, she greeted us with a smile.

When we had settled down to the usual glasses of tea from the samovar I found myself sitting next to her. She was young, dark and rather tall, with an indescribably attractive face. The sadness in her almost Eastern eyes only added to this attraction. She had that type of face and expression and colouring which belong only to her country and which give the impression that underneath lies something untamed, something that might be primitive and relentlessly fierce if brought to light.

I had heard of her husband's death at the hands of the Bol-sheviks, of her escape disguised as a peasant, her adventure into Persia to join Ivanoff.

The conversation became general. Sonia sat quietly listening. Those glittering eyes of Ivanoff's, the little pig-like ones of Borodin, the stolid face of his wife, I can see them still. Where had I come from? Was I going to stay in Turbat? Had I any musical instrument, or gramophone records? Then came vodka, and really good Russian vodka it was. As we left Sonia's fascinating smile accompanied her words, "Venez diner chez nous demain soir."

Back again in my quarters after this long day to dream of swashbucklers, camels, that grim iron post, and perhaps of slanting, smiling eyes. The southward-bound convoy had left, and with it the officer from whom I had taken over command of the post.

I found my squadron comfortably settled in a large serai. They were employed in escorting the convoys up and down the line, in patrolling the country east and west, and visiting the outlying villages and water-holes where news might be obtained from our agents who occupied these places. This was still being done although probably no hostile party would venture to penetrate into Afghanistan so far south as this. In the squadron I found very few of the men who came out on the original Cordon or who had been with me in 1916.

They had been all this time down south of Robat where the climate, the conditions, and that appalling water had been responsible for sending so many back to India. Very few ever returned.

I was particularly delighted to meet again gallant Sheikh Haider, who saved my life in the ambush and who had now been promoted to commissioned rank for his bravery on that occasion.

It was disappointing to find ourselves, although almost at the farthest end of the line of communications, separated from the regiment, of whom we had only the news that one squadron was still in Meshed while the other two had left that place for the Russian frontier.

No question makes of ayes or noes

There was a great deal of official correspondence to deal with: the rationing and quartering of the garrison itself, of the many details and convoys which came through. There were spies' reports and general information to be collected and diaried, and most distasteful of all to me—accounts. Accounts military have always seemed to me a maze of complications. It appeared that the correct way to deal with them was the one most fraught with difficulty and toil. Looking back to Sandhurst days that seemed so often to be the case, in fact, il fallait souffrir to achieve perfect accomplishment.

Having assumed what seemed a really comfortable position with one's rifle so placed that it seemed that one's sight could be indefinitely and immovably fixed upon the bull's-eye, up would come one of those amazing Staff-Sergeant instructors and with great but assumed severity force one's arms, body, rifle, head and everything else all at completely different angles to what they had ever been in before. But of course they were quite right. And how they drilled us. I can see now Staff-Sergeant Ham of H.M. Grenadier Guards looking down the front rank of a company of cadets. "Now then, 'old your 'ead up there, Mr. James. 'Oo's movin' there on the left?" "Yus, I thought so, stand *still!*"—the King of Siam! Monarchs and misters were one to this great man.

Still, all this office work had to be done. My little friend the Signals Corporal brought in the morning's telegrams, of which many had to be deciphered. It soon all became routine.

My first day in Turbat was a busy one, and I was glad when the time came to find my way through the bazaar to the Russian Consulate.

I found the same four, the Borodins, Ivanoff and Sonia, in the best of form and spirits. They had two guitars and two mandolins, and were playing and singing as if they had no care in the world. What were they doing there, since every trace of a Russian subject had long since disappeared? Ivanoff was the perfect host, Sonia was charming. After dinner, a typical Russian one, at which we were waited upon by well-turned-out Persian servants in the Consulate livery, I was initiated into the correct way of drinking vodka; then came more music. The room was cleared, and we danced to a gramophone. I was dancing with Sonia, and as we passed Ivanoff, who was sitting watching on the divan, I thought I caught a flash in those glittering eyes of his that just for a second unseated the "perfect host" expression.

However, all seemed well when I said good night to them, and the icy stillness of the bazaar as I walked home seemed strangely at variance with the evening I had so much enjoyed.

I arranged to ride with them and Borodin in the morning; they promised to show me the ways round and outside the town through the walled and now frost-bitten orchards.

I rode with Sonia, who told me that her mother and her own baby daughter, who had escaped, were now en route for Constantinople, where she hoped to rejoin them with her stepfather when news came of their safe arrival. She had been in some small Russian town when the Revolution broke out. Apparently it suggested setting a match to a cask of gunpowder. In an instant there had been an orgy of murder and loot, the gutters literally ran with blood, while the frenzied revolutionists and soldiery massacred all the bourgeois that they could find, Sonia herself, a stranger there, had borrowed peasants' clothing and managed to make her escape unmolested. Her husband, a Russian officer, was shot dead. It seemed incredible what that girl had seen, what she had suffered.

And so we rode on, Ivanoff and Borodin leading, then Sonia and I, then the Persian Cossack escort—the picturesque swashbucklers. A memorable morning, with sharp, crisp air and sunshine—the last thing I had expected of Persia. Yet Turbat-i-Haidari is the threshold of civilization, the first signs of it I had met since leaving far-away Quetta. I thought of the day in early 1916, when I had ridden out from Robat for the first time over that corner where three empires meet, Persia, Afghanistan and Baluchistan. Little did I think then that one day I should ride on into the Russian sphere; far less so that it would continue in due course over the Russian frontier and on to within marching distance of the Oxus.

I looked at this fascinating Russian girl who sat her horse so perfectly. She wore a long Cossack coat with a white Astrakhan Cossack hat slightly tilted and soft leather boots. I wonder if she realized how it suited her.

All too soon our ride came to an end and I was taking my leave. Borodin and his wife went on to their own little house adjoining the Consulate, and the Cossacks were leading the horses away to the stables.

As I turned the corner leading up to the bazaar I waved to Ivanoff and Sonia, who still lingered outside their wooden gate. Ivanoff called me back.

"Mon Capitaine," he said, in excellent French, "we shall be extremely disappointed if you do not dine with us every night."

Sonia smiled and Ivanoff glittered at me through those spectacles.

I could only say that they were too kind, and that I should be charmed to come that evening, if they would return the compliment on the following day and excuse the poor hospitality that I could offer.

"And bring your mandolin, Capitaine, and your gramophone records," laughed Sonia.

And I rode back to my duties, which had somehow become a great deal less tedious.

CHAPTER 3

A Hanging

On the following day I rode eastwards with one of my patrols to visit a water-hole and to gain an idea of the country, leaving early in order to get back in the afternoon. It grew colder every day, but as yet no snow had fallen. The exhilaration of that dazzlingly bright morning was amazing, especially as we turned out from the bazaar to cross the "public square." There stood the grim, iron "tree," but with a difference; a stout rope hooked to the bottom passed up and along the transverse piece, through the pulley-wheel, to end in an ominous and obvious noose.

My non-commissioned officer rode up alongside me.

"They are hanging a murderer here this afternoon, Sahib," he said.

Life meant to me that day freedom in the glorious sunlight, happiness; what must it be meaning to the man doomed to grace that gallows, cowering heavily guarded in the Persian prison cells? The thought sapped the freshness from the air, the brightness from the sunlight. Fate itself was present in the faint breeze that swung and turned that horrible noose.

The usual story came from our spy at the water-hole. No sign of any suspicious character had been seen. Dismounting, we off-saddled, watered and fed the horses, and spent half an hour sitting under the little clump of date trees that marked the place. I was watching the horses. Every now and then a stamp of hoof in the sand, a tail swished, an ear would be suddenly cocked forward in response to some sound that we could not hear. "What on earth do they think about? " Surely those handsome faces and patient, intelligent eyes, and all their grace and beauty are not merely a screen for thinking of when they will get back for their next feed.

Trotting quietly homewards, as we entered the town we noticed an unusual noise and stir, and realized from the densely packed crowd, through which we could not possibly force our way, that the iron tree was about to claim its victim. Not a trace of feeling could be detected in the faces of that mass of eagle-featured and Mongolian onlookers.

Sitting on my horse, I could see over their heads; a small space round the gallows was kept clear by Persian Cossacks. Discordant sounds of a primitive band heralded the approach from a side street of the principal character in this horrible act. He came into view surrounded by guards who held him on a mule. The almost green pallor of his face, and his look of imminent collapse, showed that he was beyond walking to his doom.

His appearance was the signal for imprecations and savage cries of rage from the crowd.

They reached the foot of the gallows and lifted that tortured wretch from the mule, they bound his hands behind his back; his feet and legs were left free. Then fell a deathly silence as the local Chief of Police read out in stentorian tones a list of the crimes of which the condemned had been found guilty.

In hopeless despair the victim's face turned from side to side, only to meet eyes furious, bloodthirsty, mocking. I had a sudden longing to force my way through with my patrol and rescue him, cut down and shoot any who opposed us. It was a ghastly thing to see a human being meet his end at the hands of his own kind.

The noose slid round his neck, the rope gradually tightened, and his head went back. "Allah!" he shouted once. I could not keep my eyes from that awful, convulsed figure jerking and swinging at the end of the rope. Soon he drooped motionless, and the crowd dispersed. We rode on to my quarters. I went in and sat down, muttered, "God, how awful!" and was violently sick.

Something had to be done to escape from this horror, and I thought of the Signals Corporal who brought in the morning's messages and transmitted my own.

Serving, as I did, all my time in an Indian Cavalry regiment, I missed that great element, the camaraderie, friendship and loyal support of the British N.C.O. and soldier. It was only on occasions like this that one had the privilege and the pleasure of associating with them. In saying this I am by no means belittling the great ties of friendship and loyalty that exist in an Indian regiment. But it was to this little man that I turned for help.

Snow had begun to fall as I walked out to his quarters, so thickly that it was not easy to see my way through the driving flakes.

As I groped along memories ran through my mind of a Christmas Eve in the Mediterranean in 1915, coming back from France to rejoin my regiment in this country. We had a gun mounted aft manned day and night by Marine Artillerymen, watching for the hourly expected submarine to offer a target, and I had spent the whole night at the gun with the N.C.O. in charge. He, too, like the little man I was going to visit, was the old-fashioned type of soldier. I don't know what we talked of, but it left a kind of warmth. He told a friend of mine afterwards that we had seen Christmas in together. "Yes," he said, "that there Captain James seems to be always laughin' under 'is skin." In two months it would be Christmas, 1918.

Signals had his own little Persian house. By some means—it was no business of mine—he had actually married a Persian woman according to the rites that existed. How far this was known had even less to do with me. This inscrutable little man may even have accepted the Mohammedan faith. Suffice it to say that this woman looked after him and kept house for him. I knocked.

"Come in, sir—you don't look 'arf bad, neither," said my host.

I told him of my evening's entertainment.

"Them things is best left alone," said he. "You didn't never ought to have went."

The stove was burning brightly and I sat down while my host rummaged for a suitable tonic to disperse the "horrors." Failing to find what he wanted, he went to the stairhead to summon his keeper of the house. Now, in the Persian language the word pronounced Qanoom means "lady," a respectful form of address to the opposite sex. In Hindustani "lao" is the imperative meaning "bring." In that language, too, "shiràb " means "wine." "Jaldhi" means quickly. This is what I heard. "'Ere, Kannum, lou up the shirrab and get a juldi on it too." And a right good "juldi" she got. I am afraid I was disappointed in his taste; but at any rate she was a buxom, smiling creature, and, having filled our glasses, she sat in the corner listening with all eyes and ears to what she could not conceivably understand. Looking out from his little window, one could see the snow falling and the neighbouring roofs like a collection of birthday cakes. "Kannum" refilled the glasses and returned to her corner—the warmth and comfort were beginning to dispel the "horrors."

"Yus," said my host, gazing reflectively and with an air of great wisdom at the glowing stove, "Yus, since I come 'ere I feel I somehow took Turbat in 'and, so to speak. Anything as you might want to know, just come along 'ere of an evening and arsk me."

He held the Russian Consulate in utter contempt.

"That there Ivanoff, what's 'e doin' 'ere, any'ow? That's what I want to know, and now he starts coming in on the telephone talking 'is damned bãt (language) in our time, and God knows who to."

I was interested to hear that, and began to wonder myself what was going on. But of Sonia, who incidentally had the title, "Marquise," he also spoke.

Removing his pipe, he gazed at the ceiling as if seeing some far-away vision.

"No, I don't 'old no brief for Ivanoff, but the Markwiss"—he drew in his breath—"coo!"

And so passed the evening in great content, while this amazing little man entertained me and "Kannum" wielded the jar. It was time to go. Ivanoff and Sonia were coming to dine in my quarters. The interest in all this was heightened by its unusual setting and surroundings. And who could have recognized the dapper little corporal who presented himself with the next morning's telegrams with a salute worthy of the smartest guardsman?

My guests arrived by a short cut, on foot, covered with snow. Old Suleiman had done his best.

They were marvellous company. We laughed, talked, played the gramophone, and Sonia sang to us with her guitar accompaniment. I told them of what I had witnessed that afternoon, and was interested to see how it affected them. Ivanoff was frankly bored. I saw for the moment a kind of gleam in Sonia's eyes, of curiosity at the same time savage and cruel, the Eastern for a second breaking through the Western veneer. That is the secret of the attraction that Russians undeniably possess.

The snow ceased, and I walked with them back to their house to find out their short cut. Again I was asked to promise to dine with them every night. "N'oubliez pas," said Ivanoff as he disappeared through his wooden gate. "Do svidània," smiled Sonia as she followed him—the Russian au revoir.

The snow lay inches deep as I trudged back thinking over the quaint sequence of events of the day. What an attractive girl Sonia was; what a corner of Asia to find oneself in! The moon turned this Eastern town into a veritable fairyland; but the frost was so severe that even my nostrils were stiff with the cold, and I drew my sheepskin coat closer and increased my pace, paying little attention to anything except getting back as soon as possible.

A shadow came between me and the moon—the gallows, from which still hung that poor body. All the horror seemed to have gone as I stopped to look upon this grim picture in the loneliness of night. The head was covered with snow, the toes pointed downwards. The torture and agony were a thing of the past—the spirit which had animated that lifeless burden had gone where no one could jeer at it or curse it any more. A gust of wind started it turning now this way—now that. Good night to it, and good luck to the departed soul. In the morning the iron tree was empty—the noose had been taken away. It awaited—the next.

Very little news reached us concerning the outside world. Beyond the fact that our troops had actually crossed the Russian frontier to the north, we heard nothing except that there had been some fighting. It was already November. We knew that things were going well for us on the far-off French front, but everything seemed such a long way off, so remote from our own way of existence.

That single strand of wire was humming with activity every one of the twenty-four hours, but the short span allotted for our use, when my old friend Signals reigned supreme, hardly sufficed for the necessary orders and messages concerning our own affairs.

The road southwards became daily more efficient as a motor road. A road of sorts existed from Turbat for the hundred miles or so northwards to Meshed, between which places had plied for years Persian horse-drawn vehicles for passengers and Russian kaliskas—much the same thing—but the journey had been hitherto extremely rough and precarious. The Sapper Officer at Turbat was busily transforming this into a proper track for motor transport.

Not very long ago, in one of the London night-clubs, I found myself, after a regimental dinner, watching the cabaret show. The head waiter seemed to be taking a most unusual interest in me, so much so that I was beginning to wonder in what way I, as a more than usually silent person, might have transgressed. We were a cheery party, as befits such an occasion, and this interested me.

Then somebody ordered drinks, and as this worthy proffered me my beaker he said, "Excuse me, sir, but I am sure you must be Captain James." Seeing my bewilderment, he added, "Don't you remember that evening in Turbat-i-Haidari?" Memory began to work; I recalled, among those who passed through that post on their way north, a certain party of about six of the queerest-looking beings I had ever seen disguised in a soldier's khaki uniform. These men could speak Russian, and had been sent up the line to act as interpreters; they gathered in that room of mine to report their arrival after a bitterly-cold trek. They had all been waiters in London hotels before the war, and here they were, of all places, in Turbat-i-Haidari.

They had halted for a day before going on, and I had done all I could to make them warm and comfortable. Crowded round my stove, old Suleiman sensed something out of the ordinary, and was handing round hot drinks—we now had rum as part of our rations. One or two of my de Groot records reduced some of them to tears. One of those ex-waiters was actually from the Piccadilly Hotel.

Here was one of them back again at his old calling, and I was glad that he remembered me. And so, in his own particular "holy of holies," in that club, we reconstructed the first meeting in manner befitting.

Individuals of various kinds kept coming through Turbat, spending the night there and travelling on north. Sometimes an officer who was a qualified interpreter; sometimes non-commissioned officers of the Supply and Transport Service; perhaps an occasional Indian medical officer. Supply convoys were constantly moving up to Meshed, where a depot was being formed. One car brought a most unusual type—an expert pigeon fancier, and accompanying him was a lorry filled with crates of his charges. A most interesting afternoon I spent while he showed me his birds, which incidentally proved of no value at all. They were released later from time to time, but never found their way back to India. Perhaps they took a fancy to some place like my little hill-side temple in Kain and are by now an enormous colony.

Every night I dined at the Russian Consulate. Sometimes Borodin and his wife were there, and we would play Russian folk-songs together, dance to the gramophone, laugh and make merry, then back I would go through the silent bazaar in the cold which was becoming ever more and more bitter. I could not fathom Ivanoff. If I was not there in time for dinner one of his Cossack bodyguard would arrive at my quarters with a message to escort me.

One of the hobbies of this strange man was boot-making, and at this he was a real expert. He endeavoured to teach me the craft, but my products would hardly have withstood one of those Persian stages. In a little room at the Consulate with the usual stove we would make boots together after dinner, and often I laughed at the dreadful mess I was making of my job, while Ivanoff remained busily intent on his work, too busy to look up. The red light from the stove was reflected in the polished samovar and its glasses, in the little ikons high up in the corners. The silk carpets hanging on the walls seemed to assume an extra richness of colour. Opposite me on a divan Sonia would play her guitar and sing, as only she could, fascinating little songs of her country. When she paused for a moment with her slow smile, I would pretend to go on with what I was doing, postponing the moment when I must say good night. But what was the use of pretending? Had it not been for Sonia with her smile and those haunting Russian melodies, should I have been there at all?

I had been in Turbat for about a fortnight. Routine proceeded smoothly, my squadron employed in convoy duties and patrols, the infantry taking their turns at escorting. The supply depôt with its N.C.O.s was rapidly filling up, and ceaseless work under the supervision of the Sapper Officer was swiftly transforming the camel track into a more or less level surface. A tremendous contrast, all this, to the previous year, and to the year before that!

One morning, the twelfth of November, in came my old friend Signals with his very smartest salute, and handed me the usual sheaf of telegrams which came to all post commanders in this long line of communications.

I looked at the first. "Press Bureau announces peace signed with Germany at 5 a.m. on eleventh, all hostilities ceased."

I called the old man Suleiman.

"We must do something about this at once," I said.

A twinkle came into Signals' eyes which met mine over the rim of hit glass.

"And here's your very best health, sir," said that very excellent Corporal.

CHAPTER 4

Mensheviks

News then arrived of events over the Russian border in Turkestan.

The Mensheviks who had been preparing their plans to overthrow Bolshevism in Transcaspia had acted prematurely and allowed their revolution against the extremists to break out before its time, but for the moment appeared to have been successful.

The Bolshevik army based on Tashkent came down the Transcaspian railway in force, by train, and attacked the Mensheviks' position near Bairam Ali. The situation then became desperate, and as it was obvious that something more than moral support was required on our part, the detachment of Indian Infantry with machine-guns already posted on the frontier was ordered to join the Menshevik forces. On arrival they saw the Mensheviks streaming towards their trains in retreat. Their arrival certainly succeeded in holding up the Bolsheviks, but meanwhile our allies were actually moving back in their trains, and it was only on the very last of these that our detachment managed to scramble with the alternative of being completely deserted.

The Mensheviks now retired to a defensive position farther westwards on the railway, and here the Bolshevik advance was checked. It was decided to stiffen the Mensheviks with more troops, so three companies of the Punjab Infantry were sent. The Bolsheviks' three attacks on this defensive position were beaten off, thanks to the staunch behaviour of the Punjabis.

Two squadrons of my regiment were sent as reinforcements to join the Punjabis in assisting the Mensheviks. As far as I could gather, the Menshevik forces consisted of about eight field-guns manned by ex-Russian officers, some five hundred Turkoman Cavalry, twelve hundred Russian and Armenian Infantry, and two armoured trains. The Turkomans were apparently of little value as a fighting force, and the Russian Infantry, chiefly railway workmen, were most unreliable, the Armenians totally so.

Of the enemy rank and file more than half were recruited from the mass of German and Hungarian prisoners of war who had been interned in Turkestan. These unfortunates were deluded into the idea that by joining the Bolsheviks they would be able to fight their way home. Officered by Germans and Russians, of the latter some even ex-officers of the old Imperial Army, this was the most efficient part of the force opposed to us. The remainder consisted of low-class Russians, in addition to a most unreliable following of local Mohammedan renegades and villains. One of their units was made up entirely of felons from the Tashkent jail, and at that commanded by an ex-convict.

On both sides the morale was indifferent, as could only be expected among revolutionary troops hastily raised, and with little respect for their superiors.

Our two squadrons arrived in due course at the Menshevik defensive position to find their allies very jumpy.

It was decided to attack the Bolsheviks' main force which lay at a station on the railway, Dushak, about twenty-eight miles away.

The Punjabis, the Russian Infantry and guns with five hundred Turkoman Cavalry were to attack from the left flank whilst our two squadrons attacked from the right. The cavalry made a wide detour to the right and found themselves on the enemy's flank at dawn. Gunfire was heard from the direction of Dushak, and the squadrons advanced on the station. The enemy were to he seen lining the railway embankment, but began to retire to their trains when the cavalry were viewed.

The Cavalry Commander galloped straight for the railway station with his command in extended formation under fire from the Bolshevik guns, which fortunately used H.E. and not shrapnel. The small columns of his command under their respective Indian officers during their advance acted independently, accounting for many scattered parties of enemy infantry, using their lances and swords to great advantage.

The enemy had been completely driven out, so our squadrons took up a position with the Punjabis.

It was then found that during the night our Russian allies had gradually faded away, until at daybreak barely seventy were left to carry out the attack with the Punjabis, who had received the enemy's concentrated fire and had suffered heavily in their final advance over ground almost entirely devoid of cover. On the enemy's retirement the Turkoman Cavalry fell to looting right and left, and were well on their way home laden with booty. This left our Indian troops "in the air," a fact which the Bolsheviks were quick to appreciate and take advantage of by counter-attacking in great force.

The only course now open was to retire, the cavalry to cover the retirement of the infantry and guns. This was carried out and the Bolsheviks kept at distance, but with a heavy casualty list amongst men and horses in that bare, open desert.

Thus was lost an opportunity, thanks to our allies' defection, of following up an initial success and pushing the Bolshevik right out of Transcaspia beyond the Oxus where he could have been kept. As it was, the enemy retired eastwards beyond Merv, where they took up a position, followed shortly by the Menshevik-cum-British forces who came into position facing them.

A kind of stalemate ensued. The Mensheviks had not the initiative or courage to press forward without us. We had distinct orders to "stay put" as we were, and to resist only in case of attack.

And that was how matters stood to date. Our third squadron was soon to cross the frontier to join the other two in their forward position facing the Bolsheviks. It was hard to be out of all this, but we were to follow in due course.

In Turbat-i-Haidari life continued with the customary routine work well into December. In the evenings I usually went to see my friend Signals and "Kannum." Sometimes, finding the supply depôt N.C.O.s at his house, we would sit there sheltered from what had become the most abominably piercing cold I had ever known. Apart from the few passers through on the convoys, we saw and heard practically nothing of the outside world. We were just a collection of individuals doing our respective jobs and all minding our own business. We got on well together, and nothing jarred. What a pity that all life cannot be like that, but then again I suppose it is just as well, there is such a thing as stagnation. That domed bazaar drew me daily, like a magnet, and I longed for the artistic ability to transfer to canvas that picturesque, multi-coloured Asian, Eastern life. India, which is picturesque enough, faded into a collection of picture post cards. I liked the way in which the owners, the families, and even the muleteers and camel men of the convoys, which were always coming down from the north, would look one straight in the face, their curiosity naturally roused at the sight of an Englishman riding through the bazaar. And those circles of camels all facing inwards to the blazing log fire of an evening, their masters and attendants passing in and out of the flickering shadows, sitting smoking their little porcelain-bowled pipes, and drinking tea from their samovars; the women-folk coming and going with their inimitably graceful walk and carriage carrying great earthenware jars of water—charmed the eye, and recalled vividly the illustrations in fairytale books which had filled one's childish hours of dreaming.

From these people I bought several carpets and small prayer-mats, and many a time sat patiently while rug after rug was produced and exorbitant prices were demanded. I was becoming fairly fluent in Persian by that time, enough to make those hawk-faced robbers laugh—but with that inimitable courtesy of the East where a guest feels that he is being laughed with, not at.

As usual, I often dined at the Russian Consulate; but sometimes my friends would come and dine with me. I noticed when I went there that Ivanoff frequently excused himself on account of having business and writing to attend to, and again I sometimes intercepted a gleam in those glittering, spectacled eyes which puzzled me. Sonia, with her guitar and charming old Russian songs, entertained me, and at times would tell me of her experiences in Bolshevik Russia.

She had met Rasputin, and nothing that she ever told me of

that man's life—and death—was other than his worst enemy ever imagined of him. His death at the hands of Prince Youssopoff has since been written of, and is at the day on which I am writing the subject of a lawsuit of world-wide interest. The man himself undoubtedly exercised a most extraordinary power, especially over women. He would organize parties, and be a guest at others; would merely beckon to a woman to get what he wanted, return, and an hour later beckon to another; this to be repeated an incredible number of times during the course of the evening.

That his vitality was amazing is evident from the known fact that he refused to succumb to enough poison to kill several beings, that even a succession of revolver-shots failed to part what he called his soul from his body. That body was eventually recovered after having been pushed through a hole in the ice on the Neva.

I asked Sonia what was the matter with Ivanoff, and if I had done anything to offend him. The atmosphere had changed; we were not the cheery party of previous days; yet I was always upbraided and even sent for by him if it seemed that I was not coming.

The fact was that Ivanoff was desperately in love with his stepdaughter. Hence jealousy had arrived to spoil what was too marvellous to last. I liked this queer-eyed giant, Ivanoff, and much more so Sonia, and now this demon had come and ruined everything. The situation was not improved when a cipher message came ordering me to see, with what tact I could, that Ivanoff's communications did not interfere with the small time that was allotted to us in Turbat for the use of the telephone.

This meant the disconnection of certain wires in the Consulate, and I explained to him as best I could what had been decreed. His sphere, the Russian, of course no longer existed as far as we were concerned. In fact these unfortunate people were already exiles.

"Very well," he said.

The following morning, having instructed Signals to report at the Consulate and to carry out the disconnection according to orders, I went out with one of our patrols to visit a distant oasis, returning late in the evening. The little Corporal awaited me in my quarters.

"I goes down to the Consulate, sir, and finds Ivanoff there," he reported. "'E sez, 'What do you want 'ere?' 'I come to disconneck your telephone,' I sez."

I thought of the indomitable little Corporal facing that giant, and kept a straight face.

"'And 'oo's orders is this?' 'e sez. So I sez, 'Now look 'ere, Ivanoff, it's the Captin's orders, and I'm 'ere to carry 'em out.' Yus, I was talkin' Russian at the time!"

With that astounding statement off went Signals. And now what was to be done? It was done for me. A knock on the door, and in strode Ivanoff out of the snowy night, asking me to come back at once with him to the Consulate. He said that he had been deliberately rude to me, and apologized; they had arranged quite a new diversion, and the Borodins were coming. I was only too delighted to return to that house.

Sonia and her guests seemed in the best of spirits. There they were, that little party of exiles, in what had so lately been a Russian garrison, trying so hard to keep their ends up, knowing all the time that for them all was finished.

"What is to-night's diversion?" I asked Sonia when I had a chance to speak to her alone. She was looking more attractive than ever, her slanting eyes smiling and gay, as if she had never found life as she would term it "too interesting."

The diversion was that we were all going to see what opium was like. As far as I was concerned, I would see what anything was like if Sonia was there, even if the master of ceremonies was that extraordinary man, Ivanoff.

After dinner we found that charming little room all ready laid out with the necessary implements. And as we became more drowsy the music came to an end. A sensation of general well-being, but at the same time of senses being dulled, quite different from the feeling induced by alcohol, came over me; the room seemed stiflingly hot. Outside lay at least two feet of snow, but into this we dragged the divans and there we stayed until the early hours of the morning, quietly talking; later they sang again their haunting songs one after another. It became like a kind of dream under that Arctic, starlit sky—one was wide awake and yet not awake, one's body seemed to have vanished somewhere in the snow to freeze without communicating the fact to oneself. There was an uncanny pleasure about it all. I was watching Sonia's face, quiet now, and sad. Ivanoff and Borodin were arguing in that way that only Russians do about something quite trivial, weaving into the argument an immense importance, and below the sound of their voices, as in a kind of refrain, were heard the footsteps on the far side of the high wall of the Cossack sentry on duty.

A grey light crept into the sky. Sonia fell asleep, all of life that had been "too interesting" for her forgotten, with her head resting on my shoulder. Borodin had disappeared. Ivanoff was quietly and steadily gazing to where the sun was soon to rise.

He looked at me and laughed. "Porà (it is time), Monsieur Jimmy," he said.

Sonia opened her eyes." Kak eto builò Karashò." (How good it has all been.)

In the dawn I walked back through the snow, wondering if it had been a dream, that moonlit, drugged Arabian night; but I had adored the dream, the drug, and the night. And if I did feel an hour or two later that my head was most assuredly about to divide into two portions, never to join up again, it was my own fault. Had it split into a thousand pieces, I should still have counted it worth while, It has always seemed to me such a mean outlook on life to grumble if one does not feel some mornings like I pictorial advertisement of Sanatogen or Phyllosan. I am only speaking from the point of view of a careless soldier Into whose life come many occasions for cheer. One must pay in some way or other for happy hours or even moments—be they offered by or sometimes even snatched from Fate itself.

I spent the morning with my men and horses—the finest tonic in the world to me. Sheikh Haider opined that we should soon move on to the holy city of Meshed. Those horses looked well, and the mere rhythmic sound of them feeding brought to a horse-lover a great contentment. Many old friends among them still surviving pre-war days; here they were, in this battered, but now clean serai. There was old No. 18 which I had been riding when I stuck my last boar in India; next to him No. 91, a famous mare for tent-pegging, excitable, but once on the track she never deviated one hair's breadth; others, great jumpers, trick-riding horses; all with their different characters, and so plainly showing it as one walked through the lines. Old 18 stolidly kept his muzzle in the manger, looking contentedly at one as one passed. The excitable mare raised her head, snorted, shook herself and shivered, as if to say, "For God's sake leave me alone to feed—I will take you straight past that peg at any other time as fast as you like—and don't you miss it."

Others seemed to stop feeding and talk among themselves; all kinds of heads, some lean and well-bred, others coarse and clumsy. One could almost hear their conversation. "That's only Jimmy James, he won't hurt you." Then a really wicked chestnut mare with eyes showing far too much white and little lean ears laid back would hunch up her back and say, "Yes, I don't mind Jimmy James, but I put him on his back all right at that General's inspection." Then that head would come out playfully and a hind leg would be lifted, but she would change her mind as I stroked her silky nose, and get back to her feed in great content. My trumpeter's Arab at the end of the line, with broad forehead and narrow muzzle, with the best mouth and manners of them all, would just stretch out his beautiful head and ask to be made much of. He was, invariably.

I wondered whether those survivors ever remembered the march pasts of peace-time days to celebrate His Majesty's birthday. Trotting daintily past the saluting base to the strains of the Keel Row, then wheeling by squadrons to canter past again with their feet beating time to Bonnie Dundee, the gleaming pale blue and silver uniforms, the red and white lance-pennons. There used to be something so noble and inspiriting, something which affected me like beautiful music, in the sight of those proud, tossing heads and their perfect line. And here they were on their way to Russia.

"Excuse me, sir," broke in upon my reverie the voice of Signals, "orders is just come for you to take your squadron on to Meshed the day after to-morrow."

CHAPTER 5

Parting

A hasty summoning of the four Indian officers—Sheikh Haider and the other three troop leaders. We had two days to get ready for our march north; child's play to us, accustomed as we were to turn out at immediate notice.

The news ran like fire through this Mohammedan squadron, who had for some time been eagerly awaiting the expected move to the holy city. No reveries now; we were going on, in the direction of the Russian frontier too. An atmosphere of life, of excitement, seemed to spread, even to the horses, who seemed to know that something unusual was afoot. I broke the news to Suleiman, and told him to get everything ready. "Where are we going, Sahib?" he asked. Hoping at last to see the old man really excited to hear that we were off in two days' time for that great Mohammedan rendezvous of pilgrims and worshippers, I found myself, as ever in his case, grievously mistaken. "Bahut accha," (very good) was all he said, but the wrinkled little face did go so far as to smile at me.

The weekly camel convoy had come in, which would be accompanied by my squadron after its day's halt. To my great joy, the only British passenger in it was W., my old friend the bank manager at Birjand. W., the complete soldier in khaki, was on his way to Meshed, now the centre of all east Persian interest, there to discharge his duties as F.T.C.O. (Field Treasury Chest Officer) to all troops between far-away Nushki and the Bolshevik front. Easily and well he carried on this complicated work; for on him fell the onus of seeing that everything financial down to the pay account of the humblest member of that force was correct and in order.

Farewell, then, to my romantic and picturesque city of the Arabian nights, Turbat-i-Haidari, and good-bye to Sonia, to the Russian Consulate. I sent a note to tell them the news, and forthwith proceeded with the next senior officer of the post to hand over the confidential papers, the accounts, and all things incidental to the process. But a cloud persisted in intercepting the brightness and anticipation of action in an ever new sphere; a cloud "no bigger than a man's hand," but able to blot out the sun or the moon. This particular cloud shortly concentrated itself in the form of an answer to my note. Sonia wrote that Ivanoff was furious with me again, and that I had better not come that night; but would I meet her at the corner of the Consulate garden wall, so that she could explain.

It was snowing hard as I found my way through the darkness to the rendezvous. As I waited I imagined that I could see, and hear, human beings creeping not far off, beings that would not show themselves.

Sonia was waiting, fearless as she always proved herself to be; she told me that Ivanoff had completely lost his temper, and said that I was never to go there again; he had rejoiced to hear that I was going, and they were to leave as soon as possible for Constantinople via Meshed, the Russian frontier, and the Caspian Sea. All the time those unseen creepings and movements in the shadows went on.

"Nichevo, Jimmy," said Sonia; "these are only the Cossacks Ivanoff has ordered to spy on me."

One of those Cossacks, however, she said, would stick to her whatever happened. And so it turned out later. She did not trust Ivanoff; but we agreed that I should come to a farewell dinner next night whether Ivanoff minded or not. In any case, they would pass through Meshed later and on to the frontier town of Askhabad. We should meet again, as she could always write and let me know where she was. I felt full of misgivings for Sonia as I watched her walk down to those wooden gates and saw her turn and smile in the light of the lamp that burned above them. Those unseen figures seemed to dog my footsteps all the way back.

I didn't mind if there were hundreds of them. I simply felt that tragedy lurked not far away. We had been happy together; was this the end? I had liked that crazy giant Ivanoff, and if I had liked Sonia a very great deal more, I could not help it; who could?

The snow was still falling as I turned into my quarters to find my old friend W., to talk with him far into the night.

The morrow was full of preparations for departure, but interrupted by a visit from Ivanoff! I must at all costs come to dine that night. We would have a "cocaine evening," he said. I didn't care what sort of an entertainment it was so long as I went there, especially if he invited me.

Everything was ready for the march. So, for the last time, to the Consulate. Why he had asked me I neither knew nor cared. I came to the conclusion that the man was mad. Down the white-mantled by-ways and through that silent bazaar I walked, through all that had become to me in those few weeks a kind of personal possession that amounted almost to a dream.

The Borodins were present, and all seemed as it was on that first night when I dined with them. After dinner the giant mixed his dope in fluid form. For all I knew he might have given me any poison. He was particularly charming to me that night, and they played and sang for me my favourite songs. Cocaine is quite a different dope from opium; as it has its way it seems to affect only the eyes; they seem to be very wide open; a sort of calm never experienced in ordinary life pervades the spirit; peacefulness seems to take possession of one's body, which, as the time goes on, disassociates itself and minds its own business. Yet there is no dullness of imagination and no sleepiness, and what wits one may have are sharpened to an unusual clarity. Sonia grew silent and thoughtful.

The Cossacks swung open the gate as I went out for the last time, after promising to come to say good-bye in the morning.

For the last time, wrapped tightly in my sheepskin coat, I walked back, past the forbidding iron tree, on through my snow-covered, moonlit, Arabian night's bazaar.

What was going to happen to Sonia? Sorrow, of some description, I felt. That lunatic Ivanoff could not be trusted to see her out of this merciless country to Constantinople, where her mother and her child awaited her.

What if he failed her? What if Sonia were by any chance left alone, penniless, at the mercy of the Persian Cossack guard, who were not to be trusted for a moment? Yet she had said that there was one of them who would befriend her. But surely Ivanoff would see the whole thing through. I distrusted that man.

All was hurry and bustle in the morning with the camels, sinking grumbling and complaining to their knees while our kits were being loaded. Old Suleiman with his accustomed efficiency took charge of this; W. and I had breakfast with the other officers of the post meanwhile. The moment of departure drew near. The squadron were mounted outside the wall; my trumpeter was there with my little chestnut mare, christened by Sonia "Adski-dushka" (diablement chéri), and another horse for W. who was to ride with us.

Into the saddle again, all in heavy marching order complete with rifle, lance and sword. . . . What a picture that squadron made in the snow with their long, pale blue cloaks, turned out to a nicety which suggested a pre-war manoeuvre parade.

"Half sections left, walk—march!"

W. went on ahead and I sat on my little mare with my trumpeter behind me watching them go past, winding their way out northwards through the town. Little Adski-dushka pawed the snow in impatience and snatched daintily at her bit.

Followed by my trumpeter I trotted away in the snow with a heart like lead. I had not even time to dismount. A handshake for Ivanoff and Borodin and a joke about last night's cocaine, thanks for their hospitality; then Sonia. "Don't forget us," she said, turned quickly, and went into the house. As if I could.

Then about and away, with a backward glance as we turned the corner to catch a last impression of them all. Sonia was waving to us. Round the corner and out of sight of them we met the Cossack who was to prove eventually so faithful. He understood my indifferent Persian as I told him to look after the Qanùm at all costs, whatever happened, and that I should most surely come back and then God help him if he had not done what I asked him. "Ba chashm" (By my eyes) said he. Childish, stupid, what you like; but I had a lump in my throat and those shapeless mud walls seemed hazy as I trotted to catch up my squadron. There was good old Signals to say good-bye too, looking more fierce and guardsman-like than ever.

"One for the road, sir," said this inimitable little real man.

The "road" was even then becoming more obscured by snowflakes.

"And here's your very best health, sir." Once again over the rim of a glass.

"Thanks ever so much," was all I could say as I climbed again into my wet saddle, and we settled down to a steady pace. Twenty-five miles to go before we crossed that great open desert space where the track wound into the hills to our first halting-place. We hit it off just about the same time as the squadron, and found a large serai to accommodate the men and horses, and a little mud rest-house for W. and myself.

The sky cleared, and a huge, brilliant moon illuminated the scene—stars which appeared gigantic, like electric lights hanging from invisible strings, added to this splendour. The hills surrounding the little rest-house stood out jet black, touched with dazzling white where the snow clung on their jagged and precipitous sides; they seemed so close that one could almost stretch out one's hand and touch them. The deathly silence only added to the attraction and beauty of the scene. W. took over the duties of cook and upon a large wood fire had a cauldron in which a fowl, his contribution, was boiling. One or two glasses of vodka had entirely failed to remove that infernal cloud of apprehension.

"Come on, Jimmy. I think it's done now," said W.

It was, but he had forgotten to clean the wretched thing first. And that was the first time I managed to laugh on that day.

The following morning ushered itself in with a vicious sleet shower and intense cold as we wended our way up through the first of the passes that divided Turbat-i-Haidari from Meshed. Here came the beginning of east Persian civilization as regards roads. This one was to the Persian mind fit for wheeled traffic, although to anyone unused to Persian standards of carriage travel it would not appear so. Yesterday's ride had been over a section already put in order by our Sapper friend in Turbat.

The summits of the mountains were enveloped in dark banks of ominous cloud. Up and up we climbed. It proved too cold to ride, so we stumbled along on foot, trying to keep warm, leading our horses. All the better to go so slowly, as it would not mean such a long wait for the camels at our destination. At the top of the pass the north wind blew in a furious gale laden with sleet and hail. The horses could hardly be made to face this stinging blast, whipping round and showing their hindquarters to it at the slightest opportunity. A merciless country, with its bleak and desolate uninhabited outlook, that shrieking wind; yet something magnificent and untamed about it appealed to me.

In due course we came to the village where we were to halt for the night.

The customary mud houses were slowly dissolving in the wet whilst their inmates shivered over their braziers in a stupor. No wide doored serai here. It was an absolute necessity to get our horses under shelter from the howling gale. The entrances to what cover was available had to be enlarged, and it was dark long before the last horse had been pushed stampeding and snorting into its night's billet, rubbed down and fed. And we were able to find what shelter we could in their abominable place.

Things were better the next day over the desert which connected to the second pass. At the near side of this, after the customary twenty to twenty-five miles, we found the usual snow-bound Persian village, with, luckily, a large serai where the men could be accommodated in rooms, of a kind, above their animals.

I was glad to have the company of W. in one of those little dirty rooms above the horses. In any case one felt perfectly ready to fall into a tired sleep in a cold so bitter that one's own clothing plus a sheepskin coat and anything else in the way of Persian rugs or blankets was barely enough to hold a semblance of warmth.

From this particular place ran a so-called track for wheeled traffic westwards, skirting the northern edge of the great Lut desert and connecting up with its hundreds of miles to Teheran. Only a few miles down that track from where we were spending our night lay Nishapur, the birthplace of Omar Khayyám, the place, too, where his tomb is reputed to be. It was somehow a comforting thought as one drifted into sleep to think that just those few miles away lay the remains of that immortal poet and philosopher; for in that country, his country, every one of his well-known words fitted its setting like a jewel into a ring.

Over the second pass we went in glorious sunlight, snow sparkling under a blue sky on a windless morning. The blizzard had blown itself out and left us this gorgeous day to traverse that pass and view, from its highest point, the wide valley where lay the holy city under its white mantle. In that perfectly clear atmosphere its many-domed clusters of buildings, the little dots indicating trees, a line of them, an avenue, which for a mile or two bordered the road by which we should enter, could be easily distinguished. The famous Mohammedan shrine was plainly visible as the sun's rays were caught and reflected by that great gold painted dome—

And lo! The hunter of the East has caught
The Sultan's turret in a noose of light.

CHAPTER 6
Slaughter

It was a short march into Meshed on the next day. This allowed us a comfortable start and opportunity to turn out as well as we could. The weather favoured us again as we filed out from Kafir-Killeh, our last halt before entering the only town of real interest in the whole of bleak and barren Eastern Persia, a rendezvous for thousands upon thousands of devout Mohammedan pilgrims. The road improved, and at a distance of about two miles we found ourselves in an avenue of stately poplar trees; here and there were outlying properties enclosed in the usual high, mud walls, the bare and winter-bitten branches of fruit trees showing above giving an indication of what must be the beauty and freshness of the country-side in other seasons.

Turning a corner, riding to meet us came G., the cheery companion of days in Khwash in the raider-time, and the one whom I had relieved in Birjand so long ago.

A high wall encloses the whole town, and we made for the southern arched gateway which would admit us. G. told me that he was due to leave Meshed on the following day with the squadron which was already there, and whose place we were temporarily to take before we, too, crossed the Russian frontier. As we rode on together he related stories of this fairy-tale town, and we exchanged reminiscence about south Persian days, about raiders, about the East Persian Cordon, now a line of communications. One incident which came under his own notice was typically and cold-bloodedly Persian. We happened to be passing the very spot where he had witnessed this horror.

"Riding back to Meshed past here one evening," he said, "I came upon a small crowd in the open, and from my position in the saddle saw over the heads of the bystanders an unusual sight. A post had been securely fixed in the ground, to which was tied a bearded Persian, deathly pale and bare-headed. Facing him in neat brown overcoats and circular fur caps stood a party of half a dozen Persian gendarmes. As I arrived on the scene the gendarmes raised their carbines and aimed at him. The sharp command of an officer on the flank coincided with the discharge of those obsolete muzzle-loaders. To my horror, I saw that the miserable victim was untouched. He began to scream for mercy and to try to wriggle free from his bonds. Those awful screams were answered by another volley, the result of which was to score one hit on the wretched devil's hand. The officer in charge went up to the almost collapsed wretch, and after speaking a few words, summoned one of his men, who placed his weapon against the man's chest, pulled the trigger, and mercifully blew him out of existence. This was the end of a murderer. The firing-party and escort then marched away, leaving this gruesome corpse as a warning to others. The relatives were not allowed to remove the body until the following day."

Following the line of the wall, we reached the southern gate; passing in, we found a wide, cobbled highway leading into the centre of the place. On the right was the opening to a large, well-kept serai which harboured our cavalry. My men filed into this to take over their quarters and horse-lines from the outgoing squadron.

G. and I rode on along this broad way, which led to a large square of most imposing buildings. On the left stood the post office, and beyond it well-kept municipal gardens; in front the buildings seemed to be barracks with obsolete pieces of artillery here and there. Then came the fringe of the Meshed bazaar and the shops, such as they were. Entering the square, we turned by the wall which bordered and enclosed the prison, at the end of which stood a small building which constituted the quarters of the British officer in charge of our troops. This consisted of two rooms, reached by a short flight of mud stairs, above an arch; underneath was the main entrance into the prison.

We decided to get the taking-over business through as soon as possible, the counting of moneys, signing of receipts for confidential documents, in brief the customary routine on these occasions. After a visit to the serai, where the squadron were now comfortably settled, we returned to our eyrie free to spend the rest of the day together and to talk of old times.

From this vantage-point one was able to witness Persian methods of dealing out justice, and heard almost daily the shrieks and yells of the victims. Sometimes these unhappy ones were strapped to a triangle and beaten with a leather thong across the shoulder-blades; or they would be pinioned with the soles of their feet upwards to receive the punishment. In either case each blow was followed by sufficient time to let the agony take its course before being excited once more by the next.

In a large house situated in a beautiful and spacious garden opposite our quarters, beyond the farther side of the square, we found the British Consul-General, a perfectly charming diplomat. No one will ever know to what an extent his personality, tact, and brains formed the chief factor in preventing, earlier, what might have been a massacre there of the European population, when the Russian troops defaulted and left for their frontier.

I felt somewhat dazed with all this civilization and excitement, but shall always remember that evening in the Consulate and the kindly, perfect manners of our host, who asked me to dinner on the following night to meet the European contingent.

From the Consulate we went to see some old friends of mine who had been in Birjand—the Boulatoffs—who had gravitated to Meshed and occupied a fairly respectable Persian house not far from the British Consulate. What they had to live on, how they managed to exist at all, was a mystery. Like the remainder of their compatriots, owing to the Revolution they could only count themselves as exiles. It was terribly sad, but the brave front they showed, buoyed up with their characteristic Russian optimism in face of trouble, evoked one's respect. The evening passed with talk, vodka, talk, more talk—and vodka.

With G. the next morning I rode along that snow-covered way leading northwards. In the far distance could be seen the Elburz

Mountains, which had to be passed before reaching the Russian frontier. A cloudless sky and a brilliant sun lent enchantment to the view. After a mile or two I said good-bye, and turned back over the snow-blanketed country-side to take stock of my new surroundings. The view of Meshed was striking in the extreme. Countless domes and minarets glittered in the bright sunshine. Dominating the whole place was the huge cupola of the "Imàm Riza," the famous Mohammedan shrine, which, seen at closer range, is coloured gold and blue. Across all possible approaches to this holy of holies are suspended chains at a height sufficient to touch the chest of a mounted man, and none but Mohammedans are allowed to penetrate beyond them. It would be as much as one's life was worth to pass beyond this barrier.

Yearly thousands make Meshed an annual place of pilgrimage, and from great distances corpses are brought to be buried within the environs of the holy city. Trotting quietly "home" with my orderly, I wondered how long it would be before we moved northwards.

The duties of my squadron were similar to those which held good at Turbat: convoy work, and patrols to visit outlying oases. My duties as officer commanding the British troops differed little from those I had undertaken in my last post. Yet this was the end of the line of communications, and it was only a matter of time before we went forward over yet another frontier, into another country. But Meshed held one's keen interest, being a large city of one hundred and twenty thousand inhabitants, of which some six thousand were Caucasian Turks. The European population numbered about fifty, and was very cosmopolitan, the chief factors, of course, being the Russians and the British.

On my return a letter from Sonia awaited me.

They were preparing to leave Turbat and come north through Meshed and on to Askhabad on the Transcaspian railway, thence across the Caspian from Krasnovodsk and so to Constantinople. Pleased with this news, I looked forward to seeing them, but felt distrustful of Ivanoff. Turbat-i-Haidari or Meshed, or any Persian town, was no place in those times for a girl like Sonia. I missed Turbat-i-Haidari badly, and everything connected with it.

"Don't forget us, Jimmy," Sonia had said. The appeal was not needed.

For the British Consul-General's dinner-party Suleiman had been working overtime to turn me out in what was left of my best khaki uniform. Attired in this, I walked across the great square to the Consulate, where I found practically all the Europeans of the place—the Russian bank staff, the regiment-less officers of the Semiorichenski Cossacks, the officers of the Persian Cossack Brigade, the Belgian Director of Customs, his countryman of the Excise Department, and a Swiss in the same service; other minor personages; and last, but not least, the Chief of Police, late of the Swedish Horse Guards.

It was a most picturesque gathering. The Russian officers present wore full dress uniform, with medals and orders galore, but it was sad to see uniforms and medals of a regime now past worn by a gallant company buoyed up by an optimism that one could not but admire. The Russian Consul-General was (as usual, I discovered) very late, and I found myself rather dazed with all this civilization, but interested to a degree. Talking to a young Cossack officer, we discussed Kain. I told him that it was a marvellous place. Did he know it? "Yes," he said. He had been there, but was at a loss to understand my enthusiasm. His gay and laughing manner charmed me, and he had the hardly perceptible Eastern look which is one great attraction of the Russian—who is just as fair in complexion, and often even fairer than we English.

A commotion without. ..."This must be our Consul-General," said my new friend, Youssopoff. From a window we watched a carriage drawn by a pair of prancing greys flanked by an escort of galloping Cossacks. This was indeed their Consul-General, keeping up to the last the dramatic air of the old Tsarist régime.

"Sit next to me at dinner," I said to Youssopoff.

Followed the kind of evening which to my lazy mind is the most perfect. Later on, the big drawing-room was filled with the guests.

"Are you going to sing, Youssopoff?" I asked.

"Yes," he said. "Of course, if I am asked."

He was asked, and so were many of the others. Apart from the individual performance, Russians seem to inspire each other with enthusiasm; and their unaffected, perfectly natural way of losing themselves in the enjoyment of what they do seems to remove a mental barrier, which would be only half lifted or removed in a similar gathering of Westerns. But a note of sadness came with the thought that they knew they were playing a losing-game, that their old régime was ended. Who could tell what personal tragedies were hidden behind it all? "It is just like this for Sonia," I thought. I wished she were there.

It was here that I had my first insight into Persian affairs military of the period. The weekly parades of the dejected-looking and ill-clad infantry took place in the square in front of our quarters. Round and round they marched and wheeled accompanied by the most villainous brass band that it has ever been my lot to hear. From what I gathered the rank and file were constantly in arrears of pay—and wretched pay it was. The officers seemed incredibly old, and all carried small whips. Every now and then, incensed at some mistake, they would rush up to the perpetrator and hit him across the face! The parade ended by the formation of a ragged square, when the individuals composing it would present their motley collection of firearms in salute.

Except the Russian-led Persian Cossack Brigade, the only troops of any military appearance were the artillery. About three hundred strong in Meshed, they possessed some forty guns. Of these two were breech-loading field-pieces for which they had no ammunition and would not have known what to do with it if they had. Next came a few mountain guns, and the remaining muzzle-loaders apparently were used only for salutes and the blowing to pieces of criminals who were lashed to them.

The annual artillery practice consisted of the expenditure of about ten rounds per gun.

Some of our officers were invited to attend this function and it seemed that the shooting was excellent.

The Persian Governor inspected the targets, and left filled with justifiable pride at the result. It was, however, discovered later that the holes had been made beforehand. On one occasion the Governor ordered a movable column of his troops to set out to Lushk, some twenty miles distant in the mountains, where for some time past brigands had been harrying the countryside.

The brigands were at home, and fire was instantly opened by both sides at a range of well over one thousand five hundred yards. For three entire days in this manner and at this range hostilities continued without a single casualty on either side. An invitation to the brigands to a peace conference was issued. Strangely enough this invitation was complied with; the result was that the Persian Army returned victoriously to Meshed with cartloads of these brigands who had been promptly arrested and who were deposited in the central jail.

There followed a few nights later an unusual uproar of shots and yells. It almost seemed that something really serious had happened despite the fact that shots and yells were a frequent occurrence in the night-life of the holy city. But the uproar soon died down, and the morning revealed its reason. Outside the entrance of the jail, lying in the snow, were the bodies of most of the brigands who had been brought in by the victorious army the day before. Riddled as they were with bullets, still one or two moved in this ghastly row of human game.

They had been, in a way, hostages. Whether their fellow tribesmen had broken their vows was never known. It appeared that their guards had been "tipped the wink " to get rid of them, and at a given signal had turned them out of their cells into the moonlit open quadrangle. Then mounting the walls from out-side, they had indulged in an orgy of rifle-practice upon these helpless prisoners.

I can only presume that this disgusting piece of brutality called forth strong protest from the British and Russian Con-suls. At any rate it was not long before a new Governor was appointed in Meshed, also a Swedish Chief of Police—the one whom I had met at our Consul-General's dinner-party.

This, however, was not the end of those luckless hostages. Thirty-six had been laid out for dead in that horrible morn-ing's exhibition after the firing. Several died under the floggings which had been previously administered, but still a number remained for destruction.

A day or two later, on its way to the southern gate, a procession passed headed by that abominable band and a large escort of Persian Infantry. In the midst shuffled a dismal gang of closely guarded men with a look of despair on their faces, on which even a short incarceration had imprinted a ghastly prison pallor. About twenty of them, each chained to his fellow by the neck, staggered along under the weight of huge poles painted a vivid red. These were the last of the brigands of Lushk, bearing to the place of execution the materials for a gallows to accommodate six at a time, on which six daily would meet their death. On the following day a huge concourse assembled at the gallows and the first six were brought, accompanied once more by that discordant brass band. According to the usual custom their misdeeds were read aloud to them before a vast crowd of spectators. Then, entirely unfettered, the nooses were slipped over their necks and slowly they were hoisted high above the ground. There for several minutes they swung and twisted before becoming motionless, hideous bundles.

One of these wretched victims tried with his unbound hands to swarm up the rope which was choking him, only to be beaten back by men who lay aloft on the crossbeam to frustrate such attempts. One broke his rope and came heavily to the ground. In spite of his agonized appeals he was ruthlessly drawn aloft, struggling, a second time.

So perished in daily batches all that remained of the brigands of Lushk.

As a result of the Curzon agreement England and Russia had consented to the Persian Police and Gendarmerie being officered by Swedes as subjects of a disinterested power. These members of a virile northern race certainly achieved remarkable success considering the extremely poor material at their disposal. The Chief of Police, who styled himself M. le Majeur S., was a blond giant of imposing figure, and liked to describe himself as "un bon camarade." A fine picture he made in his fawn-coloured tunic covered with gold lace, shining leather top-boots, and magnificent Astrakhan hat with a huge gilt badge of the "Rising Sun of Persia."

He spoke a vile form of French with great speed and fluency, declaring that he did not know a word of this language when he had come to Persia three years previously. However, he managed to make himself understood.

At his invitation I went one day to inspect his domain. Entering the gloomy portals he informed me, "Aujourd 'hui nooze avong line mash de brigands dong la prishong, shing sont déjà morts." I was taken to see a batch of unfortunates who had been condemned to death. They glared at us out of hopeless eyes from the far side of the iron bars, and those pallid and despairing faces haunted me for weeks. Then with great pride M. le Majeur showed me his new invention to ensure more rapid strangulation than was offered by the customary bight of a stout rope. He handed me a silken noose to examine. "Shest plus rapide," he said.

The police appeared a comparatively well-dressed and disciplined body in contrast to the soldiery of the place. This, I gathered, was the result of a generous application of the "Punitiong Suédois," during which the individual suffering correction did not receive the next blow until ceasing to complain of the preceding one.

"Il faut battre cette purple," said M. le Chef, whistling his cane through the air in a manner which seemed to bring on a slight attack of nerves to two neighbouring policemen.

He occupied a large house on the outskirts, where in real bon camarade fashion he dispensed hospitality to us. The whole of one of the end walls was covered by a magnificently made silk Persian carpet, the centre portion of which was a full life-size representation of himself. "Fait par mes prisonniers," he informed us with a smile.

For a week or so routine work kept me busy, on occasional days patrolling the district with my squadron. In the evenings I visited the Boulatoffs. Occasionally some of the Russian element would come to see me. Of those the Polkovnik (Colonel) Kyznatzoff, who commanded the Persian Cossack Regiment quartered in Meshed, was a most striking figure, well over six feet in height. He would come clanking into my room in his dark blue and gold Cossack uniform faced with scarlet. Debonair and invariably cheery, his conversation was always amusing. Occasionally I dined with him and his wife, a charmingly attractive type of Russian. With Kyznatzoff it was considered a crime not to drain one's glass of vodka to the dregs. ..."Zalpòm" as the Russians have it. That little fair-haired wife of his derived much entertainment from my serious but successful attempts not to draw upon myself the wrath of her scarlet and gold husband by transgressing his excellent custom.

A saturnine Russian doctor—a most sinister-looking little man—and his wife sang to us charmingly at our Consul-General's weekly dinner-parties.

These people and the remaining Europeans lived in houses just off the great square, which itself was flanked by very indifferent merchants' shops, a few ragged cafés, and one or two wine-booths. Into the actual city I did not go at all; in fact I had not the time during this short winter stay.

The indifference of the population to human suffering, life, and death is appalling. One snowy morning, walking through the public gardens, on one side of the chief pathway I saw lying in the snow a young Persian woman, obviously dead; a poor little child was crawling over her body and crying piteously. Not one passer-by even took the trouble to look at this tragic sight, and it was an effort to get a Persian policeman, even though threatened by a report to M. le Majeur, to do what was required.

January had come before I heard again from Sonia. The Borodins had left in one of our convoys to India, thence to be repatriated. Ivanoff continued to postpone their journey north. I had been looking forward to seeing them in Meshed, and felt that her immediate future was not promising.

The months in Kain seemed already a far-away dream; Turbat-i-Haidari with its unexpected happenings had more than usurped that dream. Meshed, the great East Persian Mecca, left me cold. I wanted to see Sonia safely out of danger, and could do nothing.

Then came news that the Headquarters of the lines of communication were to be transferred to Meshed with a battalion of Indian Infantry. I was detailed to move northwards to the Persian frontier, over it and down to Askhabad in Russian Turkestan.

"We leave to-morrow, Suleiman," I said.

"Where, Sahib?"

"To Russia."

"Bahut Accha," (very good!) said that cheery little gnome in exactly the same way that he would have answered if I had told him that he were going on ten days' leave to the Lahore Christmas week in India.

1919

"Where I made one—
turn down an empty glass!"

CHAPTER 1

Into Russia

In due course we filed through the narrow by-ways of Meshed, out by the western gate, to change direction northwards in bitter cold over the snow-covered plain. We had to cover a distance of about one hundred and seventy miles to Bajgiran, the Perso-Russian frontier post, and then onwards into Russian territory another twenty to Askhabad. The stages were longish ones, averaging about thirty miles, but by this time a few hundred miles here or there meant little to us. Now, however, we had a distinct advantage, for our transport, by which is naturally governed the pace of a unit trekking in this country, consisted of horse-drawn vehicles, known as fourgons, a type of Russian troika. The drivers were Russians, mostly of the peasant class, and a fine, hearty, willing lot of sheepskin-clad blond giants they were. The road itself, though very rough, had originally been a surveyed one and fit for this kind of travel; but at this time of the year, of course, it was rather more than usually in a state of disrepair. It was a comfortable trek; there was no more sudden stopping to get some reluctant camel on its legs again after reloading it in the snow while the whole of the convoy waited.

The night halting-places were serais in their usual state of filth, but we found our way into them eagerly out of that abominable snow. Past masters long since at settling down in far worse circumstances for the night, we counted ourselves lucky to be under cover at all. Once arrived, we had barely time to get our horses rubbed down and fed before the great wagons came rumbling and lurching in with much shouting and cracking of whips by their drivers. As darkness came on little fires began flickering where the squadron were cooking their meal, and in the drivers' quarters, throwing their red glow on the snow-covered court-yard, here and there were heard laughter and song. Later, Sheikh Haider would come to my little room to discuss the doings of the day and take orders for the morrow. Then to bed, clothed and wrapped up in everything that one owned, to fall slowly into a sleep lulled by the noise of the Arctic wind without, a sleep made the more sound after the day's trudging and stumbling through the snow, more often leading our horses than riding them. Morning seemed to come immediately, and by the time my bedding was rolled up and I was tightly belted in my sheepskin coat, the fourgons were parked in the courtyard, the last horse was being led through the archway from the stables. My trumpeter was waiting there with my little chestnut mare in front of the squadron, his little Arab stretching out a dainty head just as if asking a question: "Aren't you going to say good morning to me as well?" Then "Mount—column of half sections from the right—walk march!" Off the track outside the serai I would watch them file past, and when the last half section was clear canter up to the head of the column. The day's march had begun.

Under these conditions horses seem to show their characters much more than in dull routine garrison life. They throve, too, and kept in splendid condition, not fine drawn at all as might be imagined, but hard as nails. Some of the old stagers just went steadily past as if realizing that it was ridiculous to waste energy when a long day's work was in front of them. The famous tent-pegger would come sidling out, fretting and snatching at her bit; this walking business just bored her. Some turned their quarters to the biting wind, passaging sideways until they settled down; others, after a playful buck or two from pure enjoyment of life, got down to the day's march. All different characters—just like men, only so very much more good looking! A hard-bitten, cheerful and efficient picture the squadron presented. They were finishing the last stages of a ride from India to Russia—they would have filed out just as purposefully and indifferently if we had been under orders to go on right through Siberia.

After three days on the level we came to Kuchan, about half-way to the Russian border, a small, uninteresting walled town with nothing approaching a European element closer than a few Armenian families who traded there. Beyond and north of this, snow-covered and rising into the clouds, lay the Elburz Mountains, a bleak though most picturesque range rising at the highest point to some 8,000 feet. From here onwards for three long marches the road twisted and turned ever slightly upwards, sometimes through deep gorges, crossing and recrossing a mountain stream which had generally to be forded, the bridges being in ruins. Not a sign of life did we see on these daily struggles from one walled serai to another. It was not so cold riding through the gorges, sheltered by their steep sides from that tearing wind which swept unceasingly down from the north.

At last the frontier village of Bajgiran was reached, lying just on our side of the pass, over which the track left Persia and led down into Russian territory. Our destination, Askhabad, lay about twenty-five miles beyond the frontier post. The next day was blessed with a lull in that infernal wind, and by a gorgeous sun which glittered on the snowy country-side—a good omen for our crossing yet another frontier since leaving far-off India. The view from the summit of the pass was superb. In the distance could be seen the town of Askhabad, an oasis beyond, and on each side of which stretched, as far as the eye could see, the great uncharted wastes of the Kara-Kum desert. Right and left ran the jagged ridges of the Elburz, and like a snake winding away to the north gleamed the road we were to follow. But on this far side of the pass, instead of being an ill-kept rough track, it changed to a perfectly good metalled highway, on which it was almost uncanny to be riding. Some six hundred yards down stood a little walled, civilized fort—unoccupied. It became more interesting to me later, when the red flag fluttered over it. Ever descending, we went on, leading our horses in the gorgeous sunlit freshness. Looking back when we had at last reached level ground, that long, frowning ridge of Elburz heights was a magnificent sight, stretching from east to west.

It was January, 1919; I was thinking of that day when from

the south, hundreds of miles away, I had first crossed the frontier into Persia in the winter of 1915-16. Long ago it seemed, but I vividly remembered the thrill, and how I conjured up on that occasion dreams of lovely carpets, Comforting philosophies of Omar Khayyám, gardens with fountains playing in the moonlight, roses, wine . . . yes, it had all come up to my expectations, and exceeded them.

But this marvellous, level, and thoroughly European metalled road was almost a shock. At our midday halt we came to a kind of farm-house distinctly superior to, though in some ways resembling, the well-known mud-built Persian homestead. Its grounds were roughly fenced in; it had a real door and glass windows. And there were distinct signs of civilization in the "washing," fluttering and drying in the morning breeze.

Sitting on the bank alongside the road and watching the little dots representing our transport, clearly discernible on that winding way by which we had come, I suddenly became aware that I was not alone eating my midday meal. Three little children had approached me, and were watching me with the greatest curiosity; dazzlingly fair little Russians, with bright eyes, sunburnt skin, and flaxen hair. How I made those little devils laugh. They were suddenly swept away by a stalwart, short-skirted and barelegged peasant woman; a fine, handsome type, with her strong, well-made figure, her coal-black hair neatly plaited and framing a typical Russian face. A few halting words in Russian from me, despite their appallingly bad pronunciation, and I was invited to take tea within. I gathered that her husband was fighting against the Bolsheviks, her brother had been killed, and life was more than hard. The memory of those few minutes, the strangeness of those laughing, staring children, so very much like our own, hanging on to my tunic, trying to pull out my revolver, lingers with me. It was as though I had been suddenly transported on a magic carpet into the West—except for those slanting eyes and rather high cheek-bones.

And then good-bye—all smiles now in that brave Russian family as they saw us mount, and waved till we were out of sight on our way to the first Russian town over that frontier.

As we drew nearer the road became fringed with an avenue of poplar trees, occasional well-built houses with gardens standing on either side. The next surprise was to find ourselves riding on cobbles. In the centre of the road were tram-lines. So this was a Russian outpost, after some one thousand five hundred miles of east Persian nothingness, infinitely more civilized and Western-looking than the best of our Indian cantonments! Down the main street were shops and cafés, a theatre, a cinema, even pavements. The people were well-dressed men and women. It might at first glance seem almost to be a small French town. This illusion went as one noticed the tall figures of the real inhabitants of this country, Turkestan. The Turkomans are magnificent men physically, and their natural height is emphasized by their national costume: a tall, sheepskin hat, rather resembling a guardsman's headdress; a long, plum-coloured Cossack riding-coat, belted and close-fitting at the waist, where hung the usual dagger; the outfit completed by soft leather top-boots. I was riding along entranced with all this novelty. It was like nothing I had ever seen before, and so utterly a change after the wilds of Persia. But I liked those best. Would Ivanoff and Sonia come through here? We would dine in a café and go to the cinema; we would laugh. ... I missed them, somehow. . . .

"Hullo, Jimmy!"

I turned in my saddle to see the neat figure of one of our old friend the Sphinx's Staff Officers, who had overtaken us.

As we rode along together he gave me a rough idea of the situation relating to Askhabad. Up at the front beyond Merv there was more or less a stalemate. The Bolshevik army based on Tashkent knew perfectly well that as far as British troops were concerned there was to be no further advance; but how long we were to remain there they did not know in the slightest. It would take them a long time to forget the stiff resistance of the Punjab Infantry, whom they had never been able to overcome, and a wholesome respect for the lances of the Indian Cavalry went a long way to keep them quiet for the time. Yet that did not prevent them from spreading their propaganda once more along the Transcaspian railway down to Askhabad.

The question of a Turkish advance was now, of course, since the Armistice, an impossibility. The Bolsheviks wanted to swarm through Transcaspia and chase the hated Mensheviks into the Caspian Sea northwards through Krasnovodsk. But to tackle the British element, which they must do to achieve their desire, was by no means to their taste.

Askhabad, then, was at the moment overrun with Bolshevik agents and propaganda. The principal factor in Bolshevik favour was lack of funds to keep the Transcaspian Republic solvent. The railwaymen, the chief Russian element, were clamouring for pay. Needless to say, full advantage of these conditions was being taken to organize a first-class revolt. In order to pay those railway-men and officials the Mensheviks had been printing and issuing paper money to an amazing extent, so much so that the notes were rapidly becoming in value worth the extremely in-different paper on which they were printed.

It was to counteract the danger of a rising in Askhabad that we had been moved up. My orders were that the squadron, after feeding and watering, were to parade the town by troops under their Indian officers.

The quarters to which I was directed to lead them were bar-racks, the like of which they had never seen before. One could almost imagine oneself in Aldershot.

In this place, Askhabad, was accommodation for a large army, of a style which made one think of poor old Indian canton-ments as cowsheds. This, the nearest Russian garrison of any importance to India, was most interesting to examine.

My troops filed out in the afternoon to march through the streets, and I went to find my quarters in the most modern dwelling I had seen since leaving England, a well-built house in a turning off the main square which held the church. The windows were double, and each group of four rooms was heated by a central stove, ceiling high, which offered one quarter of its bulk and warmth to each room. A modern bathroom, too, seemed incredible! Here lived the few British officers whose duties for the time kept them in this place.

After a welcome bath and change, followed by a glass of excellent wine with the dwellers in this house, I went into the square in the dusk to take stock of my surroundings.

Past the church one of my troops was making its way back to barracks. There was an absolute silence which seemed to hang like an invisible screen, a screen which one felt at any moment might be rent by the rattle of a machine-gun, by a series of shots punctuated by cries. A kind of menace, a brooding danger. It could be felt; but how the Askhabadis disliked those lances!

Lights were burning in the church. In the dim illumination the outlines of the domes and the lines of the golden chains which connected them could just be seen. I walked in and sat down in a secluded corner to listen to the service.

The choir were singing as only Russians can sing; the lights were reflected on the picturesque vestments and head-dresses of the priests and on the highly coloured decoration of the church. Here was something real—and beautiful. I sat there enchanted by the music, by the atmosphere, by the sincerity and the charm of those voices. This very morning we had come gaily trotting down over the Elburz Mountains—over those mountains down into this civilization.

I could have listened for hours to the cadence of those perfectly attuned voices in this gold domed, chain hung, Russian church.

The last church I had been in was centuries old, tiny, of grey stone, in the heart of the Cotswolds, a church in which my father preached!

Out into the cold again, back to that comfortable house and a dinner of the best. Then to a kind of café, with a filthy Armenian proprietor, Balalaika music, dancing, that same feeling of furtive danger, but good wine. A young Russian officer to whom I spoke seemed to think that my capacity was endless. Bright eyes and laughter.

But what was happening to poor Sonia?

The Russian officers at this café were our allies against the Bolshevik; or perhaps it would be more to the point to say that we were theirs.

The whole atmosphere was unnatural, the presence of these

Russians of the old régime in this place cheek by jowl with an assortment of Turkomans and Salts and Kurds, an assortment with whom I am quite sure they would never have associated in pre-war times in such intimacy. After my long day I felt in just that mood of sleepiness, not tiredness, in which I could appreciate the strangeness, the novelty, and the interest of it all. Who was Bolshevik and who was Menshevik? Who was spying upon whom?

My glass was being refilled by my officer friend while over his shoulder laughed at me the almost yellow eyes—cat's eyes—of the very attractive girl whose arms were twined around his neck. The Balalaikas thrummed and chattered; the grave Turkoman faces, so unnatural in these surroundings, with an air of being more than the equal of any Russian or Englishman with this new doctrine rampant, seemed to be taking in and sensing the possibilities of personal loot, of indulging their favourite pastime of robbing their victims—victims dead with a furtive dagger-thrust in the dark. Cartridges are expensive and noisy; a knife, a silent but agonizing messenger of death was their way.

I suppose I ought to have walked out across the square to our absurdly civilized and heated house, but I chose to accompany my friend who, incidentally, was not wearing the insignia of his rank. Few of them dared to. A few minutes' walk brought us to a disreputable-looking hotel, into which we went—my friend, cat's eyes, and some few other friends of his with their attendant harpies. The inevitable vodka was produced, doors were locked, and with the customary hopeless optimism there followed a succession of songs and speeches upholding the old régime.

By degrees the room emptied. I knew perfectly well that I ought not to be there, but it had been a day of such contrasts, a day of such interest. I was drowsy, but at the same time kept awake by the very clash of impressions. The Elburz mountain pass, the little Russian farm children, civilization such as it was, the singing in the church, the café with its Balalaika music, those cat's eyes, the shifty Turkomans.

I knew that I must go back to my quarters, and at once. I must have dropped asleep, for I suddenly found the room empty;

those cat's eyes were looking into mine and warm arms were round my neck. "Bang—bang—bang" on the door. ... A look of terror in those eyes. "Bolshevik, Bolshevik," she almost screamed. A trying moment, if you like!

The girl dashed to a door in the corner of the room, beckoning me to follow her, and disappeared up a staircase. I went out by a side door into the snow, and along a narrow, high-walled way which led me into the main square opposite the church; then I knew my bearings.

Looking back, I saw two figures going down that road and banging at all the doors. I wondered who they were looking for, and whether they would find their quarry. An absurdly theatrical proceeding in any event; but everything there was so theatrical, and the importance of life and death became almost completely obscured. But I wished that Sonia was in Askhabad. Then came sleep, preceded by visions of church choirs, cat's eyes, Balalaika orchestras, Armenians, Turkomans and Bolsheviks—my God, I was tired!

Chapter 2

Deserter

On the following morning I walked down for a more detailed inspection of my squadron's quarters and to give them my orders, which were to take it in turns by troops to patrol the town. Before the war Askhabad had been the seat of the Transcaspian Government, and the Headquarters of a Russian Division. I found my little command highly delighted with the comfort and warmth of barracks, which were a novelty to them, accustomed as they were to Indian conditions and Indian troops' accommodation, with a much lower standard. It was interesting, though, to recall that years ago this was a possible jumping-off place for a Russian invasion of India. It certainly was the nearest point from which operations could have been launched on our Dominion.

Dreams must have been dreamt here. Budding Napoleons must have made this place the nucleus of visions leading to power and conquest. Less picturesque secret service agents must have found well-paid material here for their adventurous schemes and courageous enterprises.

A garrison, barracks of which Aldershot itself would not be ashamed, were available for at least a division. One could imagine the legions of fur-capped soldiery—one could picture the gaiety of other years. Came 1914, came that inevitable war; came to this far Eastern frontier the devastating Russian Revolution.

And now it was deserted, except for a squadron of Indian Lancers, who sat their horses like graven images.

A little ride of fifteen hundred miles—some shots—some

deaths. Sheikh Haider smiled at me. I realized that I had been day-dreaming.

"Carry on, Sheikh Haider Sahib, march the troops off," I said.

Once again through those absurdly French streets the four troops quartered their way; and so high, at that time, stood the prestige of the Indians that their very presence ensured law and order. As ever, the grace and beauty of well turned-out horse and man as they wheeled and rode off brought a feeling of gratitude that my unimportant life had been linked with these men, and to no small purpose.

I thought of them in the districts in India where they were recruited, and where I had myself shaken hands with their fathers and grandfathers who had served in the regiment. I remembered their national games, when they ran stark naked except for their little loin cloths—perfectly modelled bronze statuettes in the glory of their youth vying one with the other. What a privilege to serve with such men—real men.

The route being open northwards from over the Caspian Sea, we were daily expecting reinforcements to garrison Askhabad, and to ensure that this base of ours should be kept in a peaceful condition. To this purpose three companies of the Warwicks were already on their way. This was a relief, as one squadron of Indian Cavalry could hardly be expected to keep the peace unaided.

Here, then, was the base of this rather remarkable sideshow of the Great War. Here was the capital of the province of Transcaspia. I rode out with the last troop of my squadron, whom I had detailed to patrol the sector which included the railway station. Adski-dushka, my little chestnut mare, was just on the tips of her toes in the crisp morning wintry air after a night in stables such as she had never known.

I was anxious to see the Transcaspian railway, which before the war had been an important and well-established line running trains through to Tashkent and Moscow, via Orenburg, complete with luxurious dining saloons and sleeping-cars, and manned by the best oil-fuelled engines. Their importance and efficiency were obviously things of the past, things pre-revolutionary. It was sad to see their decline.

Trains, of sorts, were running, but could only go eastwards as far as Merv, fifty miles away, beyond which lay the opposing forces of Bolshevik and Menshevik. Northwest the line ran to Krasnovodsk, where it ended on the shores of the Caspian Sea. The route in this direction, however, since the Armistice, was open right through via Baku, Batum, Constantinople, and thence to Europe. Hence the arrival of the British Infantry force, the Warwicks.

I went into the station, as pleased as any child to see the "puffers," but the air of shabbiness and dilapidation drove me to the refreshment room. This was occupied by a motley crowd of Russians, Turkomans and Kurds. I felt in my tunic pocket for my note-case. Gone, of course, into the hands of that yellow-eyed little thief of the night before. What of it? Merely the price of an absent-minded, lazy, but thoroughly enjoyable and extremely interesting night's experience.

The few roubles which I had I spent on a bottle of beer, which I carried to a secluded corner, where I could observe the scene without interruption. It was easy to pick out the different types, but impossible to know which were the Mensheviks and which the Bolsheviks. In any case there they all were, the Russians rather drunk, the Armenians slightly more so and more noisy, and with a quite indescribable but most apparent "yellow streak." The Turkomans, like hungry wolves, slunk in and out, superior, but not unlike the Kurds and others, with an air of absolute readiness to sink their long knives into anyone for the price of a postage-stamp. The place seemed a rendezvous of the down-and-outs of the town. Curious glances were thrown in my direction from time to time, and I could plainly hear the vodka-hoarsened voices whispering behind cupped hand into dirty ears the Russian word "Anglichanin" (Englishman). Presently the daily train from Merv ran into the station, and from it alighted an officer of the Punjabis with his arm in a sling, an old friend of mine. It was years since we had met, probably away back south in Seistan.

"Hullo, Jimmy James," said he. "Delighted to see you again. I'm on my way back to England and on sick leave."

I looked at the sling. "Nothing really bad, I hope?"

"No, just an ordinary bullet wound, but it unfortunately went through my elbow."

On his way back to England, he said. And what a way! He was going up to Krasnovodsk—across the Caspian Sea, over the Caucasus, through Constantinople, and thence into the calm civilization of the Mediterranean. That way was now open. We entered the bar; the Armenian waiter hovered in the background.

"Well, here's luck, Jimmy, and may our next meeting be not too far from Piccadilly," said this cheery pal.

I asked for news of what was going on eastwards in this struggle between the Mensheviks and the Bolsheviks, and almost as I spoke, into that dingy restaurant came a party of half a dozen bearded fellows in practically worn-out field grey. One could see in them the soldier, but not the Eastern; they had no Russian fairness in complexion, no slant to those blue eyes.

"God Almighty," I exclaimed, "what on earth is this outfit?"

And this is what my friend told me. Here we were, in January, 1919, with the Armistice already more than two months old. The Bolshevik army, against whom we were supporting the Mensheviks, had been and still were drawing recruits for their fighting forces from the odd twenty thousand Austrian and Hungarian prisoners of war who had been interned in Russia.

It was almost incredible, but the knowledge that the war in Europe was over had been concealed from those unfortunates, who were being induced by varied propaganda on the part of the Bolsheviks to believe that their only chance of fighting their way home was through the British forces. Meanwhile, we had been making every endeavour by means of our agents and spies to spread the news of the German débâcle among those prisoners of war, to try to make them realize that the great struggle had ended.

Our propaganda was, at first, successful. Austrian and Hungarian deserters were coming in at the rate of fifteen to twenty every day. Passages home to all ex-war prisoners were offered as an inducement for them to desert the Bolshevik cause. Hence this party in field grey, whose appearance in the station had excited my curiosity. The actual front line eastwards beyond Merv, where we were shortly going, was a waterless and pitiless waste; the no-man's-land to be crossed by would-be deserters an area of this inhospitality about two miles across.

The fact that parties of well-clad, unarmed Europeans were crossing this strip of desert almost daily was too much for the Turkomans. After a time desertions from the Bolshevik ranks ceased altogether. Several parties had been caught by these wolves of the desert, stripped of their clothes, and massacred.

These loathsome murders provided excellent propaganda for the enemy, who noised it abroad that the English were merely enticing them into the desert, where death was a certainty. That put an end to what might have been a complete disintegration of the Bolshevik Tashkent army.

My friend told me of a patrol which found ghastly evidence of Turkoman atrocity.

Out in no-man's-land lay the body of an obvious Austrian, naked, the head and trunk abnormally bent back, the face contorted with agony. No wound was found, but a sharp wooden stake had been driven up between the legs, and there it remained for all to see.

All that I had gathered, up to date, was the fact that a temporary stalemate existed at the front.

It was exceptionally interesting to hear, somewhat against time, from my friend, what roughly had been happening since the Dushak battle.

The Mensheviks and Turkomans had left us in the lurch during that battle, and hastened back loaded with what loot they could carry. Our infantry and guns had been forced to retire, covered by our cavalry, in face of overwhelming numbers of the counter-attacking Bolshevik army.

The Bolsheviks, however, having learnt to their cost what it meant to come to grips with our Indian troops, not only did not press this advantage, but came to a standstill when our retirement ceased on rejoining what was left of our Menshevik allies. Counting discretion as the greater part of valour, they retired again eastwards to Merv.

In this warfare, retirements, or the moving up of troops to reinforce whatever part happened to be the actual front, were governed entirely by one factor—the Transcaspian railway. This line ran eastwards from Askhabad through the almost impassable and completely waterless Kara-Kum desert. Its advantages and disadvantages were equally shared by both sides. Whatever fighting took place had to be confined practically to the rail route; thus conditions climatic and geographical combined to make any outflanking movement, on any effective scale, an impossibility. Both sides lived in their trains, never more than a mile or so apart, with steam up constantly to move forwards or backwards.

On the retreat of the enemy the Mensheviks got into their trains and went forward to a place Tejend, this side of Merv, which was suitable for a defensive position; our infantry and guns accompanied them, followed by the cavalry. Again the two sides found themselves facing each other. The advancing Mensheviks had taken heart—the enemy were obviously shaken. The Mensheviks force, which included our quota of Indian troops, was under the command of one Oraz Sirdar, a magnificent old Turkoman chieftain whose word was law as far as his savage warriors were concerned. The real work was done by his Second-in-Command, an ex-colonel of the Imperial Army, a graduate of the Russian Staff College, and a most able soldier. Their plan now was to make an immediate attack on the enemy and drive him out of Merv, beyond its small oasis, and into the desert that lay between that town eastwards to the Oxus river.

The officer commanding the Indian troops having experienced what it meant to be let down by our Russian allies, and with his small command sadly depleted by casualties, would not agree to this until he had received reinforcements from Meshed, or elsewhere; and quite rightly. The Mensheviks refused to move forward a yard without British support.

Eventually it was decided that a cavalry flank movement alone would put the fear of God into the Bolsheviks; therefore one of our squadrons, accompanied by four hundred Turkoman Cavalry, was detailed to advance north of the railway as a feint, a kind of reconnaissance in force.

This mounted party by sunset were well away on the Bolshevik flank. Here, however, the Turkomans insisted on a halt in one of their villages in order to hold a consultation. They would not go on, they sat there with their leaders arguing as only Easterns can. And there among them sat the one Englishman, who commanded the Indian Cavalry Squadron, doing his utmost to urge them on—alone with these savage Turkomans who knew quite well that their only hope of future existence lay with a Bolshevik defeat. They hated the Russians, both white and red, before whose annexation of their country they had been rightly counted as hard to equal in ferocity and cruelty throughout the savage races of the world.

Eventually it was decided to fall in with the British officer's wishes and go forward.

Patrols were pushed out, and the advance continued. It was soon learnt, however, that the enemy were retiring with all speed eastwards from Merv, which town our mounted force entered, to be shortly followed by our allies in their trains. Two days' halt here, and the British force, leaving a company of infantry to maintain order, moved on farther eastwards to Bairam Ali while our allies, now again in high fettle, pursued their enemy in armoured trains. All these incidents took place successively along that Transcaspian railway which led down from Krasnovodsk on the Caspian Sea southwards to Askhabad, thence eastwards parallel to the Persian and Northern Afghan frontier through Dushak, Tejend, Merv, Bairam Ali and out through the desert, over the river Oxus, and on to Tashkent.

It was time for my friend to leave on his homeward journey across Asia. More remained to be told, but trains wait for nobody, and a minute or two later I stood watching his cheery face out of sight as he waved from his carriage window, then turned to where the impatient Adski-dushka waited to trot back with me to Headquarters.

Things seemed to have fallen flat—I had missed all this adventure. I might even miss going forward to see this new country. The Warwicks were due at any moment to make good peace and order in the town. After all, the British force, now that the

Armistice was signed, could hardly remain for ever mixed up in this Russian quarrel. I noticed several more parties of those field-grey clad Germans and Austrians, lucky in freedom, having escaped the attentions of the desert Turkomans. They looked in curiosity at my orderly and myself in our pale blue Light Cavalry greatcoats. Some actually saluted and smiled. They had every reason to do so. There was now no obstacle between them and their country. No less amusing and interesting was it to see well-dressed and attractive women, Russians and others, and men clad in normal civilized European clothes, all part of the population of this capital of Transcaspia.

CHAPTER 3

Skirmish

For me, personally, things took a definite turn for the better on the following morning, when into my room at British Headquarters came a young officer of my regiment, one of the many most efficient temporary officers, who had been posted to us for the duration of the war. He had been sent down from the front to take over my squadron for the time being at the base here, and brought orders for me to proceed at once to the Headquarters of the regiment at Bairam Ali.

Many officers of this kind had been drafted to us. It was a difficult matter to take up duty with an Indian regiment for a "civilian" soldier; not only from the point of view of the novelty, but to find that the men knew not one word of English, and there were no "sergeant-majors" and other disciplinarians. We had no time for that kind of thing.

Young Indian civilians, tea planters, members of Indian business firms, they were all represented. There were even a few young Yeomanry officers, and it was astounding how soon they settled down, learnt enough of the language to be able to carry on, and fitted into the scheme of things even on this somewhat unusual campaign. We had an excellent lot with us, and got on well together. More important still, the rank and file recognized in the new-comers the genuine article.

I was to leave by the evening train which would take me as far as Merv.

"Bahut accha, Sahib," said my little gnome Suleiman and went off to the squadron billets to arrange for my orderly and the horses to be at the station at the appointed hour. He did not even ask me where we were going.

No further news of Sonia had reached me. I wrote telling her my destination and asked her to let me know what was happening; if there were difficulties I might be able to help, if only by means of the British Consulate in Meshed. The outlook for her was none too good. Already that strange life of Kain and Turbat-i-Haidari with its solitude seemed to have happened in a dream.

Evening came; at the station waited my orderly with his horse; Suleiman in charge of Adski-dushka was in one end of a covered-in goods truck, rather like the French ones pour-hommes, pour-chevaux. The chevaux were tethered at one end; in the middle the old man and the orderly had their bedding and a small stove where my dinner was cooking; the other part my camp-bed occupied, with a hurricane lamp on an empty up-turned packing-case.

The train rumbled off eastwards towards Merv, due to arrive on the following morning.

It was curious to wake up in the middle of the night with all that rattling and clanging, to see the lamp swinging from a beam in the middle of the wagon with those two men sleeping underneath. The horses, fidgeting, changed their weight from one leg to another. I sat up; my little mare looked round, shook her head and snorted. I went across to her and talked to her for a little while. She was upset and put her silky muzzle right in my face, as horses will when they want comfort from human beings. Soon all was quiet again. Bright daylight brought us to Merv.

Very much like Askhabad, it appeared; porters and officials, all Russians, resembling those of England, except that there was an air of decay, the impression of vanished prosperity. Here was the same Turkoman element slinking furtively about, the same mean-looking sprinkling of Armenians. The Bolsheviks had passed through this station and town and had been driven back through it without having had time to do much damage. The station buildings, the whole ensemble, were efficient enough to look at, in fact about as uninteresting as any European provincial building of the railway order.

The click of heels and the sharp clap of hand on rifle reminded me that I was not in Europe. I turned to see a fine specimen of the Punjab Infantry saluting me; behind him the remainder of the Sikh guard stood to attention, perfectly turned out and as imperturbable and at home as they would have been on one of their own Punjab parade grounds. They immediately took charge of my last night's railway wagon, horses, orderly, and old Suleiman, and one of them was detailed to show me the way to the Headquarters of their Company who were "keeping the peace." I had the whole day before we could be hitched on to a train bound for Bairam Ali, the present location of the British Menshevik supporters.

Merv itself, a quite modern town, has no special interest, the old Merv, the Merv of romance and the Turkoman raiders' lair, was a mere heap of mud ruins, a few miles away. The Company Commander's headquarters were in one of the many little modern Russian houses. We decided to lunch at the Grand Hotel. This comic caricature of an hotel was in the main street, which was lined with small shops of all descriptions—tobacconists, grocers, general stores, and even milliners. Here, as in Askhabad, were to be seen Russian civilians and their women-folk, Russian officers and their wives. Mingled with them in the traffic were Asians of all descriptions—Turkomans, Sarts, Kurds and half breeds, all bearing the unmistakable Mongol brand, some being almost Chinese in appearance. Who could tell in this heterogeneous gathering who might be Bolshevik, who might be Menshevik, who was spying, who was spied? We were received at the Grand Hotel by a real waiter with black waistcoat, tie, white shirt front—even a bald head. This was too amazing.

However, an excellent lunch was produced, partnered by a wine that one could tell immediately was to be no enemy. Here was another old friend of pre-war Indian days. Our last meeting had been years ago in Seistan. Around us parties of gay young Russian officers, with laughing and bright-eyed girls, looked as if they had not a care in the world. The whole atmosphere was one of gaiety.

What a race of optimists and how likeable—even if they had yellow cats' eyes and dug for gold with the best of them! These were our Menshevik allies, who, I gathered from my host, were becoming a trifle too much inclined to leave the front line and gravitate to the liveliness of Merv.

"And what has happened up there," I asked him, " since they pursued the Bolshevik in their armoured trains and the British element moved to Bairam Ali?"

What had happened was that the Menshevik armoured trains had forged ahead beyond Bairam Ali for some seventy miles into the desert, where the Bolsheviks made a stand. A defensive position had been made across the railway by the Mensheviks, where they had been reinforced by a company of our Punjabis and half a squadron of cavalry from Bairam Ali. Without this support they refused to stay. Definite orders came that we, the British element, were not to advance farther. Without us the Mensheviks declined to move—hence the stalemate. The company who lived in their trains at this "front," and the half squadron who lived alongside in Turkoman "kobitkas" (huts) were relieved at regular intervals. The Bolsheviks soon got wind of this situation and planned an attack which, had it not been for the staunchness of the Punjabis, would have succeeded. Fortunately it occurred on the day when the relief was due.

Our Turkoman Cavalry, who were supposed to be watching the front and flank of the position out in this desert, gave no news of what was to happen. Without any warning the Bolsheviks suddenly arrived at practically point-blank range in greatly superior numbers under cover of a sand-storm. The armoured trains opened fire, and the company of Punjabis, led by a young officer, went for the Bolsheviks with the bayonet. The cavalry who had been sent out to the flanks, split up into small patrols—a fatal mistake which the Russian Commander was ever too prone to make—were out of reach.

Our Punjabis were suffering heavy casualties, and were being rapidly surrounded, when fortunately the relief train arrived. The first intimation that the officer commanding the relief received that something was wrong was a hail of machine-gun bullets into his carriage. Out the men tumbled, and, fixing bayonets, followed the first company into the scrap.

This was too much for the Bolsheviks, who retired in disorder. There was, of course, no question of following them up. It would have been an easy enough matter to have pushed them back into the river Oxus, and to have made a strong position overlooking the river at Charjui. Transcaspia would then have been swept clean. Our orders were definitely to stand fast.

Yet that last attack had been a close thing. Had it not been relief day, and had that second company not been so soon on the spot, the affair would have gone hardly for us.

Burial parties sent out on the next day counted one hundred and eighty-four enemy bodies, including two women. During the night our Turkoman allies had stripped them of all clothing.

That evening I entrained once more, for Bairam Ali, only a few miles farther east on the fringe of the Merv oasis. My train might go at any time during the night, and in any case was not going any farther than this place. Once more we settled down, the horses, my orderly, Suleiman and myself. I was awakened in the dead of night by the clanging and clashing of buffers as we were hitched on to the eastward-bound train, and again on the following morning where we were drawn up in a siding at our destination.

Here were encamped the greater part of the Punjabis and my own regiment; this was the base now of the British element, who took it in turns to go up to the front line in support of the Russian armoured trains twenty miles still farther eastwards towards the Oxus at Aninkova. Many old friends greeted me, and to be one of such a veritable army after the last few years of wandering with twenty or thirty lancers seemed strange and bewildering. Bairam Ali was an amazingly civilized little place. It had been founded, under the Tsarist regime, as a kind of model colony, with the idea of encouraging the Turkomans in cotton production. In the centre of the village lay the Palace, a smallish but artistically designed shooting-box built for the occupation of the Tsar should he at any time wish to visit the place. Equipped with every modern luxury, this "palace" formed a nucleus round which was grouped the village, consisting of electrically lit houses for the employees bordering the excellent roads. These houses, well built, with properly fitting doors and windows, provided good quarters for the British officers. The church was most picturesque with its green roof and golden cross and ornaments, and possessed an excellent choir.

The Bolsheviks, in their advance and retirement, had done little damage beyond the removal of most things which might be of immediate use to them—chiefly foodstuffs.

The population consisted chiefly of Transcaspian railway employees and their families, older members of Russian families of the Tsarist régime, retired army officers, in fact, very much the same kind of society as inhabited Merv and Askhabad. The predominating influence was undoubtedly red, not quite so red, perhaps, as the Tashkent and Bokhara pundits could have wished, but rather hostile than otherwise, and quite prepared to wave farewell to us. Those who were definitely anti-Bolshevik, quite a fair proportion, still had the way open back through Askhabad, on to the Caspian and westwards, should occasion arise.

It was the indigenous population, the Turkomans themselves, who stood to suffer most from a Bolshevik invasion of what was their own country. Only two courses were open to them should this happen: to put up what would certainly be a hopeless resistance and take what would come to them—a massacre; or to fade away into the depths of the Kara-Kum desert where none could, or would, follow them.

The Headquarters of our troops was in the Palace itself; beautifully carpeted, and furnished in the best of taste. Little damage had been done here beyond the destruction of a statue of the Tsar which had stood in the front courtyard. The china and glass, all intact, bore the Russian Imperial crest; evidences of the utmost luxury were seen. In this picture of Russian colonization, what struck me was the pathetic sadness, waste and uselessness of it all. Comparatively few miles away, at the bridge head of the Oxus river at Charjui, lay an army of discontented revolutionaries waiting for the British to go, as go they must in the circumstances; waiting to swarm over this like a hideous, destructive disease spreading cruel tentacles and merciless destruction to all who dared to oppose their wishes.

In the meantime they did not relish those Punjabi bayonets; our lances and swords were equally distasteful, not to mention the streams of lead which Punjabis and lancers were willing to direct with a venom and accuracy which would no longer have to be feared from a Menshevik army deprived, as it soon would be, of its British allies.

Of the Menshevik army the infantry had now completely disappeared, despite the overheard telephone message of Russian Staff Officers calling up such and such a battalion or unit. They were never seen again. Attempts to train Turkomans in this role had proved worse than useless.

The Turkoman Cavalry had been augmented up to two or three thousand. The only reliable element of the Menshevik army consisted of the armoured trains. The British Commander, after the action just described, decided that the defence, as any forward movement was forbidden, should be carried out by the British, the Mensheviks, with the exception of the armoured trains, being completely ignored.

A chain of strong posts, protected by wire, had therefore been formed twenty miles east in the desert by Aninkova, each garrisoned by infantry, and each so placed as to be covered by the fire of at least two others. The cavalry were to act mounted and attack the enemy as they came under fire of the posts.

Operations of any importance, as I have already pointed out, were confined to the railway, which led out from Bairam Ali through the centre of the line of posts, and along which reinforcements could be sent at immediate notice.

I left for Aninkova that night.

CHAPTER 4

Armoured Trains

The same wagon that had transported me and my retinue from Askhabad via Merv had been hitched on to the train which ran up to the "front."

The country lay under snow and the cold was intense, but the dryness of the atmosphere went a long way to mitigate the discomfort of an amazingly low temperature. Wrapped in my sheepskin coat, I sat on the wagon floor at the open flap with my legs dangling over the permanent way.

There were but twenty miles to go. Here again was a real little temporary "home." What more could be desired?—a home that contained one's belongings and personal servant, one's bodyguard—the orderly, and one's transport—the horses. Beyond Bairam Ali and the fringe of the Merv Oasis came a country of unending sand-dunes, the view being restricted by these to within a hundred yards or so of the railway track. Just Kara-Kum desert and nothingness. At the end of the short journey we drew up in a siding. Alongside were picketed the horses of the small detachment of my regiment who were always there, and who were relieved at regular intervals from Bairam Ali. I noted at once that at least one third were saddled, ready to go into action at a moment's notice. Looking farther eastwards, the railway disappeared into a haze between those unending sand-dunes on its way to Bokhara and Tashkent.

My little retinue was at once absorbed into the cavalry lines, while I was diverted to our Headquarters by one of our Indian officers. Several trains complete with every class of carriage stood in sidings with their engines headed westwards towards Merv. In one of these, and in a carriage fitted with far more comfort and conveniences than in the best of Indian railways, I found the British Officers' Mess. This was our home at that front, and the officers who occupied it had adjoining carriages for sleeping-berths; in fact it was rather like living at sea, the chief difference being that our sea consisted of sand. Farther down the train lived the Punjabi detachment. Other trains housed the Russian staff with the few troops who still were in evidence. To complete the rolling stock were the Menshevik armoured trains.

The actual engines of all these always had steam up to allow of a retirement, if necessary. In fact, with the exception of the cavalry, the army lived in their trains. With the greatest interest I listened to the latest news of that front—sitting in an absurd railway carriage in the middle of that desert, once again back with my brother officers, many of whom I had hardly seen since the beginning of the war. Although we had been on service in the same country, since the inauguration of the East Persian Cordon, our ways and adventures had been separated to such an extent that we might almost have been at opposite corners of the earth.

The Bolsheviks, only a mile or two away on that railway line, lived also in their trains; even the cavalry boxed their horses at night and jumped them out again in the mornings. Every now and again there came a familiar sound which I had not heard since leaving France—the droning whine of a shell and its subsequent explosion.

"That's only the daily duel between the armoured trains," I was told.

The Bolsheviks, despite their advantage in possessing better armament, were very poor gunners, and the few shells that they threw over in our direction, far from causing any damage, were a source of great amusement to us.

Of paramount importance was the maintenance of a water supply. Aninkova was entirely waterless and all supplies had to be brought up from the Merv Oasis by train.

I have mentioned that the Russian-led Turkoman Cavalry had been augmented by two thousand. A certain number of those were to be seen, but, very rightly, in the British troops, Commander's plans had now been ignored. From the point of view of reconnaissance and protection they had proved useless, and had always failed when cavalry work was to be done. The job of cavalry in warfare is to locate an enemy, to be the eyes of slower moving troops, the tentacles as it were. When the main armies have joined battle, they should use their mobility to get round and on the flanks of their enemy to cut them off or pursue. The only experience we had up to date of these swashbucklers was their ability to come in when the dirty work was over and to indulge in an orgy of murder and loot.

Yet, to look at, they were a fine body of men, and properly led and trained, would have made first-class material. In the days before the Russian occupation of Turkestan, these Turkomans had been the terror of Northern Persia, to which fact the innumerable forts and towers still visible all over the country-side bear witness. A splendidly picturesque lot, they were men who specialized in knife-thrusts in the dark, in cutting defenceless throats, in finishing off the wounded. To see them as they moved in long columns, usually two abreast, winding in and out of the sand-dunes of the desert in their long, dark plum-coloured coats or at speed with the hair of their tall, sheepskin head-dresses flying in the wind, one could imagine that here was material for cavalry second to none.

A walk round our cavalry lines and to meet the Punjabis. To renew acquaintances which dated back in some cases even to pre-war manoeuvres, so far had we been scattered apart; and then sunset, and a glimpse of the armoured trains crawling home. The hour of the most arduous work had come—work to ensure that this little force might relax until another dawn.

The Bolsheviks, only about two miles distant eastwards, living in their trains on this same railway line, had grown careless as regards their own protection and outposts, knowing that the British section of their opponents was now acting entirely on the defensive and would not advance. As far as the Mensheviks were concerned, they knew well enough that without British support they would not advance a yard.

Yet a careful eye had to be kept on the Bolshevik position. As long as no reinforcements were forthcoming via Bokhara from Tashkent, which could only come by train, so long did we know that we were immune from attack. In order to keep in touch with the situation a strong cavalry patrol of my regiment stole out of Aninkova just before sunset every evening, past the sand-dunes, and spent the night on the flanks of the Bolshevik position, returning in the morning to report the number of trains present. In this way we obtained a good idea of enemy dispositions and possible movements. So lax had the Bolsheviks become that some patrols actually penetrated the enemy outposts and returned with lamps, etc., which they had managed to take off the trains. It seemed that the nights were spent in great conviviality. To every carriage were attached a number of women, some of whom had even taken part in previous attacks. Shouting and singing in an uproar of drunkenness seemed to be the programme.

Not always, however, did our nightly patrol get away with it without opposition. One very fine cavalry action took place. There had been one or two minor scraps on the patrols' journey back home, but this affair gives an idea of the spirit of our Indian Cavalry. They were on the return, a patrol of thirteen men commanded by a non-commissioned officer, tired and cold, visualizing the warmth and comfort of our Headquarters. Passing two sand-hills they found themselves confronted by a party of one hundred and fifty Bolshevik Cavalry who stood between them and home.

Realizing that their only chance was to break through, they closed their ranks and galloped hell for leather straight at the enemy. This caused hesitation in the enemy, who expected men outnumbered by ten to one to surrender at once. The lancers of our men jolted, stuck, some into and some through the squirming bodies; those whose lances were wrenched from their hands, whipping out their swords, hacked right and left at human faces, arms, shoulders. The trumpeter, the only one without a lance, accounted for one man with his sword and crashed in a face with a bullet from his heavy revolver as he galloped through.

The Bolsheviks, recovered from their surprise, gave chase; but our patrol was well through and had broken up into small parties which found their way back independently. Three of their men, however, were missing. As our patrol had been long overdue a reconnoitring party had gone out, to discover, where this gallant charge had taken place, pools of blood and confused horse tracks. Some months later one of the missing men, who had been taken prisoner, escaped and crossed the border into Persia. He reported that all three of them had been captured and sent five hundred miles north of Tashkent to Vyerni. Disguised as a Persian, he had eventually boarded a train which took him within reach of the border, an easy enough matter at that time when in Soviet Russia the trains were the property of the people and tickets were not required.

Two years later, to our amazement, a second man reported himself at our Regimental Headquarters at Lucknow. He had escaped from Vyerni and actually walked from there to Kashgar in China, where he had reported to the British Consul-General, who had sent him along to India via Gilgit and Kashmir. A remarkable feat for an illiterate Indian soldier with no knowledge of geography, probably not even of the direction of India!

The third man, he was able to say, was alive at the time of his own escape, but unfortunately no further news has been received of him.

The Russian Commander of the Menshevik forces immediately wired to General Denikin, commanding the white forces in south Russia, recommending that all members of this patrol should be awarded the St. George's Cross.

It was now getting dark and the cavalry patrol had left some time ago to keep their nightly watch on the Bolshevik front position. The armoured trains had come to rest, and I suggested paying them a visit.

Stumbling and slipping in the snow over the tracks of the improvised siding, we came upon a covered truck, part of one train, and found its men delighted to see us. We clambered up from the ground level and soon were comfortably settled down around the glowing stove. Hot rum and vodka were handed round, and under cover of the general laughter and conversation, from my corner in the shadows, I observed with interest this one unit of our Menshevik allies which was of any value at all.

The personnel consisted of about a dozen ex-officers, a hard-bitten looking lot. Time and again they had proved their worth, and were now the only remaining actively offensive Russian unit whom we could depend upon to see a show through. The one fixed impression that I gained in this country was that as far as the male population was concerned, there was no balance, no half-way. The Russian seemed to belong to one or two definite categories. He was either a kind of almost fanatical hero who would shrink at nothing and court death with complete uncon- cern, and with an almost unnecessary bravery, or on the other hand had a yellow streak in his composition which showed him as a coward, and no man, in a tight corner.

The ordinary hum-drum character did not seem to exist. It was just cut and thrust and forward and to hell with everything, or back, back, excuses, anything to put off the crucial moment. These fur-hatted hosts of ours belonged without any doubt to the former category. Next to me, absurdly young in appearance, sat in silence a rather undersized, boyish member of this unit. He drank nothing, nor did he smoke; he merely gazed, as though hypnotized, into the light of the stove, taking no interest in what was going on. I learned to my surprise, later on, that this was an ex-officer's widow, who, dressed as a man, shared in all the fight- ing. It was said that she had formerly belonged to the famous "Battalion of Death," but had now joined the Mensheviks to avenge her husband, who had been killed by the Bolsheviks.

I have written my impression of the Russian man. No one qualified by experience to give an opinion on the Russian woman would hesitate to say that here is the courage, here is the character that knows no half-measures; here are the mothers of those death-defying, gallant, fearless allies that we knew during the war. It was not the women's fault that all were not cast in this mould, not their fault that ordinary, mediocre fighting men were lacking.

Beyond our nightly cavalry patrol the only touch that we

had with the Bolsheviks was the morning duel between our respective armoured trains. Eastward towards' our enemy the line ran on a curve between the sand-hills and through a cutting. A curve and a cutting are great points to the advantage of an armoured train; the first makes ranging difficult to the enemy, the second provides cover. The usual proceeding would be for our train to steam out to the curve, let off a round, and reverse immediately. The opposition employed much the same tactics, but on both sides the gunnery was indifferent.

On one occasion our allies actually hit the Bolshevik train and brought it to a standstill, but such was the enthusiasm engendered by this direct hit that they ran off the rails. By the time they got going again nothing was gained.

There were three Menshevik armoured trains. Number one, which I visited, was the only real effective unit which performed the daily duel. Numbers two and three waited in support of this. Number one was well built and armoured with steel plates. In front were coupled two flat trucks; next came a truck to accommodate a howitzer; after this a large, armoured wagon containing a field-gun—its sides being loopholed for a couple of machine-guns. Height did not matter, as there were no tunnels. On the top of this last vehicle a kind of bridge was built from which the commander directed his fire and controlled the engine by signal. The locomotive, and behind it two wagons for the crews' quarters, completed the outfit.

Between these opposing trains a considerable amount of ammunition was daily expended. "Wides" and "overs" would wing their way back to us, but the damage was negligible.

The Menshevik Air Force consisted of one aeroplane, and its one appearance was a fiasco. Flying low over our front position, it was seen to be in obvious trouble; it dived earthwards and crashed into the telegraph wires close to which several of our trains were standing. The two airmen were rescued from the débris uninjured, as the engine had fortunately parted company with the rest of the machine. Such an incident might be expected to rouse interest even in an Eastern mind. But our troopers, seated cooking their food, did not allow it to interfere in the least with their imperturbability; just turned their heads, per-haps, and remarked, "Hawai Jehaz-Bhai" (an aeroplane, brother), and went on with their work.

This reminded me of arriving at St. Omer, in France, early in 1915, when the tranquil old Suleiman and I tumbled out of a troop train to join the Indian Cavalry Corps at the front. The 'planes ever ascending and descending on reconnaissance work thrilled me, but the old man stood holding the horses utterly unmoved. Somehow I found it difficult to meet those queer little eyes in that Sinbad face, looking at me as a great-grandfa-ther might look at an over-excited great-grandson. Illiterate he was, ignorant, and probably dirty, yet for him I had unbounded respect and affection. He certainly had affection for me; possibly respect also, though I had no reason to expect it.

And here we were together again—in Central Asia.

"Salaam, Sahib," said the little man as I turned in that night.

I smiled, thinking of his funny little legs hanging over the dashboard of a lorry at Abbeville.

"Salaam, Suleiman."

CHAPTER 5

Withdrawal to Persia

So passed the days at Aninkova. . . . The morning duel between the opposing armoured trains, the nightly cavalry patrol.
Any reinforcement that might reach the Bolsheviks would be
known to us in time to rail up infantry from Bairam Ali, and to
supplement the permanent cavalry garrison at this little desert
station. My personal job was to get a thoroughly clear idea of
the country on both flanks, which would be occupied by the
infantry in case of a Bolshevist attack, so that I could lead out
the cavalry should it happen to be my day to be cavalry commander. We took it in turns to seek the comfort and security
of Bairam Ali, and in the meantime spent the day, while at the
front, patrolling and reconnoitring through those unending, infernal sand-hills. For a change one might go with the armoured
train and take part in those artillery duels.

The actual Russian staff of the Menshevik force lived in trains
at Aninkova alongside ours, and we used to visit each other in
the evenings and pass the time of day.

The Turkoman Cavalry units, supposed to be several thousands
strong, were for the most part conspicuous by absence. In any event
we did not take them into consideration. We knew that in the case
of an action they would be ready enough to come in when the
dirty work was over and do their looting act, one which did not
entail the expenditure of costly ammunition, and one in which
they excelled. They were just supposed for the present to be guarding the flanks of our position. Previous experience had taught us
exactly how much such guardianship could be relied upon.

It became increasingly obvious that the Bolsheviks did not intend to attack us. They could "bide their time," knowing that the hated Punjabis and lancers would go. Also they were aware that we should not advance farther, as we found by the reports of our nightly patrols. Any pretence at defensive arrangements in the form of outposts was growing slacker, and the nightly orgies were becoming more uproarious. There was no sign of any reinforcements reaching them via Bokhara from Tashkent.

Behind us the way was clear up to Krasnovodsk by rail, over the Caspian, across the Caucasus and on to Constantinople.

No news of Sonia had come from Turbat-i-Haidari, and I naturally thought that she and Ivanoff had long since taken advantage of that route to escape from this Asian muddle. All that strange Persian life seemed to be of the past. But I did very much want to know that she was out of it and back in civilization with her family.

"Don't forget us," she had said. I had not forgotten.

Early March arrived, and with it, along this route from Constantinople, came the British Commander-in-Chief of the Black Sea Army. His train drew up in our siding at Aninkova, complete with himself, Staff, and appurtenances. He was somewhat surprised when he realized in what a strange position the British troops found themselves, and the complimentary manner in which his surprise was worded was appreciated by us all. I believe that his first question to the quite junior officer who happened at the moment of his arrival to be in command of the British contingent was, "Have you any machines?"

"Sewing machines? No, sir," said that graceless one to a most amused General.

We were the very last feeler on the very last tentacle of his command. It was obvious that the time had arrived for our departure. The Turkish menace, with its infiltration of enemy agents into Afghanistan from the north, no longer existed. We had no further right to interfere in the Russian quarrel. Also, this tiny British force of two regiments was here in a most dangerous position, opposed many months after the Armistice to some twenty thousand ex-prisoners of the Central Powers, in addition to the mass of felons, renegades and rebels of whom the Bolshevik element was composed.

Shortly after the General's departure, orders were received for the British troops to evacuate Transcaspia and make their way back over the Elburz Mountains again into Persia—to Meshed. Then began the arrival of the white Russian forces who were to take our place, from General Denikin's Army of the Caucasus. First came some thirty field-guns and five aeroplanes, then cavalry and infantry.

The greater part of this force consisted of Dagestanis, a most picturesque but useless body of men, not unlike the Turkomans in appearance. I remember watching sotnia (squadron) after sotnia of their cavalry coming into Bairam Ali on their way up to the front. They had similar tall, sheepskin head-dresses, curved swords, and rifles slung on their backs. Here seemed material for a first-class fighting force, but it wasn't. Yet they made a brave sight as they came in, and we could but wish them luck. They were full of confidence. They even sent their guns to the workshops in Bairam Ali to be repainted. As far as the Turkomans were concerned they by no means shared the confidence and optimism of the newcomers. Oraz Sirdar, our commander, made a personal appeal for a contingent of a hundred British troops to be left, even if they were not actually to fight, merely to hearten the Mensheviks by their presence. This, of course, was an impossibility. It was the real inhabitant of the country, the Turkoman, who stood to lose in the event of the Bolsheviks overrunning Transcaspia, as they wished, up to the Caspian. The Russian element still had a way open, a line of retreat.

The fears of Oraz Sirdar and his countrymen were only too well justified, as matters eventually turned out.

It was on April 1st that we began our evacuation. I was in command of our first two squadrons, who entrained at Bairam Ali with Dushak as destination, a small station about half-way to Askhabad, the scene of one of the major actions in Transcaspia, in which our troops had taken the leading part. From Dushak we were to march through a pass in the Elburz Mountains with camel transport for the five days that it took to reach Meshed from that place.

The remainder of the regiment were to follow at one day's notice. The Punjabis were to train right through to Askhabad, and march on to Meshed with our one squadron which I had left behind there. In the meantime the troops which had come up to relieve us, from Denikin's army, had taken over our defensive line, the chain of strong posts which lay across the railway at Aninkova.

It was only a matter of days before those posts were in an indescribable condition of filth; and our cavalry standings became an abomination of desolation.

The complete mastery of Transcaspia now obviously lay in the hands of the Bolshevik army. One could imagine the Bolsheviks rubbing their hands with glee, only waiting till the hated Indian troops were well away and southwards over the Persian border. The last horse had been boxed, and the last man had entrained on the Bairam Ali platform.

Our horses were so accustomed to jumping and crawling into shelter that this commonplace entrainment was carried out in record time. As we steamed out I watched with great interest the Russian railway officials who were present in force to witness the departure. One might have thought that there would have been an atmosphere of regret at losing the only troops who had kept them free from the Bolshevik yoke. Not a bit of it. One felt glad to get out of it when they laughed and spat on the train as it moved off. There were, of course, exceptions, but the general impression was that our departure was welcome. Not so, however, with the Turkomans, who had every reason to wish us to stay. Out over the desert steamed our train as we left the Merv Oasis. The Russian colony of Transcaspia henceforth became the Russians' affair. Despite the arrival of those thirty field-guns and the aeroplanes—the Dagestani swashbucklers, both horse and foot—we knew that it was only a matter of time before the Transcaspian political pink became red, and a rich red too. It would seem that our wanderings were over, and that we should concentrate in Meshed prior to the long, many hundred miles ride back to India and peace-life in cantonments.

We left our train at dawn on the following morning, when

the old familiar business began once more. The grunting, grousing camels loaded, we would traverse the usual forlorn and stony mountain pass—into the usual dirty serai; then, in a few days, back once more in Meshed.

April the first, 1919. . . . What a lifetime it seemed since Boxing Day, 1914, in Quetta, when I was Adjutant to my regiment. The war then was going to be over in a few months! Four or five officers of ours had left since the beginning of hostilities for France to replace casualties in the Indian Corps. On that day had come a wire from Army Headquarters to the effect that a captain and twenty rank and file were to proceed immediately to Bombay en route for Marseilles. We had then only two available captains—myself and another, who was married. The Commanding Officer told me that I could settle the matter over the toss of a coin. The rupee spun in the air, and I won. As the coin fell I had a momentary glimpse of my friend's wife's face. What it meant to her! But what a horrible disappointment to me had I lost!

The Transcaspian train was lulling me to sleep as one by one came impressions of the years which had gone since that rupee spun.

France—a great massing of cavalry up behind the line—two divisions of them waiting day after day to the accompaniment of the crashing guns—saddled and ready to pour in a human mass through the gap that was to have been made in the German defences. Again and again we had awaited this moment which never came—at Neuve Chapelle—at Loos—elsewhere. And then that ceaseless stream of whining shells. That was no cavalry amphitheatre. And what a holocaust, had we been loosed on that mission. . . .

Odd spells in trenches with stammering machine-guns, and dank, cold nights lit with the flares of the ever ascending and descending Verey lights. . . .

Seven days' leave to England, the channel boat packed with tired but happy soldiers. Seven days, each of twenty-four hours, and each hour to be lived. . . .

There was that dear old, grey-headed cashier with an office not very far from Waterloo Place, who did all that his famous bank would allow him to make those seven days worth while. Then had come Persia, with its thousands of miles of trekking, dirt, and solitude. And the romance of it all, of everything that had gone to make these last few years something which one could never forget!

There was that clattering gallop down the stony nullah to come to conclusions with Juma Khan and his raiding army . . . that sickening crash in the ambush afterwards when poor Strawberry and I fell in a heap, and my wonderful luck in getting away with it. . . . Kain, the temple, month after month of its attractive loneliness. . . . Turbat-i-Haidari with all its Eastern charm, and the nights at the Russian Consulate. . . . My friends must be well out of all this muddle and safely in Constantinople. I wished that Sonia had written to let me know. At any rate, here was the end of the adventure, and only a thousand-mile ride lay between this and tranquillity in an Indian cantonment. So I imagined; but my forecast was a little premature.

The springtime of this part of the world was becoming evident in a comforting warmth of a sun that began to evoke signs of life and greenness in the shoots of the camel thorn bushes and other rough vegetation in that desert; but nights were still bitterly cold. We left our train and filed up and through the Elburz Mountains, two complete squadrons.

Over the Persian frontier, back in a neutral country, it was like a holiday, with no enemy to be considered, with nothing but a small quarter-guard in our camp itself. No more pickets and no more patrols to crouch the night through among the cold and cheerless sand-dunes. In this part of the world there is a certain amount of animal life of an interesting nature. Great lammergeyers winged their way from range to range, vultures of various kinds soared, ever looking for some dead or dying body to appease their appetites. Here was one of the homes of the bustard, both lesser and greater. Those magnificent birds, best described as wild turkeys, were very often seen, and proved welcome after weeks and weeks of bully beef and goat; in fact, as table birds they are excellent. Very wily and cunning they are, but sometimes we could circumvent them. The way to do this was to mark down one special bird and stalk him as one would a buck or gazelle, in circles, getting ever closer and closer, and finally run straight at him, when his inability to take the air, owing to his weight, without a succession of long, flapping hops, gave one a chance to get within range. The few that we secured were a great addition to the extremely limited menu in what we were pleased to call our mess.

The Bairam Ali Oasis had contained a few woodcock, also a few pheasants of Mongolian origin, preserved in times of peace to provide sport for the Tsar, when he should pay a visit to his palace in that colony now torn to ribbons by avenging rebel fingers.

Land turtles of all sizes we found, but how these creatures existed, and upon what, it was hard to imagine. Old as time they looked, moving across the sand with their scaly reptilian feet, or cautiously extruding a queerly wrinkled head to feed. The little jerboas—mice in the form of kangaroos—seemed to make a point of coming into one's tent at night, running and hopping with their long hind legs over anything and everything; quaint objects, with beady eyes and bat-like ears far out of proportion to their size. Marmots, too, burrowed and dug into those sand-hills, making the going treacherous for horsemen.

A day's march behind us followed the rest of my regiment, with the exception of my squadron in Askhabad, who were converging also on Meshed with the Punjab Infantry, who had railed down to join them from Aninkova. The three companies of British Infantry in Askhabad were moving up to Krasnovodsk on the first stage of their homeward journey to Europe, over the Caspian.

Behind us, in Transcaspia, the reinforcements from Denikin who had taken our place opposed their Bolshevik enemies with their newly painted field-guns, their aeroplanes, and over-confident Dagestani soldiery. I could not help wondering how they would fare.

The spick and span infantry posts on the defensive line across Aninkova which we had handed over to them had been converted into latrines by the newcomers almost before our troops were out of sight, and lost all semblance of efficiency or cleanliness. One could imagine those sotnias of Dagestani Cavalry just not being bothered to do the nightly reconnoitring act, could picture the boisterous optimism of their officers back in the sordid cafés of Merv and the comforts of Bairam Ali. "Nichevo, Nichevo," (Never mind, n'importe). That word sums up the Russian character so well!

Our five days' trek was coming to an end, heralded by the sight on the horizon of the gleaming cupola of the Meshed Mosque. Ugly clouds, banking up on the west and south, foretold rain. Uglier clouds, but invisible, were banking up northwards behind us; human clouds, red-fringed, inexorable and merciless.

CHAPTER 6

War with Afghanistan

Circling the walled town of Meshed, we came to the site of our camp to the south of the city gate, in the open desert, chosen to accommodate the units concentrating there. During our absence a whole regiment of Indian Infantry and a Kashmir Mountain Battery (Imperial Service Troops) had arrived from the south to garrison Meshed. With the addition of my regiment and the Punjabis this made a compact little force. Just within the city gates, in the serai formerly occupied by our cavalry, a large supply depot had been stocked by local purchase as regards fodder and rations, and clothing and equipment had arrived from India by the Ford lorries which now operated regularly along that motor track, that line of communication which had originated in the nothingness of the old East Persian Cordon.

We settled down to the re-equipment of man and horse. Both badly needed a complete rest, and the conditions of the clothing and saddlery after the past few months, or in some cases years, of roughing it can be imagined.

As though to spite us, there came a veritable deluge of rain lasting for several days, turning our desert camping-ground into a morass where man and horse soon forgot what it meant to have dry clothing or dry skin. The discomfort and dirt of this downpour were partly mitigated by the increasing warmth of spring, but it became ever more difficult to keep our tents standing on this swamp, and to fix the horses' picketing-pegs in the ground. We moved, then, into a high-walled Persian garden about a mile outside the town, an ideal camp with rows of fruit trees to shelter the horses, a large tank of water, and a little rivulet which flowed through it. At the top of the garden stood an avenue of small poplar trees bordered by the main stream, and this offered a delightful situation for the officers' tents and the mess. There was only one entrance, by huge wooden doors. Above these were the living apartments in which our permanent quarter-guard found comfort which they had not known since leaving India. The horse lines, flanked by the perfectly aligned tents of the respective squadrons, all sheltered from the glare of the sun by those blossoming fruit trees, made a pleasant picture.

For the first time since 1915 the regiment were all together once more, as we thought for a brief rest and equipping before our long ride back to India.

To my great surprise a letter came from Sonia, from Turbat-i-Haidari. Ivanoff had left some weeks earlier for Meshed, she wrote, ostensibly to arrange for their long-delayed journey up through Turkestan and across to Constantinople. She had no news of him. Would I inquire, and let her know what had happened?

We were able to go into Meshed to renew our acquaintance with that charming Consul-General of ours, who had begun again to give his weekly dinner-parties to officers of the British garrison. The foreign element had practically disappeared, with the exception of a very few, among whom were my old friends the Boulatoffs. The ex-bank manager of Birjand still remained, his duties as Field Treasury Chest Officer greatly augmented by the reinforcements in Meshed, and those who occupied the little posts far apart which divided that desolation southwards and which we all knew so well. I was delighted to have news of Sonia, but felt that the cloud of trouble which had oppressed me in the old Turbat-i-Haidari days was now to become an actuality. I could not imagine Ivanoff so inhuman as to desert her and leave her to fend for herself in loneliness, and what was worse, in want, in such a place. Surely he must have arranged for them both to get out of this tangle back to Constantinople, to safety. I made all possible inquiries and traced his movements. He had passed through Meshed and gone on through Askhabad, by himself. Something had to be done at once. I knew that life must be hard for Sonia, who would be too proud to acknowledge it. Russian refugees from Meshed had left in large numbers for India in our southward-bound motor convoys, thence to be repatriated. Perhaps, I thought, some friends of hers going southwards in one of these convoys might be found who could look after her.

My application for a few days' leave was readily granted, and I boarded an empty lorry bound for Turbat. With the motor road now vastly improved, it was only a day's journey; but this was not the Turbat-i-Haidari that I had known. Near its northern side stood a regular fortified camp of neat, mud-built buildings in which lived the garrison. Gone were the days when we lived in the midst of the town, when our wanderings led us by that domed bazaar and through picturesque, untouched Eastern life. There was nobody I knew except the officer-in-command. An unusual bustle and confusion went on in this horrible, rectangular, civilized and most warlike mushroom of a fort, from which the orchards surrounding the old town were visible a mile away.

"Hullo, Jimmy," said my friend the CO. "Put your kit in my room."

It was very queer, this excited atmosphere.

"Thanks very much," I said, "but what on earth is all this song and dance about?"

"Haven't you heard?" he asked. "News has only just come through that we are at war with Afghanistan."

As in all the posts on that long line, defence was being prepared. Troops were concentrated in strong posts, while the actual protection of the line, or rather its patrolling, was to be undertaken by the Seistan levies. This was one of the strong posts; hence the excitement.

As we happened to be about a thousand miles away from our base in India, and as this intervening space consisted of a now hostile country round two sides of which we must trek to regain our base, the situation was not without interest. Behind us to the west lay the formidable Lut—north lay Turkestan with its inevitable occupation by the Bolsheviks; east lay the now hostile country of Afghanistan. The south, the way by which we had originally come, was open to attack by the Afghans. It would seem an easy task for an Afghan army to have cut through our line of communications with India and segregated our main force in Meshed. This would be numerically inferior to theirs, and could easily be cut off from all supplies even if the enemy hesitated to attack.

My orders were to rejoin my regiment immediately in Meshed. So much for plans to get Sonia to India with a refugee convoy. So much for the refitting of my regiment and a return to India.

It was beginning to get dark as I rode out of that horrible mushroom fort on a borrowed horse with an orderly and came once more into that well-known bazaar, past the house which was once my own headquarters, across the square with its iron tree of death, and so to the Russian Consulate. This wore a forlorn aspect as I knocked on the great wooden doors. No Persian Cossack Guard appeared to do its swashbuckling salute. After some time the gate swung open to the hand of the Cossack whom Sonia had trusted, Akber Ali. He was delighted to see me, and assured me that he would convey at once my "salaams" to his Qanùm. He returned to lead me through those rooms that I remembered so well, now stripped of every ornament, of all furniture. My heart sank. At the end of the verandah, in a room I had seen before, I found Sonia, gay and gallant as ever, but with a strained, nervous manner which did not deceive me. There was no time to waste. I told her my news of Ivanoff, about the Afghan trouble, everything.

She was terribly pale, but she smiled and said, "Nichevo, Jimmy—Nichevo." And then she told me that the Borodins had gone to India, of how Ivanoff had gone north, and of the desertion of the Cossack bodyguard, the faithful Akber Ali only remaining.

Fumbling for matches in my pocket, I looked for a lamp or a candle with a lit match in my hand. There seemed nothing to light. Sonia laughed, but her laughter turned to sobs, and the dying flicker of the flame showed me a heart-breaking thing. That splendid Russian girl was crying as if her heart would break.

"No, Jimmy," she said through her tears, still trying to smile, "there has been nothing to light here for weeks, there has been hardly—anything—to eat!"

Akber Ali led my horse to the Consulate stables while my orderly did record time back to the fort with a letter that produced visitors to the Consulate doorway who made Sonia laugh again. The visitors were five mules, loaded with the necessities of life, not to mention some of the luxuries. Within half an hour we had the lamps aglow and were sharing an amazingly good supper, waited on by the old Cossack. Why had she not told me about all this before, I asked? Why had she not written? It was no good arguing—a Russian woman has a pride and courage that cannot be argued with. Somehow or other, I promised, we would get her back to Constantinople malgré the Afghans—malgré the Bolsheviks.

Happily we sat there making plan after plan, remembering the days when I had come stamping through the snow to dine with them all, the little room with the stove where Ivanoff and I had struggled at our boot-making, the music, and above all that freezing night when we had sat in the garden till dawn. . . . Time to leave her; I had to return to Meshed on the following morning. I promised to find a spot where Sonia could live and be looked after—she, to be ready to leave Turbat-i-Haidari in two days' time. My good friend the officer commanding the post helped me. A smiling and brave Sonia said good night, but I felt somehow that she would have to pay. There is a limit to all courage, even that of a Russian woman.

Akber Ali begged to be allowed to come to Meshed. Of course he must escort his Qanùm, I told him. He reminded me of the time I had said good-bye before; was I pleased with him now? Yes—good fellow, Akber!

The short ride back to the new fort was filled with thought. How strange it seemed, with Bolsheviks to the north, Afghans between us and India.

"There has been nothing to light here for weeks, there has been hardly anything—to eat." Brave Sonia!

"One before we go to bed," said my friend the O.C. "Jimmy James is a bit pensive to-night."

Later Afghans, Bolsheviks and Cossacks chased through my sleeping imagination, and a voice echoed, "No light—hardly anything to eat."

I just had time to canter down to the Russian Consulate the next morning to tell Sonia that arrangements had been made for her to leave Turbat and come to Meshed on the morrow. I had anticipated that my good friends the Boulatoffs would be delighted to look after her, as of course they were when I explained matters. Akber Ali in his enthusiasm assumed his full-dress uniform, and he opened the gates to me with a real Cossack salute.

I found Sonia in her little room, and we were talking together when Akber Ali knocked on the door and informed us that a certain Armenian wished to see the Qanùm.

"Who is it, Sonia?" I asked.

She told me it was a man who had been pestering her ever since Ivanoff had left, and who was claiming money which he affirmed that Ivanoff owed him; in default of which, in the manner of his kind, he had been daily suggesting that poor, defenceless Sonia could liquidate the debt in the only way which would appeal to such a scoundrel.

"Show him in," said Sonia.

The visitor appeared taken aback to find me present. As I had expected, he was one of those very mean Jewish types, a half-bred, over-fat, shifty-looking individual, truculent, dressed à la Perse in flowing coat and round, felt, brimless hat. There are splendid Christians, and admirable, intelligent Jews; there are also loathsome Christians and equally detestable Jews. This man belonged to the latter category. He started a torrent of Russian far too quickly spoken for me to understand a word, and then switched on to Sonia, who signed to me to do nothing. I longed to kick him out. Sonia just looked steadily at him, saying not a word, with something in her slanting, dangerous eyes that boded ill for this unsavoury intruder.

Her right hand was slowly feeling under a cushion behind her. The Jew became noisy and it seemed to me insulting. In a flash, out from behind that cushion came an automatic, and

I was just in time to snatch it out of her hand while the visitor made the quickest exit out of that room that the highest paid music-hall acrobat in London could ever have hoped to achieve as the result of a lifetime's training. That delighted me, but I was not keen on being mixed up in a murder case. There seemed to be quite enough difficulties to surmount without that.

The faithful Akber was already busy packing as hard as he could. I had to get back to Meshed. Sonia was still laughing as she said good-bye to me.

"Now, for God's sake don't go shooting anyone," I said.

She was to leave on the following morning.

"All right, Jimmy; do svidània (au revoir)."

The Boulatoffs were delighted to know that Sonia was coming to Meshed to stay with them. They, however, were considering departure through Askhabad while the way was still open. Sufficient unto the day among a good many evils and difficulties! The immediate problem of the well-being of Sonia was solved.

Any idea of the British troops returning to India was countered by this Afghan trouble. We were re-equipped and resharpened, and could but remain in Meshed. Should the Afghans cut our thousand mile line of communications, turn northwards and attack us—well and good. We were in first-class fighting order and prepared to take on anybody.

After all those years of trekking and fighting in Central Asia, the present situation did not excite us over-much. It was like a link in a chain of "what nexts."

As it turned out eventually, the northern forces of Afghanistan, based on Herat, showed their lack of enthusiasm by remaining within their own frontiers. There were certainly incidents along our lines of communications to India, but these were chiefly affairs caused by local brigands, ever ready to take advantage of a situation such as this. Yet we were a tempting bait in our small numbers, cornered as we were by the Bolsheviks from the north and the great Lut desert westwards. It was not for us to make a move; there was nothing to do but just "stay put" ,and ready.

A character who took the place of the faithless Sandy, the Saluki dog, is worthy of a place in this record. Sandy, with the rest of

223

his kind, wandered and followed up to the Bolshevik front, where he transferred his allegiance to a Turkoman camp. After all, they were his people, among whom he had been bred. Good luck to him, with his long, flat head and those exceedingly grave eyes.

The new character who then attached himself to me was a white dog. His father or his mother must have been a bull terrier, hence his typical wedge-shaped head and muscular body—covered with scars, which one hoped were honourable. He ended up with a short tail, which I never saw lowered in fear, however many enemies surrounded him. This queer one had run the whole way from Quetta with some detachment coming out, had been right up to Aninkova with our troops, and returned to Meshed. He was a delightfully vulgar dog, and I made friends with him one night in our mess tent when I looked down to find that great fighting, ugly face on my knee, with its pleading eyes, and that absurd little stiff tail which never seemed able to wag. It just shivered.

Every dog must have a name, and this one had a name which suited him down to the ground. "Smith" he was, and if there was time, "John Smith." Smith took complete charge of my tent and slept on my bed. To make more room we had excavated the ground below our tents, leaving pillars of earth for the tent poles, so that we lived almost underground with little nights of steps dug as an entrance and exit. The actual walls, on this account, were first the plain earth which had been taken out, and then the canvas sides of the tent which stood above them. Through these earthen walls, especially at night, mice, marmots, and all kinds of strange creatures appeared, whose normal existence is an underground one. Smith would lie there on my bed watching for these apparitions. If a little piece of earth fell to the floor up would come that great head, and those bull terrier eyes fixed on me just as if the valiant Smith was reproaching me for my inattention and at the same time asking if he might disturb the peace by investigation. He invariably did, as a matter of fact. But no going outside the camp for this quaint character. A soldier's dog was Smith, his home my tent, his boundary the camp perimeter.

Sonia joined the Boulatoffs. We were staging imaginary battles against imaginary hordes of Afghans most of the day. We had made them attack us, these imaginary foes, at all times of the day and night, and to tell the truth were getting rather bored with it. What I had feared, a breakdown, was imminent for that brave girl. Most of us rode into Meshed in the evenings, and in the garden of the Boulatoffs' house I endeavoured to devise some plan to free her from all this muddle. Things were not improved by the sudden decision of the Boulatoffs to go while the going was good. Poor Sonia was far too ill to travel.

I found a small house in the town belonging to a Russian ex-Cossack and his wife, to whom I entrusted my charge. Thanks to the kind efforts of our medical officers she began to improve in health, but the question of leaving Persia became daily more difficult with the news that came of the Bolshevik advance along the north Persian border. There was our little force bottled up in Meshed, ever prepared to tackle an Afghan attack which never materialized. The actual fighting was taking place far away south, where troops based on Quetta were rapidly bringing the Afghans to reason. Yet the situation kept us stationary in Meshed, every week making us realize that this was not to be our war. On the roof of that little house, within call of our quarter-guard, where I used to leave Adski-dushka, Sonia and I dined and talked and discussed her chances of getting away. Akber Ali would wait on us. The ex-Cossack and his wife would bring coffee, and we sat late into the night in the warmth of that welcome Persian summer. Sometimes they sang, and the old Cossack's wife sat there sewing, making clothes for Sonia, a great full moon turning the rustling poplar leaves outside to silver. It was all uncertain, and its impermanence in some strange way heightened the charm of those memorable evenings.

CHAPTER 7

Spies

On my return, old Suleiman emerged from the shadow of my tent to take my horse, and the white, shivering form of Smith became visible silhouetted in the moonlight sitting at the top of the little stairway. The queer dog would growl with content to see me back again, and instantly assume his position on the bed, looking with great ferocity around the earthen walls for the arrival of some insect marauder. He was never happy unless he was guarding something. Good old Smith!—his body felt like cast-iron to stroke, and what was left of his ears would become one with his head. I could just imagine him sitting there in the moonlight with my old man syce—waiting—sitting so straight up as he always did.

One morning as I started to inspect my horse lines our Commanding Officer hailed me.

"Be ready to move off with your squadron in four hours' time."

Giving the necessary orders to the squadron, to whom such a move was child's play, I went to discover what it was all about.

The Bolsheviks had chased our late allies right through Transcaspia up to Krasnovodsk, in fact to the Caspian Sea. The province now being clear of the hated Mensheviks, the Bolshevik armies were concentrating in Askhabad, for what purpose nobody knew; but the situation pointed to the fact that they might turn their attention southwards to Persia, so that it was essential for us to keep an eye on their movements. My orders were to proceed at once northward once more as far as the Russo-Persian border post of Bajgiran, one hundred and seventy miles away, and sit there, send back what news I could get from spies and by personal observation, not to advance one yard over the border, and in case I was attacked, to fall back. I had just time before leaving to say good-bye to Sonia. My doctor friend promised to look after her and do everything that he could.

"All right, Jimmy," she said. "I shall be here when you come back."

"Don't shoot anybody, Sonia," I said, like a fool. And then we both laughed, and I told her that I should be back again in no time to see her on her way to Constantinople in spite of everything. She had gone and I was left with an impression of two smiling eyes, but eyes from which the smile had suddenly vanished as she turned back through the door of the Cossack's house.

One route still open to her was that along the northern fringe of the Lut desert westwards to Teheran, thence to Enzeli and her destination. This was a journey to be undertaken in long, slow stages by horse-drawn transport, impossible for an invalid to make, and doubly so for a woman alone. The faithful Akber Ali and the Russian Cossack and his wife were a good bodyguard to Sonia, with whom I incidentally left Smith, content as usual to have something or somebody to guard.

Things might have been worse, I felt, confident that we should eventually manage to extricate her from all this trouble. And now I had this job to do—to go and play hide and seek with the Bolsheviks.

This was my second ride from Meshed up to the frontier at Bajgiran: this time it was in the pleasant warmth of the north Persian summer, with what vegetation there might be, and trees green with life—a most agreeable change to the snowy conditions under which I had last passed that way. These long marches in Persia had become commonplace. It was only one hundred and seventy miles this time, and our immediate duty was to get to our destination as soon as possible.

On this particular expedition I had with me one of our temporary officers, a subaltern S., than whom I could have wished for no better second-in-command or more cheery companion.

Up again we wound our way through the northward pass in

the Elburz Mountains, and one evening just before sunset filed into that last little Persian village, Bajgiran. Here the inhabitants, chiefly Persian, with one or two of the Russian poorer class families, were panic stricken, packing their belongings and preparing to flee before the Bolsheviks. While the squadron horses were being watered and fed we gathered what news we could.

It appeared that Askhabad was daily filling with Bolshevik troops, of whom already several thousands were concentrated there. This was twenty-five miles distant over the frontier.

The arrival of the squadron calmed the panic. Putting out small outposts for immediate local protection for the night, S. and I collected the one or two responsible and reliable inhabitants of the place to make a rough appreciation of the situation.

Firstly, the Persian telegraphist, to send back the news of our arrival; then the local Customs Authority. Up to date this large concentration of Bolshevik troops twenty-five miles away was all that they had to panic about. We were definitely forbidden to move into Russian territory, the border of which lay over the rising ground a mile north of the town, and over which ran that snake-like road which became so perfectly metalled and European from the border onwards. Our temporary outposts included this road, of course, so until the morrow nothing further could be done.

For our own Headquarters, and accommodation of the men of my squadron and their horses not on outpost duty, I selected an old mud barn, one end of which was walled off for S. and myself. It was in reality the remains of an ancient serai, which from long experience of such places I knew could be cleaned out and made habitable. Door-less and windowless, it furnished us with a cool living place during our stay, though it was black with flies.

Old man syce and S.'s retainer prepared a meal for us in our new quarters; the squadron settled down, and the local excitement subsided. There was no undressing that night. The horses were kept saddled and ready for action with loosened girths. Suleiman was washing up our tin plates and smiling as he always did—but no curious Persian or stranger was allowed in our new home.

I had fallen into an uneasy sleep, but was awakened in the early dawn by the most infernal clamour.

"Amadan! Amadan!" (they have come) was being shouted by the Persians congregated in the road, for all the world like a flock of pullets invaded by a fox.

Down from the sky-line from the north came galloping one of my men. It was all I could do to blast and curse my way through the mob to meet him. I told S. to get the men with us at Headquarters standing to their horses to await orders.

My galloper informed me that Bolshevik Cavalry, at a rough estimate fifty strong, were taking possession of an empty fort on the Russian side of the pass. Leaving S. in charge and sending the horseman back with orders for his post to remain under cover and watch developments, I rode up with an Indian officer and my orderly to see for myself what was afoot. Dismounting under cover, we looked over the top of the northern ridge to a scene of great activity. A red flag had been run up, and apparently transport units were filing into the fort. Sentries already patrolled the walls.

At that distance, with glasses, every detail could be seen, but we were on the high ground overlooking proceedings. All we could do was to remain where we were, as we were forbidden to set foot on Russian soil. I sent my orderly to tell my outposts in no circumstances to open fire unless an advance was made from the Russian fort, and to let them know that they would be relieved after their night's duty as soon as possible.

Sharp reports cracked from the fort, and bullets whizzed over our heads as we dropped back under cover. We had been spotted. After some time, as nothing further happened, I sent my Indian officer back for outpost reliefs from our Headquarters, and with a message for S. to join me. From our commanding position we watched the Bolsheviks settling into their fort and posting their sentries. No further shots were fired.

It was a precarious situation for one squadron of cavalry separated from its main force by one hundred and seventy miles, the first fifty of these through a twisting mountain pass.

It seemed unlikely that the Bolshevik army would actually

make war on Persia—they had quite enough, it would appear, to occupy themselves in their own territory. Yet our squadron must be a tempting bait to these ruffians, who had every reason to hate the British troops, and to wish to get a little of their own back.

Here we were, literally face to face, and the most careful plans in case of an attack by day or night had to be made. It was not only from the direction of the fort that we might expect trouble. There was nothing to prevent a Bolshevik force making its way by night through the mountains and cutting off our retreat. In fact, as George Robey used to say, "Hast heard of mashed potatoes?"

Our orders were definite enough; we were to remain there on the frontier and keep our Headquarters informed of what was going on.

Our scheme of defence kept at least half of our force constantly on outpost duty, and these outposts were arranged to ensure as far as possible that the main body of the squadron could get away in case of trouble. The dispositions of these posts kept us busy most of that day. By the evening S. and I were back in our mud serai.

As the sun was setting, unexpected and most welcome reinforcements arrived from Meshed—Lance-Corporal A. and Private B., both telegraphic experts, to take over the local telegraph office. Last but not least came a Caucasian Turk, Asadulla Khan, deputed to assist me in organizing a system of spies, and as a kind of local political officer. The two British ranks were soon installed in their office—a good pair.

Asadulla Khan came and sat down with me in that clean-swept room, or rather cowshed of ours. With Astrakhan Cossack cap and short-belted Russian tunic, breeches and soft top-boots, an ever-smiling and rather Jewish face, he presented a character which amused and interested me. A cartridge-filled belt over his shoulder was balanced on his right hip by an enormous automatic. Our telegraphists, getting to work quickly, reported their arrival and the situation up to date.

The fact that Asadulla knew no word of English or of Hindustani rather impeded matters. However, we managed all right, and as days went on found that my Persian and Russian, such as they were, allowed us to understand each other. Off he went while S. and I were having our dinner, to reappear shortly with several most truculent and villainous-looking Kurds, all armed to the teeth. Down they squatted, and I was given to understand that these gentlemen were willing to cross the frontier and get all news from the Russian side. Not unlike Turkomans these, but with the customary Russian fur cap and with not such a Mongolian cast of feature.

Then and there, slinking into the darkness like human Saluki hounds, they set out, promising to return in twenty-four hours.

"Tell your friends over the border that we are only the advance-guard of a large Indian Cavalry force, and God help the Bolsheviks if they interfere with Persia," I told them, and they laughed like the great big untamed babies that they were. We were to become great friends later.

S. was doing a round of the outposts, and I was left alone with Asadulla.

Filling up two good glasses of vodka and handing him my cigarette-case, I told Suleiman, who had been a most interested spectator, that he could go.

"Why are you laughing, Sahib?" said Asadulla.

"For the very good reason that I am not crying," I replied.

That occasion was the first of many when I sat talking late into the night with this queer Caucasian. At that time it was out of the question for me to take off my clothes by night, and only in the daytime, covered with a rug to keep off those damnable flies, was there now and then a chance to sleep.

"Do something, Sahib, anything, to frighten these thrice damned Bolsheviks," he said.

That was all very well to ask a squadron of cavalry, in touch and sight as we were now with a large enemy force, and, as regards our own, entirely in the blue. The night passed without incident while I considered my friend's advice. I had an idea.

Next day my men could be seen highly amused and interested, making for all they were worth two excellent dummy mountain guns. Wheels were soon obtained from broken down Russian and Persian kaliskas—odd pieces of wood and mud completed certainly a model of a small gun, which would at a few hundred yards deceive anybody, especially if they had the "wind up."

Back came the Kurds in the evening with news that they had been able to spread, certainly in the fort, the propaganda that I had entrusted to them.

They laughed hugely when they saw our "property" artillery. The curtain was timed to rise an hour after dawn, provided that we were not before then being chased back through the pass. S. and I were at our vantage-point in the morning on the top of the rise overlooking the Russian fort; behind us frowned the two "guns" with necessary complement of men. I had all my available force mounted and divided into four parties, each a few hundred yards apart and well under cover behind this long ridge. At a signal from me these advanced in single file at the canter, and as they ascended the hill and became visible to the Bolsheviks below they wheeled left and continued cantering, each party in a circle. This called to mind the old days at the White City, when the Cavalry Charge was presented and twenty men galloped across the stage, behind it, and on again, to simulate a continuous stream of horsemen.

From the Bolshevik fort the movement gave an impression of swarms of cavalry manoeuvring.

Through our glasses we saw the startled sentries and heard shouts and confusion. Then our two "pieces" of artillery were wheeled up and the muzzles slowly lowered. Within a few minutes the Bolshevik Cavalry were legging it out of that fort as if the devil was after them. We became weak with laughter as they disappeared in clouds of dust in the direction of Askhabad.

For the next two or three days the fort was unoccupied, but we could not relax our vigilance. It gave us a breathing space to settle down to a routine which protected us as far as possible, and an opportunity to reconnoitre the country in the vicinity of our Headquarters. I was shown by my Kurdish villains one or two passages through this part of the Elburz Mountains by which a Bolshevik force could cut us off from the rear, but by which also we might smuggle refugees into safety.

We enlisted one or two useful spies. In the meantime I collected news of the situation in Askhabad, of the numbers of the Bolshevik troops, guns, and any available details, through the medium of the villains who came in every night to tell their story—which my two admirable telegraphic experts wired to Meshed. At the end of this first week the Bolshevik fort was reoccupied by about double the number who had first taken it over and disappeared with ignominy. Down to them over the hill daily went certain villagers selling meat and vegetables and eggs. The greater part of these villagers, in fact practically all, were in sympathy with us, but, their first panic over, were only too ready to trade with the occupants of the fort. Through these and through our spies who also paid daily visits to Askhabad we received similar reports, to the effect that the Bolsheviks had no more intention of crossing the frontier into Persia than we had of crossing it into Russia. This became increasingly obvious as the time went on, yet still we kept on the alert. Our spies were doing good work, and all news was daily transmitted to our Headquarters in Meshed.

One morning, brought to my serai in triumph, a Bolshevik soldier arrived who had been foolish enough to cross the frontier near one of my outposts; he had been captured and led straight to me. I have seldom seen any human being in such abject terror. He looked as if he expected to be pegged out there and then on the ground and tortured to death. We questioned him, Asadulla Khan taking the chief part, but could not get a word out of this terrified youth.

I sent his escort back to their post and gave him a cigarette and a mouthful of vodka. He told us then the story—nothing doing over the Persian frontier, but instructions were to stop or kill if necessary any Russian subject trying to cross it. I walked to the top of the hill with him and gave him back his sword and pistol.

His fort below came in sight.

"Run, bolvan (idiot), and quick," I said.

He put up a good performance.

Apparently quite a different type now took charge of the Bolshevik post. They spent their nights in great conviviality, judging by the noise and the singing which were a nightly feature. I used to look over the top every morning, and on several occasions I saw small parties gallop out to intercept individuals who were making for the frontier, but off the road. Sometimes shots were exchanged, and I saw several unfortunates killed. One desperate gallop I witnessed; the refugee had almost reached the frontier and safety when his horse was shot under him and he was overwhelmed and hacked to death.

Through my invaluable Kurdish friends I was getting into touch with many would-be refugees in Askhabad.

There was a way by which they could cross the frontier at night if guided, a little-known defile through the mountains which came out south of our Headquarters. Once through this we could send them down to Meshed in our convoys. We ascertained that no Bolshevik sentry was ever posted there. Asadulla and I devised our scheme to pass the unhappy refugees through this defile guided by our Kurdish brigands.

CHAPTER 8

Refugees

The next urgent matter was to clean out a neighbouring serai to accommodate our expected refugees. These very soon started to come in, a heterogeneous lot. The courage of the women showed as clearly as ever. They arrived usually about dawn, to find samovars on the boil and ready for them. For a day or two they rested, then went on by mule transport or fourgons to Meshed, and from there usually by the long desert route to Teheran. In the evenings they used to come into my serai, men, women and children, of various types, desperately grateful for nothing. Among them were many professional musicians, and seldom did a night pass without the most charming entertainment.

In the background were those excellent Kurds, villains, but good villains. The dim light from our hurricane lamps showed vaguely their fierce faces, and, nearer the samovar, the haggard faces of men and women transformed by some haunting Russian melody, care-free for the moment as they took up the chorus. Perhaps some little girl would sing. On more than one occasion that saturnine Caucasian countenance of Asadulla crumpled like a child's as he listened, tears glistening on his cheeks. Through the door-less entrance glittered the North Star, pivot of the ever-circling wagon, reminding me of Sonia, who would never believe that it was the only star that stood still. She had sent news by convoy that all was as well, in the circumstances, as it could be.

Bajgiran in the moonlight on these nights looked like fairyland, the broken, tumbled walls of its domes and buildings presenting an Oriental scene which no master of stagecraft could ever rival, a wonderful setting for the circle of faces within, some coarse and ugly, some young and beautiful, and its frieze of cartridge-belted savages with long daggers aslant in their belts.

Asadulla Khan, my subaltern S., and I would sit a while over a glass of Persian wine and discuss what we might do to improve the occasion. Days passed into weeks, and still this queer situation remained; the same vigilance of our outposts, the daily collection of trans-frontier news, these gatherings of refugees, and last, but not least, in the background the little figure of Suleiman, "old Sinbad," with little grey beard and twinkling, beady eyes, calm as ever, and utterly unmoved by these unusual proceedings.

The up-coming convoys brought letters from Sonia. She was much better; the old Cossack and his wife were looking after her well, and among the very few Russians left in Meshed she had found some new friends.

Good and cheering news—but the problem of getting her back to Constantinople still remained. It was not much good bothering, however, about this immediate impossibility. The Afghan war was grumbling on, but as regards actual fighting was confined to the far southern Indo-Afghan border. Here on the Bolshevik frontier that seemed remote.

In the meantime a squadron of my regiment had been moved out northwards towards us, about half-way to Bajgiran, to act as support in case we found ourselves in difficulties. It was quite obvious by now that the Bolsheviks in Transcaspia were intent on their own business, in setting their newly acquired country in order. Daily reports from my spies confirmed this. After all, they had nothing to gain by an invasion of Northern Persia, and even less to gain by trying to revenge themselves on any British troops who happened to be there. Still, we were able to smuggle countless refugees out of Russian territory, and give our Headquarters in Meshed a very good idea of affairs across the border.

Our friends over the hill in their fort patrolled their side of the frontier with the object of cutting off refugees, fortunately entirely by day. The refugees used to steal through the lesser-known passes by night guided by our spies. From the fort came sounds of drunken uproar and merriment. The squadron supporting us found that time hung heavily, with nothing to do except occasional patrol work.

Hearing that pig had been seen in the neighbourhood, the Squadron Commander organized a pig-sticking expedition. This meant a trek through the hills for several miles to a wide valley with good grass going. To our Rajput Squadron the prospect of one of their first national sports was a delight.

Almost immediately after reaching the valley the local hired beaters put up a good "sounder" containing several boars, and our party settled down to a good gallop over the firm grass. Suddenly a hail of bullets spattered round our men. Thinking that this was due to over-excitement on the part of the hired beaters, the Squadron Commander carried on with the hunt. A repetition made him realize his mistake. Galloping with his men into cover of a nullah he climbed its bank to discover his opponents some five hundred yards away. He opened rapid fire on them, and the hostile unknowns withdrew at once.

On returning to camp it was discovered that there had been a raid on a neighbouring village. The raiders who had decamped via the pig-sticking arena had mistaken our men, intent on the hunt, for Persian troops whom they imagined to be on their track, hence the rifle duel. None of our men or horses had been hit, but the raiders had two men and two horses killed.

Official and voluminous apologies were sent in by the raider chief for his mistake and for having interfered with the sport! What a country! The apologies were accepted, since beyond the spoiling of a promising hunt we had suffered no losses. These raiders requested to be allowed to enlist in our forces. Had this been possible, I am perfectly certain that their knowledge of the country, their hardiness and courage would have proved most useful.

News reached us at the end of August that the Afghan war was over and peace had been signed. It seemed ridiculous to think of an uncivilized little nation like Afghanistan having made war at all to begin with. What on earth had been gained? Large quantities of public money had been expended on both sides. From our point of view the casualties (an objectionable and unfeeling term) had been infinitesimal. The Afghans had suffered comparatively to a far greater extent. On either side a certain number of women and children had been left destitute; the slayers of their breadwinners became entitled to a strip of ribbon of a certain kind to be worn as an honour. There always has been war and there always will be war, but, patriotism apart, thoughts of its result, its values, will come. The professional soldier is a professional murderer; yet there must be soldiers, and if I had my time over again I would still follow the drum. There has been, is, and always will be a vein of chivalry in all fighting. Despite the Press, despite financiers, despite everything, there is something decent in war. After all, defending the hearth is a primitive instinct. And, apart from all these considerations, the discipline, the fitness, the hearty cheer of a soldier's life are worth something.

Refugees of all types continued to arrive via our little secret passage through the mountains. Men, women, and children— Russian, Persian even, Armenian, Austrian and German. Not often were we alone at night in that serai. Sometimes I ascended the ridge and spent the night with one of our outposts. It was a marvellous view into complete nothingness by day, but moonlight would lend it mystery and a sense of unlimited space. There below us lay the enemy fort with the only visible lights, and its Bolshevik devils would sing and carouse until all hours.

We rehearsed every conceivable alarm that might surprise us, practising what our movements should be whatever happened; this became routine, and every man knew exactly what to do down to tightening the last buckle. The "wagon" circled round the North Star, the refugees came and went.

From the far side of the partition, in the night, came that most comforting sound, horses feeding, a sound which always conveyed to me a kind of content.

A week or so passed without incident. Obviously the Bolsheviks had no intention whatever of crossing the border.

Orders came then for me to march my squadron back to Meshed on relief by levies and a company of Indian Infantry from the line of communications.

For some time past printed propaganda had been sent up to me to be disseminated, as an inducement chiefly to the unfortunate Austrian and German prisoners of war with the Bolshevik army to desert, in order to convince them that it was months since the Armistice had been signed, and in the hope that they would escape over the Persian border to be repatriated by us. These leaflets were dropped nightly in the streets of Askhabad by my spies, and were the cause of a fair number of the unfortunates coming through that back door in the Elburz Mountains to safety and a free passage home. At this time, too, from Afghanistan into Meshed came members of these "hostile parties" who had penetrated the Cordon in the old days.

The Bolshevik post had been amusing itself by having stray shots from below at any of us who happened to show against the sky-line. These, of course, were not returned, but I thought it about time to give them something to think about. At night their nearest sentry was stationed at the foot of the hill, between the fort and the frontier line where we were. Asadulla got into communication with this post, posing as a Bolshevik spy from behind our lines. He told them of a strong British force on its way northwards from Meshed, and claimed to be able to hand over secret documents of the utmost value which he had managed to steal, and which dealt with the British plans. We had made up the "secret documents" in a neat parcel, which contained a large supply of our propaganda leaflets. A day was appointed for the handing over of this mysterious sealed packet, and at dawn I watched from above as Asadulla slithered down and handed it to the Bolsheviks, returning in high glee with generous payment for the same.

It seemed almost too good to be true when we saw two mounted men leaving for Askhabad at a gallop from the fort with the package, which obviously the fort commander had neither time nor inclination to investigate.

On the following day the detachment from that fort was relieved for the second time since our arrival. On this occasion, however, our friends did not waste good ammunition on us, and contented themselves with minding their own business.

Meanwhile, the company of infantry had taken over our out-posts, and we were due to march out again back to Meshed. I remember sitting up late that night with the whimsical Asadulla. September now, and the nights were growing cold.

I had taken a great liking to Asadulla, with his cartridge-filled bandolier and gigantic automatic, and his stories on our last night surpassed anything that he had hitherto told me, doubt-less owing to the extra glass of vodka to celebrate this farewell sitting.

How we ever managed to understand one another is still a mystery to me, for we conversed in a kind of mixture of Per-sian and Russian on my side, ungrammatical and incorrect to a degree. He had to be away early on a special mission on the following morning, and the squadron would have left on his return. It was time to say goodbye.

I thanked him for his good work, and promised him that I would tell the General Sahib in Meshed how well he had done. Poor Asadulla looked dejected and sad, and when I gave him my wrist-watch as a parting souvenir, he wept with gratitude, went to his quarters, and came back with his very best Astrakhan Cos-sack cap as a gift to me. I still have it.

"Good-bye, Sahib," he said, "and may you always laugh."

"Good-bye, Asadulla. . . ."

He disappeared into the night, and that was the last that I saw of him.

Once again on the road—trotting, walking, leading, hour af-ter hour. The same nights' halts in the same serais, but this time with nothing at the end of our journey of one hundred and sev-enty miles of a hostile nature. We were rejoining our regiment in Meshed, in that charming Persian garden. And what then?

It seemed an impossibility that this might be the end to our wanderings. Surely somebody would start making war, and we should be at it again. I had let Sonia know that we were return-ing, and hoped that I should find her really well again, so that some kind of a plan could be made to get her to her people in Constantinople. If we were to leave on our seven weeks' ride to India that plan would have to be made at once. S., my subaltern, and Sheikh Haider, were of opinion that it was to be "back to India"; old Suleiman was quite indifferent. He merely smiled and got on with his job.

One morning the gleaming dome of the Mosque came into sight, and shortly afterwards we were filing into camp under the arched gateway of the garden. Here I found Akber Ali, the Persian Cossack, with Smith, who nearly wagged his entire body out of its skin. I was delighted to hear that the Qanùm was well, and sent a message that I should be coming to see her that evening.

CHAPTER 9

Endings

It was good to be back with the regiment, and to see one's squadron once again take its place in those neat and orderly lines of horses bordered by the men's tents. The transport would be in later. In the meantime I reported to the Commanding Officer, and was glad to hear that our mission to the Russian frontier had produced all the information required by the General in command.

The forecast had been a correct one on the part of the cheery S. and Sheikh Haider. We were to return to India in November, marching separately by squadrons at a week's interval. My turn to go came in the first week of December. The Punjab Infantry, our old allies since 1915 on the original Cordon, then line of communications, and then in Russia, were to leave before our first squadron.

We were actually returning to peace conditions. It would be strange after the roving, lonely life that we had led for the past few years, trekking our hundreds and thousands of miles in desolate Eastern Persia. The ride in itself to rail-head in the south would take at least seven weeks, yet it seemed nothing out of the ordinary. It was merely what we had all become accustomed to. This idea of returning to civilization was a shock, like waking up after a dream. It ought to have seemed wonderful, to have been like the end of a particularly long term to a schoolboy.

Up and down the lines of feeding horses I walked, deep in thought—the one place in the world for me when things didn't seem quite right. Would peace-time soldiering in India ever sat-

242

isfy again? It would be all so entirely different from the pre-war days in 1914. Nearly all one's old friends had been killed. Unavoidable red tape and officialdom must be faced.

More still to come—the Commanding Officer told me that the new rules on service for promotion meant that I had become a Major after fifteen years' service instead of the old regulation eighteen in the Indian Army. There came visions of the life of a Squadron Commander being "divided" from his men and horses by unending Courts Martial, Courts of Inquiry and other formalities. A "Field Officer" is in constant demand as President of these wearisome proceedings. I thought of the caricatures of the Indian Army Major who lived chiefly on curry, whose face was tomato red blended with grey moustache. Of the reputed Major whose answer to the newly joined subaltern who came into mess at breakfast and wished him a polite good morning was: "Good morning—Good morning—Good morning—Good morning—Good morning—Good morning—Good morning—and that will do you for a week!"

I had hated, and loved east Persia. Peace soldiering, it seemed, would be like putting on tight, uncomfortable and hot clothes, and having a key turned on a life which one had liked and disliked, a dream which could fascinate as easily as it could repel.

I turned to go to breakfast in the mess tent cursing myself for an ungrateful fool. Had I not my full complement of limbs, to begin with? And the ragging I received at the hands of my brother officers brought a badly needed degree of common sense.

"We know all about you up at Bajgiran and your cocktail-parties and the lovely ladies in distress—no wonder the General ordered you back...." And so on.

My little tent was up once more over its particular hole in the ground, and I had been revelling, as far as one can revel, in a waterproof canvas bath. Smith was on the bed with eyes like beads scanning every inch of the earthen walls, sitting on the clean kit which Suleiman had put out for me.

"Blast you, Smith," I said.

The only answer was a short bark and the nearest thing I ever saw to a laugh in a dog's face.

Poor old, tough, ugly Smith—he was only guarding my clothes. He had to guard something, or life was futile.

In the Cavalry Quarter-Guard in Meshed I handed over my horse. Akber AH, one expansive smile, opened the door of the old Cossack's house. I found Sonia looking infinitely better and almost her old self again. The Cossack's wife had cooked a special dinner for us and had managed to find some really good Persian wine.

There was much to say. She had no further news of Ivanoff, but her mother and daughter were awaiting her in Constantinople. We were very happy, and exchanged reminiscences of Turbat-i-Haidari, the boot-making, the music and the hundred things that had happened. One doesn't always remember exactly why or how happiness comes. It's just like that.

"Is it true that the Indian troops are leaving Meshed? " asked Sonia.

It was only a matter of a few weeks, I answered, and we must seriously make plans for her to get away.

Sonia remained silent for a long time. Then she said, "Jimmy, I have made plans. I knew that this was coming—I shall be well enough in a fortnight's time, and I must go. Why not be happy? It's no use looking sad like that."

Trotting back to camp in the bright moonlight I was more than ever filled with admiration for the courage of the Russian women.

There was little for us to do in camp. Transport was collected, arrangements were being made all along that line southwards for the forage and rations required for the passage of four separate squadrons. A regular overhaul and refitting of horse gear—rugs, picketing pegs and ropes, all the necessities for a long march of this kind were attended to.

While I had been away on the Russian frontier, Sonia met among her few countrymen left in Meshed an old friend of her family who in former days had been attached to the Russian Consulate. Fortunately this delightful old man was preparing to leave by the long desert road to Teheran, en route for Constantinople. This meant travelling by horse-drawn carriage through Teheran, up to Enzeli, and thence by sea.

The north Persian winter once more threatened with light falls of snow and bitter winds. He was pleased to look after Sonia on this journey. The faithful Akber Ali was to accompany them as far as Teheran, and they were due to leave in ten days. Until then we spent cheery evenings in the old Cossack's house with a good fire going. The old man's wife would be there when I arrived, sewing away for all she was worth, making things which Sonia wanted—we had a leather sheepskin coat complete with knee boots and gloves; and never were such preparations, thanks to that dear old woman.

I joined her husband sometimes in a glass of vodka, and he told me the most impossible yarns which I only half understood when I could get him to speak slowly enough. After dinner Sonia played her guitar and sang. So the days passed, ever too quickly. When the last night came, the old Cossacks were in tears. The carriage was to call for Sonia in the morning, and I was coming to see them off.

"It's good-bye now, Jimmy," said Sonia. And she added, as once before, "Don't forget me."

I let Adski-dushka pick her way back to camp through a blindingly cold sleet-storm, than which nothing could have suited my mood better.

This was still raging as on the following morning I rode for a few miles alongside that carriage. A last goodbye as they slackened to a walk through a nullah bed, and then I sat on my horse watching until they became a speck in the distance, and vanished. Sonia's eyes had filled with tears, but she was smiling—just as she did when she would say "Nichevo, Jimmy," when things seemed at their very worst.

Adski-dushka fidgeted; I realized that we must go back, back to an empty Meshed. It felt like the end of a play; and this was the end without doubt. I could see imaginary curtains slowly closing down on a chapter in life which could never be repeated. Whatever light there was in this sleet-ridden, bitter day came from some huge lamp whose wick was being turned slowly downwards by inexorable, unseen fingers.

Those slanting, smiling eyes had gone right away across the world.

The wick of that lamp burnt to its lowest as we turned and made our way to camp. Not long after, we marched out, squadron after squadron, week after week. That line down to rail-head on the Baluchistan frontier was a track now, straight and forbidding, along which motor transport could travel. The posts which we had known as Persian village serais and some-times as merely a clump of palm trees sheltering a water-hole, no longer existed. In their place stood out in the desert well-built mud houses and barracks. Turbat-i-Haidari, Kain, all my well-known villages and landmarks, were well away from that efficient line. The old East Persian Cordon had been trans-formed out of its adorable nothingness, as we knew it, into the most efficient line of communications that ever served a force, far flung as we had been almost to the Oxus river. I believe that this fact, this triumph of staff work, has already formed the subject of a book written by the General Officer who was its organizer. Personally I was only too glad not to revisit those queer, attractive places in which I had spent so many months. Such an experience could not be repeated.

Grateful, then, that the romance of the last few years was to remain untarnished, and grateful for the comfort of this entirely new line of posts, we took our places week by week, squadron by squadron, in the trains that awaited us at rail-head at the end of our seven weeks' march, and so were carried back to the civi-lization of India, to Lucknow.

And now for one last look at the holy city of Meshed as my turn came to march out of that garden camp in early December.

The curtains had almost closed now.

Away over the oasis we filed, up to the top of the pass whence I had seen my first glimpse of Meshed, so long ago. Here the road forked away from our path to Nishapur, the burial-place of Omar Khayyám, the road which Sonia had taken out of this troublous country. I backed off the track and watched the squad-ron go past. Bringing up the rear was old Suleiman, riding my second horse.

"Khush hai?" (are you happy?) I shouted.

"Ha, Sahib, bahut khush." (Yes, Sahib, I am.)

246

And this was the first time that he had ever owned up to it.

It was on the summit of this pass that the curtain closed completely down, not before allowing, even as I had first seen it, a brilliant sunlit ray to sweep over what could be even now seen of the holy city, and to flash on the blue and gold dome of the Mosque. Was it possible that old Omar had seen this? . . .

The Spot, where I made one . . .
turn down an empty glass!

LEONAUR

ALSO FROM LEONAUR
AVAILABLE IN SOFTCOVER OR HARDCOVER WITH DUST JACKET

DOING OUR 'BIT' *by Ian Hay*—Two Classic Accounts of the Men of Kitchener's 'New Army' During the Great War including *The First 100,000 & All In It.*

AN EYE IN THE STORM by *Arthur Ruhl*—An American War Correspondent's Experiences of the First World War from the Western Front to Gallipoli and Beyond.

STAND & FALL by *Joe Cassells*—A Soldier's Recollections of the 'Contemptible Little Army' and the Retreat from Mons to the Marne, 1914.

RIFLEMAN MACGILL'S WAR by *Patrick MacGill*—A Soldier of the London Irish During the Great War in Europe including *The Amateur Army, The Red Horizon & The Great Push.*

WITH THE GUNS by *C. A. Rose & Hugh Dalton*—Two First Hand Accounts of British Gunners at War in Europe During World War 1- Three Years in France with the Guns and With the British Guns in Italy.

EAGLES OVER THE TRENCHES by *James R. McConnell & William B. Perry*—Two First Hand Accounts of the American Escadrille at War in the Air During World War 1-Flying For France: With the American Escadrille at Verdun and Our Pilots in the Air.

THE BUSH WAR DOCTOR by *Robert V. Dolbey*—The Experiences of a British Army Doctor During the East African Campaign of the First World War.

THE 9TH—THE KING'S (LIVERPOOL REGIMENT) IN THE GREAT WAR 1914 - 1918 by *Enos H. G. Roberts*—Like many large cities, Liverpool raised a number of battalions in the Great War. Notable among them were the Pals, the Liverpool Irish and Scottish, but this book concerns the wartime history of the 9th Battalion – The Kings.

THE GAMBARDIER by *Mark Severn*—The experiences of a battery of Heavy artillery on the Western Front during the First World War.

FROM MESSINES TO THIRD YPRES by *Thomas Floyd*—A personal account of the First World War on the Western front by a 2/5th Lancashire Fusilier.

THE IRISH GUARDS IN THE GREAT WAR - VOLUME 1 by *Rudyard Kipling*—Edited and Compiled from Their Diaries and Papers Volume 1 The First Battalion.

THE IRISH GUARDS IN THE GREAT WAR - VOLUME 2 by *Rudyard Kipling*—Edited and Compiled from Their Diaries and Papers Volume 2 The Second Battalion.

LEONAUR

ALSO FROM LEONAUR
AVAILABLE IN SOFTCOVER OR HARDCOVER WITH DUST JACKET

ARMOURED CARS IN EDEN by *K. Roosevelt*—An American President's son serving in Rolls Royce armoured cars with the British in Mesopatamia & with the American Artillery in France during the First World War.

CHASSEUR OF 1914 by *Marcel Dupont*—Experiences of the twilight of the French Light Cavalry by a young officer during the early battles of the great war in Europe.

TROOP HORSE & TRENCH by *R.A. Lloyd*—The experiences of a British Life-guardsman of the household cavalry fighting on the western front during the First World War 1914-18.

THE LONG PATROL by *George Berrie*—A Novel of Light Horsemen from Gallipoli to the Palestine campaign of the First World War.

THE EAST AFRICAN MOUNTED RIFLES by *C.J. Wilson*—Experiences of the campaign in the East African bush during the First World War

THE FIGHTING CAMELIERS by *Frank Reid*—The exploits of the Imperial Camel Corps in the desert and Palestine campaigns of the First World War.

WITH THE IMPERIAL CAMEL CORPS IN THE GREAT WAR by *Geoffrey Inchbald*—The story of a serving officer with the British 2nd battalion against the Senussi and during the Palestine campaign.

STEEL CHARIOTS IN THE DESERT by *S.C.Rolls*—The first world war experiences of a Rolls Royce armoured car driver with the Duke of Westminster in Libya and in Arabia with T.E. Lawrence.

LEONAUR

ALSO FROM LEONAUR
AVAILABLE IN SOFTCOVER OR HARDCOVER WITH DUST JACKET

A JOURNAL OF THE SECOND SIKH WAR by *Daniel A. Sandford*—The Experiences of an Ensign of the 2nd Bengal European Regiment During the Campaign in the Punjab, India, 1848-49.

LAKE'S CAMPAIGNS IN INDIA by *Hugh Pearse*—The Second Anglo Maratha War, 1803-1807. Often neglected by historians and students alike, Lake's Indian campaign was fought against a resourceful and ruthless enemy-almost always superior in numbers to his own forces.

BRITAIN IN AFGHANISTAN 1: THE FIRST AFGHAN WAR 1839-42 by *Archibald Forbes*—Following over a century of the gradual assumption of sovereignty of the Indian Sub-Continent, the British Empire, in the form of the Honourable East India Company, supported by troops of the new Queen Victoria's army, found itself inevitably at the natural boundaries that surround Afghanistan. There it set in motion a series of disastrous events-the first of which was to march into the country at all.

BRITAIN IN AFGHANISTAN 2: THE SECOND AFGHAN WAR 1878-80 by *Archibald Forbes*—This the history of the Second Afghan War-another episode of British military history typified by savagery, massacre, siege and battles.

UP AMONG THE PANDIES by *Vivian Dering Majendie*—An outstanding account of the campaign for the fall of Lucknow. *This is a vital book of war as fought by the British Army of the mid-nineteenth century, but in truth it is also an essential book of war that will enthral military historians and general readers alike.*

BLOW THE BUGLE, DRAW THE SWORD by *W. H. G. Kingston*—The Wars, Campaigns, Regiments and Soldiers of the British & Indian Armies During the Victorian Era, 1839-1898.

INDIAN MUTINY 150th ANNIVERSARY: A LEONAUR ORIGINAL

MUTINY: 1857 by *James Humphries*—It is now 150 years since the 'Indian Mutiny' burst like an engulfing flame on the British soldiers, their families and the civilians of the Empire in North East India. The Bengal Native army arose in violent rebellion, and the once peaceful countryside became a battleground as Native sepoys and elements of the Indian population massacred their British masters and defeated them in open battle. As the tide turned, a vengeful army of British and loyal Indian troops repressed the insurgency with a savagery that knew no mercy. It was a time of fear and slaughter. James Humphries has drawn together the voices of those dreadful days for this commemorative book.

AVAILABLE ONLINE AT
www.leonaur.com
AND OTHER GOOD BOOK STORES   SC-1

Lightning Source UK Ltd.
Milton Keynes UK
UKOW051213170512

192748UK00001B/55/P